Love, Loss, and Longing in
KASHMIR

Love, Loss, and Longing in
KASHMIR

SAHBA HUSAIN

zubaan

Zubaan
128 B Shahpur Jat, 1st floor
NEW DELHI 110 049
Email: contact@zubaanbooks.com
Website: www.zubaanbooks.com

First published by Zubaan Publishers Pvt. Ltd 2019
Copyright © Sahba Husain 2019

10 9 8 7 6 5 4 3 2

ISBN 978 93 85932 87 8

Zubaan is an independent feminist publishing house based in New Delhi with a strong academic and general list. It was set up as an imprint of India's first feminist publishing house, Kali for Women, and carries forward Kali's tradition of publishing world quality books to high editorial and publishing standards. *Zubaan* means tongue, voice, language, speech in Hindustani. Zubaan publishes in the areas of the humanities, social sciences, fiction, general non-fiction, as well as books for children and young adults under its Young Zubaan imprint.

Printed and bound at Thomson Press India Ltd.

✿

For my parents,
Khadija Bano and Syed Alam Khundmiri

Contents

Love, Loss, and Longing in Kashmir
An Introduction ix

1. Fear, Displacement, Departure
   The Experience of the Kashmiri Pandits 1

2. In the Absence of Their Men
   The Phenomenon of Enforced Disappearances 72

3. The Other Face of Azadi
   The Presence of Women in the Movement 107

4. The Mind and the Body
   The Mental Health of the Kashmiri People 162

5. The Tyranny of Silence
   Sexual Violence and Impunity in Kashmir 204

Conclusion 236

Acknowledgments 244

Love, Loss, and Longing in Kashmir

AN INTRODUCTION

Kashmir conjures up many images, perhaps the most common of them its stunning and majestic natural beauty. But there is another side to this fabled 'paradise'. In the words of a well-known local woman leader, Kashmir is a place where profound individual grief is absorbed into collective sorrow as people mourn the killings, the deaths, and the loss of those, known and unknown, who have gone.

Kashmir brought me face-to-face with a political, a humanitarian, an emotional, a psychological and a deeply personal reality. It challenged my understanding of these in light of the ongoing conflict that it has lived through for so many years. And, over the years, it not only influenced me profoundly but also transformed me, becoming what I began to see as my own place, its people, my own people. As a woman and a researcher, Kashmir has, in many different ways, been an exceptional and memorable experience for me. What I saw the first time I went there, and then on subsequent visits, the friendships that were gifted to me, the stories people shared with me – with warmth, despair, love, generosity, and hope – left an indelible imprint on me.

It was in Kashmir that I found friends who became family. Two of them, Rasheed Bhai and Sajjad, became my anchors as I tried to grapple with the complex reality I saw around me. Tragically, less than a year ago, within months of each other, both of them passed away; their loss affected me deeply. For me, they were the essence of the spirit of Kashmir – of optimism, hope, integrity, joy, and moral strength. They became my buddies, my family, my work-mates, and my companions through the years of my work and life in Kashmir. Rasheed Bhai went first, due to cancer, in early February; Sajjad went suddenly (on April Fools' Day) of a heart attack. Perhaps his heart held too much in it, perhaps Rasheed's did too, along with the smoke that seemed to have filled their lungs as much as their zest for life. They had their fingers on the pulse of Kashmir, and Kashmir and Kashmiriyat ran in their veins, the one (Rasheed) a houseboat owner living on the Dal Lake and the other from the downtown area of Alamgiri Bazaar. Their friendship and love accompanied me through each season I spent in Kashmir – and their sudden deaths led me to think about my relationship not only with them and their families but also with Kashmir and its people. I began wondering how one defines one's relationship to a place, how one grows into it. Kashmir was a place that was once distant to me but that gradually began to inhabit my everyday consciousness, my thoughts, and my memories. With each visit, it also crept in, and touched and transformed my intellectual and emotional realm. I kept returning. What I want to share with the reader in this book is not only my personal experience of love, loss, and grief, but also how, in a place like Kashmir, the personal and the political begin to converge in people's everyday lives.

Nearly thirty years after the conflict in Kashmir began, the much needed and much talked about political solution remains elusive. Instead violence continues to escalate, and people's desire for a resolution and an end to it remains unfulfilled. Worse, rather than acknowledging its role in mass violence and injustice, the Indian state denies its complicity. Instead, it encourages people to forget the past, to put injustice behind them, to not think of grave violations and traumatic events, and to move on for 'a better future'.

But while the state espouses the 'forget and move on' theory, for the people the question is different. I discovered early on in Kashmir that the pledge of the aggrieved is never to forget, and never to forgive, as well as to ensure that the next generation remembers the history of the violence and its devastating consequences. Their struggle, defiance, and resistance continue against the institutionalized impunity perpetrators enjoy. For them, the battle is for justice and accountability and they want the state to recognize and acknowledge the truth of these violations.

The state, however, denies, erases, and often distorts the truth. It is no surprise therefore that it does not provide any accurate information on the human cost of conflict, and that it refuses to acknowledge the truth of the crimes it has committed against people in the name of national security/sovereignty as well as how it deliberately denies justice to victims/survivors.

The large-scale militarization in Jammu and Kashmir to crush the armed insurgency that began in 1989 has had far reaching consequences for the people. Today there are more than half a million troops against a population of around 12 million – the soldier/civilian ratio being around 1:20, and the presence of the troops and paramilitary forces is far more visible in Kashmir where the population is 7 million. Kashmir is the only Muslim majority state in India; every man and boy is a suspect in the eyes of the Indian state and its agencies, and women are specifically targeted to punish their men and terrorize the community.

There are many coercive laws in operation in the state. These include the Armed Forces Special Powers Act (AFSPA), the Public Safety Act (PSA), and the Disturbed Areas Act. Each enables the state to ruthlessly intrude upon the privacy of civilian spaces. Thus, frequent raids take place where the state forces enter private homes with impunity, where crackdowns take place all the time and 'encounters' are carried out. With these laws, the state shields and protects the perpetrators while further victimizing the victims and survivors. No wonder then that despite hundreds of registered complaints and documented evidence against perpetrators in many cases, there is hardly ever a conviction, as prosecution cannot take place without government sanction or approval, which is consistently and deliberately denied.

Numbers tell only part of the story, for these too are disputed: official figures are always at variance with those provided by civil society organizations working on the ground. According to the estimates provided by the government officials that I met during fieldwork, since the time militancy began, approximately 30,000 people have been killed, 6,000 women widowed, 3,000 men disappeared and 10-15,000 children rendered orphans. Unofficial estimates put the figure much higher, at 80,000 killed, more than 8,000 men missing due to the heinous practice of enforced disappearances, 20,000 widows and half-widows, 30,000-40,000 orphans. These estimates also account for the en-masse displacement of the minority community of Kashmiri Pandits from their homes and mass rapes of women in villages and towns committed by the soldiers during crackdowns and cordon and search operations. I also learnt of the discovery, a few years ago, of thousands of unmarked graves that dotted the landscape of the hinterland.[1]

More recently, in 2016, in the mass uprisings against the killing of Burhan Wani, a young and popular local militant commander, more than 100 protesting men, mostly youth, were killed by the Security Forces (SFs). The killings led to such outrage among people that the government decided to 'soften' their practice by bringing in 'non-lethal' weapons for crowd control. Bullets were replaced with pellets. The result was that more than 13,000 people were injured as pellets were fired in such a way that they riddled the bodies of those who were targeted. More than 800 people were directly hit by pellets in their eyes and nearly a hundred of them have been partially or fully blinded. More than 10,000 youth were detained/arrested at the time and criminal charges framed against most of them. The disruption of ordinary lives – whether in health, education or livelihood – is beyond comprehension.

❄   ❄   ❄

This was the field I entered as a researcher in the summer of 2000. I was not a stranger to research. For two decades previously, I'd been working on different subjects in other parts of India. But nothing prepared me for the colossal human tragedy I saw in Kashmir. I initially went there as a consultant for the Oxfam India Trust, as part of its Violence Mitigation and Amelioration Project (VMAP) and later I returned with the Aman Public Charitable Trust under its Gender, Mental Health and Conflict programme. Aman was established in 2003 to continue the work that we had begun at Oxfam. The work was meant to be more in the nature of action-oriented research aimed at building partnerships at the local level with organizations and individuals working on the ground. The idea was to strengthen their efforts at mitigating the effects of prolonged conflict and violence by initiating need-based, practical interventions at the community level.

My brief was to examine, empirically, the psychological impact of violence on people's daily lives in order to understand the various ways in which they coped with the immediacy and the aftermath of violence, both at the individual and collective levels. Thus I looked at the loss of loved ones, prolonged suffering, grief, stress, the unforeseen hardships, and the intense trauma that was part of people's everyday lives. It struck me that just as violence had become part of everyday life in Kashmir, the word trauma had become part of people's everyday vocabulary even though hardly anybody was equipped to recognize its symptoms or seek timely remedy.

My first impression on my arrival in Srinagar was that I had entered an occupied state although the mainstream narrative was that it was 'an integral part of India'. It was challenging for me to make sense of such a massive presence of the Indian security forces and to see how they were pitched against the unarmed civilians – their own people – whose commitment to India was being sought through the barrel of a gun. I remember feeling ashamed and violated as an Indian citizen in their midst.

The deep sense of hurt, betrayal, anger and rage that most people felt and expressed against 'India' was quite intimidating for me. At the same time, it demanded a clarity of position from me as an Indian: could I expect them to trust me? How could I begin to gain their trust and, equally importantly, where would I begin?

I began to travel to meet and interact with people. I visited bereaved families, hospitals, schools, colleges, newspaper offices, chemist shops, orphanages and even shrines where people went to seek comfort and solace. Tragically, I did not come across a single family that had been spared; each had a story to tell of the violence they had experienced in one form or another and what it meant. A mother searching frantically for her missing son for more than a decade, a wife waiting endlessly for her husband to return, unable to overcome grief, a young widow looking after her two small children after her husband was suddenly killed by the Security Forces, a man grappling with the humiliation and pain of being let off after severe interrogation and torture, old parents displaying photographs of their sons killed, children filing past for their daily meal in an orphanage…the list of casualties was endless.

It was during my visits to the only government hospital for psychiatric diseases in Srinagar that the magnitude of the mental health problems was revealed to me. I met and interviewed doctors and also spent considerable time with patients – men, women and youth – who had come with complaints of acute depression, frequent palpitations, heartache, lack of concentration, loss of appetite, sleep disorders and bouts of intense anxiety. Children were conspicuous by their absence as both parents and doctors believed that it would further traumatize them to see the multitude of patients who waited in the poorly lit corridors and those in the two small rooms who clamoured for the doctors' attention inside. Though the doctors believed that sustained counselling was better than medication, the paucity of time made it difficult for them to engage with the numbers of patients who sat clutching their prescriptions and waiting their turn. According to the hospital records, the number of patients had gone up exponentially from 1,700 prior to militancy (1989) to 32,000 ten years later, reaching 70,000+ by the mid 2000s, and shortly thereafter crossing an alarming 100,000 a year. At the time of my initial visits, the psychiatrist/patient ratio was 1:100,000, there were only two psychiatrists at the hospital.

A senior psychiatrist at the hospital told me that more than two-thirds of the population suffered from chronic psychological disorders and what the majority of people were coping with was not ordinary but catastrophic stress, which is induced when they are witness to sudden killings, disappearances, and torture of their close relatives or loved ones. The quality of life among such people was close to schizophrenia, he said, adding that what I was seeing was just the tip of the iceberg. Even remote reminders of the actual event could trigger extreme fear among patients, leading to their refusal to go out or meet people, the fear and isolation causing further distress. An individual's psychotic state did not remain confined to him or her and could often lead to family illnesses where all members, particularly women as prime caregivers, began to suffer similar symptoms. Out of 10 cases of acute depression, seven or eight were those of women patients as they struggled to keep the family together, often neglecting their own health. Doctors at the hospital and officials in the health department admitted that it was beyond their capacity to adequately address this scale of tragedy and trauma among people, many of whom were faced with no other option than to consume a variety of psychotropic drugs on a daily basis, including anti-depressants and tranquilizers. This was their only survival strategy. A chemist I interviewed at the time confirmed that there had been a 100 per cent increase in the sale of such drugs.

❊   ❊   ❊

Given the nature of my research and the close proximity to the 'field', there was no way I could remain untouched by what I saw and heard. Thus I would like to speak of how I was impacted by coming so close to the violence, how the trauma entered my life too. The violence was unlike anything I had seen previously as a researcher and it affected me deeply. As my journey of hope and despair began, I learnt so much and unlearnt even more – a process that wasn't easy. For me, it is necessary to note this: for the researcher, coping, processing, assimilating are part of the research process but the process that I personally experienced was more than this, it was also about becoming who I am and how, in turn, that process was shaped by my intimate engagement with the field.

The challenges I faced as a researcher, an activist, a field-worker and an Indian citizen were not so much in terms of collecting data and securing testimonies as much as they were in being able to question my own ignorance about the scale of the tragedy and to absorb and understand the calamitous change I was witnessing. Alongside this, I had to try and come to terms with my fast eroding beliefs and assumptions, which I had so far held and which I had carried into the field, of the Indian state and the Kashmir conflict. The nature of the Indian state, and the nature of this conflict with its devastating implications for people were now unfolding before me. I knew I could not remain neutral or objective any more, although objectivity in research is much valued but here it was imperative for me to take a position – politically and emotionally – and it soon became clear to me where and on whose side I stood: by the side of the people and their struggle for justice.

When I first heard someone say to me that when he left home in the morning, he was not certain whether he would return alive, I took it as a stray comment, his individual anguish. But it soon became a refrain, a collective anguish of a people learning to live 'normally' in the midst of the most abnormal and traumatic situation. I remember how deeply shaken I was as I encountered that comment again and again, reinforcing how dispensable and frail life was in Kashmir and how it was taken for granted elsewhere. Women breaking down during interviews, sobbing, falling silent, left me helpless and speechless too as I tried to fathom the depths of their loss and grief. These moments have stayed with me. I remember how, in some families, young, teenaged children would try and fill in the gaps in their mothers' narratives whenever the mothers broke down. These children had grown up listening to stories of violence from their mothers, fathers, and grandparents. In a strange kind of irony, women, who were normally silent even inside families, had begun to break their silence. Now they talked all the time, and in doing so they renewed the never-to-forget pledge of Kashmir, and also somehow created a kind of healing.

I did not realise – until much later—how their pain and trauma was beginning to affect me and leave an impact on me. Was it secondary trauma that I suffered? Did I need professional counselling, as some colleagues and friends began to suggest? I remember how, in the initial phase of fieldwork, I would be haunted by images I had seen, words and sounds I had heard long after I returned home. I lost my sleep and appetite, I would break down every time I spoke about Kashmir and its people. Over the years, as it became my second home, I also found joy, confidence, emotional strength, and contentment.

What helped me deal with my own trauma – without being aware of it then – was the close friendships and relationships that I had forged over the years and most importantly, the resilience of ordinary people. They helped me to not only cope but also understand and assimilate this emotionally destabilizing experience into my everyday life through a process of shared reflections. I was struck by how much the people of Kashmir had suffered, and how they offered the utmost optimism and generosity to me even in the face of extreme hardship. They anchored and grounded me in a way that was not possible elsewhere – it had to be in their midst, in the midst of collective trauma that I could find my own emotional and psychological balance. My adoptive houseboat family in particular became my anchor. Rasheed Bhai, who I have spoken of earlier, despite having lived through violence and trauma himself, travelled with me to distant villages, took keen interest in my work, asked me questions that helped me clarify so many doubts. His family provided me a home, support, understanding and warmth that nurtured me and helped me to comprehend on my own terms how I was affected by the violence I saw, the moving narratives I heard, and how to deal with my feelings of being a victim, a participant and an observer. At the end of the day – however difficult or traumatic the day had been, I always returned to the emotional safety and the 'warm embrace' of the family, just as most people in Kashmir would – except that a home in Kashmir is not necessarily a safe haven for its inhabitants.

Today, Kashmir continues to fester given the Indian state's rigid stance and its repressive anti-people policies along with its refusal to accept its own role and responsibility in prolonging the conflict. I believe that the process of political resolution in Kashmir is contingent upon the Indian state's acknowledgement of the truth and its recognition of the urgent need for justice for victims and survivors, not just a few people but almost an entire population. The unresolved political conflict, along with the unresolved collective trauma of Kashmir's people, is not only a challenge but also a threat to India's own democracy.

❆ ❆ ❆

This book is based on personal interviews, group discussions, information and stories that women and men – young and old – shared with me over a long period of time. We spoke together about their lived experience of direct and indirect violence and how it affected their everyday lives as well as the psychological impact it had on them, their families and society. The issues of privacy and rights violation in the face of increased militarization of civilian spaces, gendered violence, women's mobilization for justice and accountability, were some of the integral features of research. Given the complex nature of the conflict, the research felt like peeling many layers to see what lay beneath. I was always conscious of the moral and political dilemmas that arose for me as an 'outsider' placed in an existential situation of violence, loss and resistance amidst those who had experienced it. Where does the researcher stand in relation to the researched – particularly in a conflict zone, a militarized zone within the borders of your own country? Does one have to be an insider to be able to understand and write about the deeply complex situation of Kashmir and its women? I did not know then how my own involvement in the field and with women would become deeper over the years. I was beginning to learn about the inherent complications and contradictions that defined the nature of the conflict.

I highlight voices from the field and privilege women's voices. Over the years, I sort of became an intimate part of the 'field' of my research, and in the writing, I now often find my voice embedded – in greater or lesser degree – in that of the people I spoke to. This journey has been both personal and political for me. I must say that I did not go into the field with the intention of writing this book. It began to take shape gradually in my mind as I met people and collected substantial material mainly through in-depth interviews with a cross section of people to gauge the extent to which their everyday lives had changed and how they coped with it. This book is also about what this sharing meant for me as a woman researcher and how deeply it affected me and shaped my own political understanding.

My personal involvement with the people and the place deepened with each visit, the closeness and proximity bringing in its wake questions that I had to address. At a broader level, the questions I was grappling with had to do with what have come to be seen as acceptable research methods: what did these mean in a context where notions of objectivity and the need for a 'scientific' methodology seemed totally redundant? The conflict had massively impacted people, its consequences were not restricted to a particular area or a particular people. I soon realized that I was going to have to let a method, if at all there were to be one, evolve as I went along; none of the existing accepted and acceptable methods seemed adequate to the realities I saw around me. In a place marked by such acute uncertainty, the outcome of every visit was contingent upon the situation as it prevailed then. At a more personal level, my difficulties had to do with dealing with my own learning and unlearning as well as my emotional and intellectual churning, and the question of how best to process what I had seen, heard or witnessed. In the eighteen years since I first began my fieldwork, much has changed in Kashmir and yet so much has remained the same. My life too has gone through many changes – both positive and negative – from the birth of my grandchildren to the deaths of close family members and friends. There was much for me to learn in Kashmir, and in a strange way, the process of learning helped me deal with my own personal loss (or gain), away from Kashmir. Other than grief and mourning, it was every individual or collective act of defiance and resistance that I witnessed on the streets or within homes in Kashmir that opened one more way for me to understand the extraordinary human spirit of its people and find fellowship in it.

✼ ✼ ✼

It was in 1999 that I began a research study on the gender dimensions of violent conflict (with Oxfam India Trust's VMAP programme). This study took me to different parts of India where caste-based, communal, or ethnic violence had occurred. I looked at the specific ways in which women experienced and coped with direct or indirect forms of mass violence and how it played out in their daily lives. A year into the study, I made my first research visit to Kashmir. What I saw there was remarkably different from what I had seen elsewhere in the country. It is not that there were no commonalities, but in Kashmir, the massive deployment of security forces created an unprecedented situation in which all men were considered prime suspects and many of them were routinely roughed up, tortured and even disappeared, leaving women and families even more vulnerable. It was as if the people were the enemy – the state's relationship with them was, and continues to be, expressed in harsh, discriminatory and military terms, with hardly any space for political negotiation or settlement.

I was reminded of the decade of the seventies when I had first begun work as an activist and a researcher. It was a politically significant time for people of my generation. Indira Gandhi, the then Prime Minister, had declared a State of Emergency and there was political and civil unrest all over the country. Indians were suddenly stripped of their fundamental and democratic rights and civil liberties. There was massive state repression and large-scale violence that led to fear and uncertainty among ordinary people, many of whom were thrown into jails or detained randomly, on mere suspicion of some undefined 'anti-national' activities. I remember how people's resistance, their sustained campaigns and mass struggles marked this turbulent period that also took me into its fold because, in a strange way, it had affected my own family in an extraordinary manner.[2] I mention it here for the simple reason that the harsh memories of Emergency resurfaced for me as I began to witness what was unfolding in front of me in Kashmir – although the fundamental difference was that while the Emergency lasted for less than two years in India, in Kashmir a state of Emergency seemed to be a continuing phenomenon, with far greater and much graver implications for the people. Yet for many years we, the citizens of India, paid hardly any attention to what was happening in 'one of the most militarized regions' of the world where the state seemed to have abdicated its responsibility towards its citizens and, where 'the ordinary processes of law remain(ed) suspended.'[3]

My fieldwork in Kashmir began in the summer of 2000; a decade after militancy had begun. At the time, I was returning to Kashmir after a gap of twenty years – the last visit had been personal, when my six-year old daughter and I came to visit my father (a professor of Philosophy at Osmania University in Hyderabad) who was at the Iqbal Institute in Kashmir University for a year. He lived on campus in a simple, comfortable home that was surrounded by tall chinar trees overlooking the majestic snow-capped mountains and amidst neighbours who were friendly, warm and hospitable. I can quite easily recall the sense of joyous wonder with which my daughter explored and absorbed the beauty and peace that surrounded us. The people we met and became friends with during our stay at the campus introduced us warmly to the tastes and textures of life in the valley. It was a new world for my daughter whereas I was aware, although distantly, of the rich and rebellious history of the place and the people who lived here. Yet, it also seemed like a new world for me in the sense that the knowledge I had acquired earlier was slowly gaining life and the images I had formed were now becoming more tangible. As I remember, there was no thought or threat of violence then. Everywhere, people worked hard to prepare for the long and severe months of winter. Life was bustling with activity, on the streets, in the fields and within homes. Children could be seen playing games in open fields and playgrounds. Cool evenings drew people out of their homes and some of the main city areas wore an almost festive look.

When I returned twenty years later, I was immediately struck by how much had changed. I still remember the sense of disbelief when I looked around me, despite the cool breeze of the mountains that greeted me on that sunny, warm afternoon. It was clear to me how two decades of militancy and counter-insurgency had wreaked havoc and transformed the landscape. Everywhere, there was widespread material destruction and, as I began to learn, enormous loss of human lives. I felt quite overwhelmed and unnerved by the heavy presence of the military and the armoured vehicles that had taken over the streets, particularly the white 'rakshak' Gypsies used by the army to pick up 'suspects' who could not be seen because the vehicles had no windows. A sinister shadow seemed to loom over everything, including the breathtaking landscape and the people who lived in its midst. On this visit I hardly knew anybody and that added to my dismay. But if anyone had told me then that Kashmir would become my second home one day, I would not have believed them.

In 2000 when I began work, my mother was in the terminal stage of cancer and I visited Kashmir soon after I had lost her to the disease – her pain was intense and so was my suffering. Personally, I was grief-stricken but also aware that the 'Kashmir project' was inordinately delayed as I had chosen to stay by my mother's side during her illness. Every time Kashmir came up in our conversations, she would remind me, half in jest, that there was no greater project in life for a child than to be with her mother when death was imminent.

Her words rang in my ears as I began to meet bereaved individuals and families where death had made its mark. It was as though the grief of my mother's passing had prepared me in a way to plunge myself into a 'field' where people were coping with unimaginable challenges on a daily basis. When I look back, the foremost memory I have of that time is of sharing my grief with people I met and in return, experiencing the warmth of their collective grief and the understanding that decades of violence and loss had generated. My personal sorrow found a new meaning and location in their midst; I felt better prepared to deal with it in Kashmir than elsewhere. My individual sense of loss had become deeply enmeshed with their collective one and drew me closer to them.

Although I had been intellectually aware and concerned about the political and humanitarian situation in Kashmir, nothing that I had read, seen or heard had prepared me to witness such a colossal human tragedy. It was the first time in nearly thirty years of conducting research and fieldwork that I had come to work in an armed conflict zone. Questions began to cloud my mind about my own ignorance, my inability to absorb and understand the calamity I was confronted with, and about my own role as a researcher. How was it that the country that claimed to be the largest democracy in the world, treated its 'own people' in this brutally oppressive manner? How was it that the women's movement, of which I have been a part for so many years, was oblivious to the reality of fellow women in Kashmir? Where was our spirit of enquiry, and our intervention? Where was our solidarity? I wondered whether it would at all be possible for me to gather the required data and secure testimonies from a people so deeply touched by human and material loss. It was apparent that gender roles inside families had drastically changed as thousands of men had been killed and many had become victims of enforced disappearances. Women seemed to have assumed new roles as protectors and providers, many of them first generation workers.

As I engaged with such questions, I realized that I had already begun to share their grief, that I had taken so much for granted earlier; that I had never realized the privilege of my own freedom of movement and speech. Suspicion, trust, citizenship, freedom, democracy, rights; all these terms began to acquire new meanings for me.

I also became aware of how I myself had, perhaps inadvertently, become a victim of the Indian state's propaganda that Kashmir was an 'integral' part of India, but it did not take long for me to realize that this was far from the truth as the people's alienation from India seemed complete. I felt both intellectually and emotionally shaken and vulnerable, as my notion of the state, my own citizenship as well as my core belief in constitutional democracy was challenged as never before. How do I make sense of the overwhelming presence of gun-wielding soldiers against unarmed civilians, 'our own people'? Have I entered a state under military occupation? I knew that as a researcher here and now, as a woman activist, it was not possible for me anymore to be non-partisan or objective – a prerequisite for 'sound and scientific research' but it was a lesson I was ready to unlearn, a risk I was ready to take, however challenging. As I started meeting people, visiting women in their homes and in public, walking closely with them in their quest for justice, I knew that I was already beginning to be on their side. And as I began to listen to their stories, my own began to take shape – the journey of my own learning and unlearning, of the alternating sense of hope and despair, of the trust and courage that I gradually gained from a resilient people, and the warm, unsuspecting welcome and hospitality that I received from them, whether in a remote village or in the city. I remember wondering how a people touched by so much violence could still be so warm, so hospitable and generous. Even though an outsider, I was beginning to feel one with them and over the years, I was able to develop an intimacy with the field that helped me forge deep friendships and become a part of some enduring family relationships.

When I began, it was quite difficult for me to begin to gauge and understand the human reality that lurked behind the political exterior. This was the first time in my life that I was seeing gun wielding soldiers everywhere—on the streets, in market places, in bunkers, among the pedestrians and atop speeding convoys that seemed to signal impending danger; a grave risk for anyone going about their daily chores, a constant reminder of their unequal status, a source of deep humiliation as it seemed to demand their subjugation through brute force and intimidation. It was ordinary people's defiance and resilience, however, that also inspired confidence and courage in me, built trust, and lent a new meaning to my own existence because life in Kashmir was surrounded by violence and death, despite the natural beauty of the landscape. That life was so fragile there and could not be taken for granted was something that came home to me repeatedly and sometimes through direct experience, as when a bomb blast ripped the wall of a building that I had left minutes ago or when I caught myself running for safety with hundreds of others on a busy street where a bomb had exploded nearby. I had just stopped to buy newspapers at a street corner when I heard the blast and was told to run. I realized how such mundane, everyday activities could also spell grave danger or even death. However, what struck me most was how quickly people resumed their activities. Incidents like this were a normal occurrence in their lives – and a rare lesson in mine. People left home accompanied by the thought of death, aware of the possibility that they may not return. I did not know then that this matter-of-fact refrain that I heard everywhere was a symptom of the collective anguish of a community about the uncertainty and fragility of life. I remember how a young man once held out his palm to me and said, this is where I carry my life, it can be blown away any moment. Women mentioned how, as dusk fell, they would wait anxiously at the door for their men to return. Some never did.

Many interviews with women in their homes were marked by silence and tears when I asked them about the loss of their loved ones. At times, it was the opposite, the need to share their grief would impel others to talk and pour their hearts out. It was obvious that hardly any family had been spared and each had a story to tell. The tragedy that they spoke of may have occurred years ago but the memory was raw and festering as women fell silent, wept, and resumed speech if they could. The experience of listening to their stories, to their silences and tears, affected me deeply. It also challenged me as a researcher. Whatever I had read thus far on the conflict in Kashmir related mainly to its historical and political aspects and was rarely about people's lived experiences. Here in the field, in the midst of people who bore the brunt of violence daily, and in the absence of any information, whether official or unofficial about the casualties or the human cost of conflict, the first priority for me was to seek information, gain first-hand knowledge, and to learn from those who were affected and those who worked closely with them. The plight of the people, particularly women and children, traumatized as a result of continuing violence, was something I had not read about then as it had not yet received the attention and concern that it deserved. One could sense and see the extent of state repression and its grip over people's lives, the extent of militarization in the name of national security and territorial integrity, and one could see how it had snatched away people's basic rights, including their fundamental right to life. To live with dignity and without fear was a goal that people had to strive for on a daily basis but the perpetual threat of violence reinforced their insecurity and vulnerability and quite paradoxically, their resilience too. The daily hardships people faced defied imagination. It seemed that people's capacity to cope with tragedy was challenged on a daily basis.

❀   ❀   ❀

In my subsequent visits, I travelled extensively, covering all the districts and my journey also took me to certain 'marked' villages such as the 'village of the raped women' (Kunan Poshpora) and the 'village of the widows' (Dardpora). Never before had I visited such villages anywhere that were defined by the mass violence that had been unleashed against their inhabitants – men, women and children. As I travelled, it became apparent that there was a near total structural breakdown of services everywhere, particularly health services in the rural areas. The security forces had occupied many of the civilian buildings, including schools, community halls and hospitals. At district level hospitals and primary health centres, the staff were often conspicuous by their absence, particularly women staff, and especially nurses. The heavy presence of the security forces on the streets, and in the lanes and by-lanes instilled fear among people and posed a real threat of violence. A block medical officer in a village casually remarked to me that although he had the authority to ensure that the staff reported for work, he hesitated, knowing that he could not ensure safety for the women staff. How could he, when he himself had been picked up once by the army and subjected to torture merely because he had treated young men who had approached him with gun wounds? Was it not his duty as a doctor to treat anyone who came to him, irrespective of whether the person was a militant or not, he asked me. If a professional doctor like him could be detained, interrogated and tortured (he described to me how each of his finger nails had been pulled out inside the interrogation centre) imagine the plight of ordinary people, the majority of whom were traumatized, he reminded me.

Through all this, a question that confronted me was: how does one measure the trauma, the psychological impact of violence? I realized that other than the records in the psychiatric hospital, the extent of trauma that people had experienced had to be elicited through narratives of their everyday lives. The word trauma was used by everyone without necessarily recognizing its symptoms or understanding the need for treatment. One look at the staggering figures of casualties explains the widespread trauma suffered by people and why they referred to it so frequently. A senior psychiatrist had mentioned to me how particularly complicated the grief of the families of the disappeared was and therefore how difficult to understand or treat as the whereabouts of these men were unknown and their bodies untraced. Their wives (half widows) and children could not claim to be beneficiaries of the official relief and rehabilitation that was available to other widows and orphans – except for a one-time ex-gratia relief which, if they accepted, would bar them officially from registering a case against the disappearance. The half widows' livelihood and survival were critical in this context. Understanding the trauma that they suffered was a challenge in the sense that they experienced their loss and the resulting grief as a constant. There could be no closure for them in the absence of the dead body of their loved ones. In fact, the majority of the population suffered from common symptoms of stress and among them 25 per cent were diagnosed with clinical depressive disorders, as revealed by the records of the government hospital for psychiatric diseases in Srinagar. This affected women's lives and their health in significant ways. Tending to those who were 'ill' in the family, as mothers, wives and daughters, women bore the maximum burden as caregivers, often at the cost of their own health. According to a psychiatrist I met at the hospital: 'Women here are biologically predisposed and psychologically more vulnerable. Conflict is one of the major reasons for the increase in psychological problems among Kashmiri women. They are the commonest survivor group that is left behind with the responsibility of their children.' As survivors, women have borne the brunt of trauma of losing their men, and this is one of the major causes of depression among them.

❀   ❀   ❀

Prior to fieldwork, I had to weigh a few options about the different possibilities of doing the kind of research I was set to undertake. Because of people's resentment and loss of faith in the government and its lack of accountability, I made a conscious decision not to collaborate with any of its agencies. This helped me, and the organization I worked with, gain credibility and trust among the people. The nature of the work demanded that I identify and collaborate with local NGOs and professionals. These were doctors, lawyers, teachers, community volunteers, who worked with the affected people. For us, it was important to build these local level partnerships. In that way we could strengthen each other's work and provide whatever minimum relief was possible; we could also document and disseminate information by working on the ground with these organizations and building local teams of doctors and community volunteers at the urban, community and village levels to deal effectively with issues of health and mental health. We included in this specialized care for traumatized children such as pediatric psychiatric care, to document their health status and create a database which we felt was badly needed. It was important to also reach out to the youth and for this I visited many colleges where teachers were often generous in providing time with students between their classes. Among the many memorable exchanges with students, I recall a few that jolted me out of my own assumptions. In one of the classrooms full of young men and women, a young man asked me first of all to spell out explicitly what my own position and understanding was on the 'Kashmir question'. Why, he asked, should he and the other students trust me, an Indian? This prompted a few others to ask me directly whether I was on their side or on the side of the 'Occupation Force'. A young woman student was more concerned about the question of peace; she did not understand the meaning of peace, she said, adding that all she had seen was violence as she grew up. 'The word peace means nothing to me. I am not even able to imagine what it means. It is an empty word for me,' she had said, and I still remember the troubled expression on her face. It was these interactions with students in different colleges that helped me later to mobilize students towards building a team for research as well as a resource centre to take up issues of their interest and concern.

Given the focus of the VMAP/Aman programme and the nature of my research, I realized that it would be difficult for me to do this on my own without the help and support of local people. This research had to be a collaborative effort. At the time of my first few visits, there were only a handful of non-government organizations that existed on the ground but I was able to identify the ones that worked with affected families – although in a situation such as in Kashmir, it is difficult to say or decide who was affected and who was not. The three NGOs that I selected to work with were the Help Foundation (HF) headed by Nighat Shafi, the Hussaini Relief Committee (HRC) led by Sajjad Hussain, along with a core group of members and thousands of volunteers on the ground and the Association of the Parents of the Disappeared Persons (APDP) headed by Parveena Ahangar and Parvez Imroz who had jointly established it in 1994.

With the help and insights I gained from these three organizations, I was able to travel and reach individuals, families and the community of victims and survivors with whom these organizations worked. Apart from conducting time bound surveys to assess the status of women, children and young people, along with the families of the disappeared that we personally visited, we conducted several workshops with different groups of people on mental health issues, particularly the need to understand and recognize the meaning and symptoms of trauma that almost everyone suffered from. Since children and young women were not brought to the psychiatric hospital, we set up a Child Guidance Clinic in Srinagar with Help Foundation with a team of psychiatrists and interns from the government medical college, to cater to the mental health needs of this vulnerable group. We managed to advertise it through newspapers and within a few months, children were being brought here from different districts by their relatives. I remember how I felt both distressed and hopeful at the same time because here was a special facility we had 'successfully' initiated for vulnerable children but their sheer numbers reflected the grim reality that was Kashmir.

As I have noted earlier, the health infrastructure at the time, particularly in rural areas, had virtually collapsed. With the help of HRC, who were well known and well thought of in the area, we were able to initiate an innovative project of health care. A group of local villagers offered us a piece of land to build a health centre that would also cater to twenty surrounding villages in Baramulla that had no health facilities. This centre became a sort of landmark as we were able to build a local team of professionals as well as volunteers who looked after it on a daily basis to provide much needed care. Within the first year of its existence, hundreds of patients, including women, had availed of the facilities. The lack of clean and potable water in the villages meant that many of the women came with complaints of skin rashes as they used the streams or even stagnant water to clean utensils or wash clothes. Some of them also suffered from gynecological problems. Another common complaint was gastro-intestinal problems as well as dental infections.

Sadly, unforeseen developments during the following years led to the closure of the health centre: HRC split vertically into three different factions down to the village level and this raised the question of ownership of the building and the medical equipment that we had managed to put together. This was a difficult lesson we learnt, we had not taken these aspects into account when we initiated the project. An additional concern raised by local villagers had to do with a 'mixed team' where men and women worked together at the centre. People suggested it would be better to have an all-male team.

The 'warring' factions ensured that the health centre was locked along with the equipment and the only options available to us were either litigation or to rent a place in a nearby village to run the centre – we chose the latter and it functioned until recently but could not be sustained, particularly after the coordinator (Sajjad) passed away.

In addition to these initiatives, a research project was initiated with a small group of students from Kashmir University to document the lived experience of violence and its impact on the educated, unemployed youth. The group of students made extensive field visits to different colleges, covering all districts, conducting discussions and in-depth interviews with 100 fellow students. This was followed by several workshops where students from different colleges participated and prepared a detailed report documenting their collective experience.[4] Following this and in the absence of any student union or forum in colleges, the students set up a resource centre for debates, discussions, film screenings and seminars in a rented space but within a few months there were objections from neighbours against young men and women meeting 'freely without teachers or guardians' until the owner of the premises was forced to shut it down.

Working with local NGOs and the community helped us understand the importance of being more sensitive to their larger concerns, especially in relation to the prevalent social, behavioural and cultural norms, and particularly within the political dynamics of a militarized state. Even as we tried to introduce new ideas and practices of working as a team in a more egalitarian manner and with a focus on gender equality, it was, at times, a dilemma to maintain that critical balance, to ensure that we did not succumb to any conservative pulls and pressures that could have a negative bearing on our work. In a team that included women, we realized how they were constantly under close scrutiny by the community at the village level, whether it was the clothes they wore or their attitude or how they related to their male colleagues. Since no work could be sustained without popular community support, it was critical for us to maintain an active link with the community in terms of both its participation and collective decision-making. In the urban student centre too, it was the community gaze that determined whether the project could be sustained or not, particularly where young local women and men had come together to work under one roof. The fact is that the student resource centre had to be shut down mainly for this reason as questions were raised as to whether it was morally correct for young women and men to spend time together away from their colleges and homes. This was considered to be an outcome of an 'alien culture' and was therefore to be resisted. There was also the issue of social and political dynamics that operated locally that could 'make or break' a project, a team, and even an organization – as we learnt through the course of our work. How do we intervene in a situation like this, which has a direct impact on our work? It has been our experience that after having worked closely with some organizations, we found ourselves helpless when confronted with a break-up of the organization and the consequent polarization among its team members. In an interesting case, a woman co-founder of an organization believed that she was the one who truly represented the organization rather than her male colleague as she was a 'victim' and therefore entitled to represent other victims. Her victimhood as well as her sense of agency became paramount in this.

We found that there was an inherent tension in attempts to resolve such a crisis and questions of loyalty and ownership became critical, where in the latter material resources were also in question. Moreover, depending on the priorities of a local organization, the design, concept and nature of a collaborative project, initiated by an outside NGO, could undergo significant and radical changes. This was our experience regarding the child guidance clinic that we had set up with a local NGO. Although the first of its kind in terms of its reach among traumatized children and the documentation of their mental health status, it was subsumed under the larger programmes and expansion of the organization over a period of time. The question we had to deal with was: do we, as outsiders, withdraw or shift our focus as well? The decision was left to the local team of doctors and the concerned organizations, as they were responsible for the implementation of the programme.

Apart from the organizations I have mentioned above, many individuals also helped me in reaching out to women in their homes: a shikara-wala ferrying me across the lake, an auto rickshaw driver, a shopkeeper, a student, a receptionist at a hotel counter, and a clerk in a government department being a few of them. Each of them took a keen interest in my work and as soon as I told them the reason why I had come, the response was usually quite overwhelming as each one would first share with me their own story or that of their family and then would refer me to others they knew. It was in this way that word had also begun to spread of an 'Indian Muslim woman' travelling around and asking questions/talking to people wherever she went. The question of trust (mutual or otherwise) often cropped up as I went along. A chance meeting with a clerk in a government department, who later helped me to reach some of the women who had been directly impacted by the conflict, comes to mind because someone later told me that it was a grave risk I had taken by trusting him and then going along with him to meet the women. Trust, as I was beginning to learn, was a casualty in the given political climate and young men were particularly suspect, not only in the eyes of the state but also amongst others, be they professionals or even family members, as they were prone to join the ranks of the militants or were militants. One morning I set off for the tehsil (district) office of the Social Welfare Board in Srinagar where I knew that many of the widows or women whose husbands or sons had been killed visited with their case files to pursue the ex-gratia relief or other state 'benefits' that they were entitled to. The office was busy with women carrying worn-out files containing details of their cases when I noticed a young girl who had accompanied her widowed mother. They had come to register her mother's claim under 'the militancy victim scheme'. They had been unaware of any government scheme until their neighbour told them about this one and they had come to see if they could at least begin the process, which was cumbersome to say the least. As I talked to them, I heard a man telling me over my shoulder that this was not the only story of this kind and that it was, in fact, 'har ghar ki kahani' (the story of every household) as violence had touched and transformed every home. As I turned, he introduced himself as a field officer whose job was to visit the women's homes to verify if a killing had indeed taken place, as reported by the women. This way he had access to many of the homes and not only that, he claimed that he had all the information that most officers did not even bother to share. When he heard of my work, he offered to give me whatever information I needed as well as to take me along with him the next day to introduce me to some of the women in their homes. 'You may not get the kind of information you need from this office except the basics', he said. As we met the next day at the appointed hour, he told me that he was taking me to one locality that was the bedrock of militancy in the nineties and that he himself had lived there for many years. Every house here either had a militant within the family or harboured one, he informed me. 'On any given day you would see militants battling the security forces from rooftops or in the by-lanes', he said, adding that the place reverberated with slogans of azadi everywhere. As we set off, this is what he told me: 'You either walk ten steps ahead of me or behind me, not along with me'. When I asked him why, he said, 'For your own safety because I am not sure what the consequences will be if you are seen with me in this mohalla.' Not to lose sight of him I decided to walk behind him, wondering about the possible consequences. The place was dotted with army camps and bunkers while people seemed to be going about their daily lives despite these life-threatening landmarks. It wasn't long before he suddenly stopped in the middle of a somewhat isolated road that was flanked by BSF and CRPF bunkers on either side with a few houses scattered in between. 'Aren't you afraid?' he suddenly turned and asked me. Before I could begin to say anything, came the next few questions in rapid succession: 'How come you trusted me so readily? Why did you agree to come with me when you did not even know anything about me? What if I left you here and walked away? Have you seen the number of lanes around here? Even a local person could get lost. Have you seen those army bunkers? Would you be able to find your way out of here?' More than what I said to him in response, I figured that the questions were his way of warning me against trusting anybody as readily as I had trusted him and perhaps the display of his concern for my own safety. However, he did take me to a few homes where I was able to spend time with the women and talk to them and make more visits subsequently on my own, and the women I met helped me reach out to others in the neighbourhood. A few days later the field officer invited me over to his house for lunch because he wanted to share his own story with me and for me to meet the women in his family and hear how they had survived through the peak of militancy when he had been picked up and tortured by the security forces repeatedly. Later, he had voluntarily surrendered as a militant, not to the authorities but on his own.

Sometimes I went to meet people along with students, some of them male. I found this often raised doubts in the minds of others. Once, I had gone to meet a district medical officer in Baramulla town along with a local research coordinator. As we met at the office and I began to talk to the DMO regarding the purpose of our visit, he asked me to first disclose the identity of 'this young man' and explain why I had come with him when 'he could as well be a militant'.

How was I sure that he was not, asked the DMO, cautioning me in the same breath that I should 'think twice before trusting a young man like him in Kashmir.'

As with trust, information too had become a casualty as I soon learnt. Obtaining official information proved to be an uphill task. Moreover, no census had been undertaken in Kashmir for the last twenty years and the provisional figures of the 2001 census did not reflect the socio-economic changes that the state had undergone since armed conflict began. The staggering figures of the number of those killed, maimed, injured, disappeared, widowed, orphaned that one heard from those working in the field were always at variance with the official figures. The centre and the state government's contribution to the human cost of conflict was neither recognized nor reflected in the official figures. People's willingness to talk and share information was in sharp contrast to the reluctance displayed by several government officials. My enquiries, based on information shared by people on the ground, were often denied or dismissed and the difficulties that people faced in their daily lives were attributed to the 'financial crunch' that most government departments were facing at the time.

I sensed a constant effort among people to come to terms with the changed reality of everyday life and the 'new' identities the conflict had imposed upon them, particularly the large number of women who were now the sole breadwinners in the family. One of the challenges was to bring together members of different local organizations as there was a great deal of suspicion among them. No one really trusted anyone else. In this sense, building local teams was as much a challenge as a rewarding experience.

Many of the people I worked with, particularly women, saw in me a fellow Muslim, embracing me with the words: my Muslim sister, an identity that I myself had not consciously carried in the field. A question that others back home often asked me was whether it helped being a Muslim woman to work in Kashmir and whether people were more receptive to me due to the fact. I, however, marvelled at what I had observed – that despite all the hardship of many years, Kashmiris were warm, welcoming and hospitable to all, irrespective of their religion.

The difficult part of any long-term research is always how to bring the findings together and structure them into a coherent narrative. Like all researchers and writers, I too struggled with this. Should the narrative be constructed chronologically? Should it be focused around themes? After considerable thought, I realized that no structure was perfect and I decided to discard the linear narrative and to put a different structure in place. Thus I begin with an extensive chapter on the experience of the Pandits – for after all, the migration, which many saw as the end of their lives, was in a way also a beginning not only for those who left or were forced to leave, but also for those who stayed behind, whether Muslim or Hindu. I trace their very complex and interrelated experiences before I move on to looking at other, equally complex, but different stories. So from the narrative of the Pandits, I move on to look at the story of women, and structure my story around one or more women who represent a particular situation or story at a given time. Although each story I tell is of a particular woman, it intersects with that of the others as well as the situation pertaining to that particular time and place. I hope that this will also reflect the many changes that have occurred over the years in Kashmir and in the lives of women. I begin by looking at the practice of enforced disappearances through the story of Parveena Ahangar's life and this is followed by the gendered aspect of militancy and women's contribution and participation in it, along with the life stories and trajectories of three women political leaders. The next parts of the book deal with the long-term impact the prolonged conflict has had on the health of the people of Kashmir. My last chapter focuses on a visit I made to Kashmir a few years after I had concluded my research, for a project that looked at sexual violence and the structures of impunity that allow for a lack of accountability. And in my conclusion I address the difficult, sometimes the near impossible, task of bringing my thoughts on this land that has given me both grief and love, together.

NOTES

1. International People's Tribunal on Human Rights and Justice in Indian-administered Kashmir. 2009. 'Buried Evidence: Unknown, Unmarked, and Mass Graves in Indian-administered Kashmir'. Available at: https://jkccs.files.wordpress.com/2017/05/buried-evidence-_report-on-mass-graves.pdf

   Association of Parents of Disappeared Persons (APDP). 2008. 'Facts Under Ground: A Fact-finding Mission on Nameless Graves & Mass Graves in Uri Area.' Available at: https://jkccs.files.wordpress.com/2017/05/facts-under-ground-first-report-on-mass-graves-in-kashmir.pdf

2. My father, Alam Khundmiri, was dismissed from his job as a professor at Osmania University due to his past involvement in the communist movement in Hyderabad. He was later reinstated after he challenged the dismissal in the Hyderabad High Court and won a favourable verdict.

3. Chakravarti, Uma. 2016. 'Introduction: The Everyday and the Exceptional: Sexual Violence and Impunity in Our Times' in *Fault Lines of History, The India Papers II*, pp 1-34. New Delhi: Zubaan.

4. Fazili, Gowhar; Kanth, Idrees; Kashani, Sarwar; Violence Mitigation and Amelioration Project 2013. *The Impact of Violence on the Student Community in Kashmir*, New Delhi: Oxfam India Trust.

chapter one

Fear, Displacement, Departure

THE EXPERIENCE OF THE KASHMIRI PANDITS

In 1989, when militancy began in Kashmir, the Kashmiri Pandits made up around 4 per cent of the population. Over the years, as the clamour for freedom from India gained ground and there was large scale public mobilization on the streets, a sense of fear and uncertainty took hold that eventually led to the sudden migration of the Pandit population. The factors that led to the displacement of the Pandits have their roots in a much wider political context but once migration began, their departure became contentious and any debate around the issue was couched in communal politics of religious identity and ethnicity.

We[1] heard many accounts during our fieldwork of how Kashmiris – both Muslim and Pandit – woke up one morning to find their neighbourhoods deserted as the majority of Pandits had suddenly left. The dark had provided them some cover, and the curfew that had been in place for several days had served to keep others inside their homes. Mutual suspicion seemed to have replaced the 'peaceful co-existence' and the harmony and trust that the two communities shared earlier.

In this chapter, I focus on the experiences and perspectives of the displaced Kashmiri Pandits as well as those who chose to stay back, even though their numbers are small. Their story is part of the larger story of Kashmir, which would otherwise remain incomplete. I write here about their lived experiences: the loss of their homes and their loved ones, and the separation from their Muslim neighbours of many long years. This story is also an account of their resilience and their struggle to regain control of their lives, whether in the migrant camps in Jammu or in rented accommodation elsewhere in the country.

Among the many implications of Kashmiri Pandit migration, their exclusion from census records as a separate and distinct community in Jammu and Kashmir, and outside the state, had a direct bearing on their demographic status. Until 1981, Kashmiri Pandits represented the categories of Hindus living in the Kashmir division. In the year 2001, at the time of the census, more than 95 per cent of the Pandits were no longer living in the Valley and therefore could not be registered there. As a result, there is no accurate information about their total population, the male-female ratio, the rural-urban distribution, the literacy status, age, income and occupational composition. In many ways they are what Dabla calls a 'demographically lost community.'[2]

Estimates regarding the number of those displaced vary vastly and even the statistical information provided by the government can be misleading: the Annual Report of the Ministry of Home Affairs (2016-2017), for example, says: 'at present there are about 60,000 registered Kashmiri migrant families in the country, out of which 40,000 families are residing in Jammu, about 20,000 families are living in Delhi/NCR and about 2,000 families are settled in other states.' Since these figures did not reflect the actual/disaggregated number of migrant families, we looked at the (2005-2006) report – the period of our research – according to which 'there are 56,476 migrant families of whom 34,088 families are in Jammu, 19,338 families in Delhi and 2,050 in other States and Union Territories.' Regarding families that are drawing relief from the government, there are 18,250 eligible families in Jammu and 3,385 in Delhi. Significantly, of the total number of migrants, '22,714 are government employees/pensioners.' These figures indicate that, despite their small numbers in the Valley the 'Kashmiri Pandits held a major chunk of all professional jobs for decades with few Muslims in services or educated even. Kashmiri Pandits dominated such jobs where 80 per cent of the seats were reserved for them. Muslims started to gain education gradually after 1947 and as they progressed, it made Kashmiri Pandits insecure about losing their privileged social and economic dominance, which happened with their mass exodus in 1990.'[3]

The majority of those who migrated came from fairly privileged backgrounds. The sudden displacement was a traumatic experience for them, both at an individual and at a community level. However, it is well known that 65 per cent of the Pandits had built houses in Jammu even prior to militancy and did not have to go to the camps once they migrated. Our research confirmed Dabla's findings that along with class differences, there was a rural-urban divide that characterized migration, with the rural poor finding accommodation in different camps in Jammu – which he termed 'shame accommodation' – while the rich and upper middle class moved to their own houses built prior to militancy, or lived in rented accommodation until they were able to construct their own. Similarly, there were class-based differences in access to education even though 'the Kashmiri Pandit migrants tried to maintain

100 per cent literacy by providing their children education despite the hardships.'[4]

While locating the phenomenon of the displacement of Kashmiri Pandits within the broader political context, I focus here primarily on the experiential aspect of their displacement although the political dynamics of displacement are closely linked to the everyday, ordinary, personal lives of the displaced as the two seem interlinked, despite the controversy surrounding the issue. The use of the term displacement here instead of the more common and official use of the word migration, that implies a voluntary and wilful action on the part of the individual or a community, is deliberate (Dabla 2004). It was instructive for us that the Kashmiri Pandits we interviewed in the camps in Jammu referred to themselves as a displaced community rather than as migrants for the same reason. In response to the National Human Rights Commission (1995) where Pandits had sent a petition demanding that the government extend facilities and rights to them as Internally Displaced Persons (IDPs) by virtue of their displacement, the government argued that the word 'migrant' was a more appropriate description of the status of Pandits since it favours their return when the situation became conducive to it.[5] Interestingly, our fieldwork showed that any talk of Kashmir and its unresolved status invariably led to the question of the return of the Pandits and their rehabilitation, and while there was controversy about the circumstances of their displacement or the numbers involved, there was unanimity of public opinion regarding their honourable return to Kashmir.

There have been many phases prior to militancy when the Pandits have migrated voluntarily to different parts of the country for personal or professional reasons, often to improve their life prospects. At the same time, a large number of Muslims have also been displaced, not only from the border areas at different times due to firing and shelling but also from their homes in Kashmir at the peak of militancy when militants selectively targeted and killed a few prominent members of the Muslim community, as well as some Kashmiri Pandits, on suspicion that they were pro-India or government agents. While figures vary regarding the number of Muslims and Pandits who were displaced, according to Balraj Puri, 'an officially estimated 20,000 Muslim families from the Valley were forced to migrate' at the peak of militancy. However, while there is much written about Pandit displacement, the displacement of Kashmiri Muslims under similar circumstances hardly figures in migration stories – nor have the Muslims been given any facilities or benefits by the government. The question then remains: both communities experienced displacement, why has the state privileged one and ignored the other? Is it just a problem of numbers – the Muslim numbers are smaller as compared to those of the Pandits – or is there something else at work?

Historically, the process of displacement and migration in J&K began with the partition of India in 1947. Our focus, however, is on the recent past, starting with the rise of militancy in the late 1980s. According to the Ministry of Home Affairs, 'the targeted attacks by the militants against civilians in the initial phases of the terrorist violence in J&K forced a vast majority of Kashmiri Pandits and a sizeable number of Sikhs, other Hindus, and a few Muslims to migrate from the Valley in 1990 and thereafter.' While the government acknowledges that such migration took place due to militancy, it does not provide exact numbers for 'others' who also had to migrate. This has also led to strong differences of opinion between both communities on this troubled question. Long past the event, and depending on their vantage point, people often expressed ambivalent views sometimes accompanied by a sense of betrayal, anger and humiliation. We found that migration stories – particularly those that related to relations between the two communities – evoked emotional responses that were both positive and negative.

According to the majority of Kashmiri Muslims that we met, the
Pandits were not forced to leave: they left voluntarily; their departure
was facilitated by the government, which is why the government
did nothing to stop them from fleeing. They believed that Kashmiri
Pandit migration took place under the then governor Jagmohan's
direction and supervision although there was no threat from the
Muslim community, which offered whatever help and support
it could. Although many innocent, prominent Muslims were also
targeted and killed by militants, they asked why there had been no
official recognition of this and why Pandits had never addressed this
issue. Kashmiri Muslims felt they had got a raw deal, and received
none of the benefits Pandits got. Was it because Pandits have always
been a privileged class compared to Muslims even though the latter
have continued to bear the brunt of the army's excesses whereas for
Pandits, their migration was a one-time suffering? According to the
Pandits, they were targeted/killed as an ethnic minority and it was
because of this that they had to flee. When this happened, the state
– the then governor Jagmohan – did not help them but did not stop
them either. They felt betrayed that their Muslim friends had not
alerted them to the movement for azadi or the 'religious' direction it
would take. Many were also of the view that the suffering experienced
by Kashmiri Muslims was of their own making whereas what the
Pandits had to endure was the responsibility of the Muslims: 'Our
suffering is greater as we became homeless in our own land.' Others
claimed that the reason they were displaced was because 'Muslims
wanted our jobs, our land and the orchards.' What is obvious from
these sorts of conflicting narratives is how they are entangled in the
politics of the day and seen differently by each side. Despite the fact
that the events that led to the departure of Kashmiri Pandits are
rooted in a much wider political context, once the Pandits actually
began to leave and their departure became contentious, the entire
debate on displacement came to be seen only in terms of community

and communal identities, and wiped out other socio-economic differences.

Since Jagmohan's role came up in almost all our conversations with Pandits and Muslims, it would be useful here to consider what he had to say regarding the situation just prior to the migration of Pandits and its implications for the Muslims: 'the Kashmiri Pandits are safe targets for militants. There should be strong-arm methods against militants to the extent of frightening the Muslim population through demonstration of the might of the Indian state. Ruthless operations in different localities of Srinagar could be fruitful counter-insurgency operations. But in some areas, there is mixed population and Pandits may become targets of security forces.'[6] When we interviewed Balraj Puri in Jammu (2006), he told us that Jagmohan had personally told him that the 'Kashmiri Pandits had become soft targets of the militants and hence they must leave as this would create a conducive environment to eliminate militancy in Kashmir', adding that 'Jagmohan started facilitating Kashmiri Pandits to leave the Valley.'

✳   ✳   ✳

Given the sensitive nature of the subject, the primary method we used for data collection was qualitative research as it has the potential to 'reveal complexities of an experience and provide vivid descriptions that are nestled in a real context.' Qualitative data, with its emphasis on people's lived experience is 'well suited for locating the meanings people place on the events, processes and structures of their lives… and for connecting these meanings to the social (and political) world around them.'[7]

As we undertook this journey, we were concerned about how our story of the 'exodus' of Kashmiri Pandits would be different from others. A review of literature at the beginning of the study (2005), though not exhaustive, revealed that, barring a few scholarly works, most studies thus far had focused mainly on the communal rather than the political dimensions of the displacement, and on the victimization of the Pandits as a religious minority at the hands of the majority community. Moreover, many of the studies originated and ended at the camps in Jammu, focusing only on the living conditions there, and did not address the rich and complex social relations between Kashmiri Pandits and Kashmiri Muslims, choosing instead to stay within the rhetoric of Islamic fundamentalism, Muslim terrorism, genocide, ethnic cleansing and the exodus. The voices and the subjective experiences of Pandit families who had decided to remain in the Valley were almost totally absent in the literature. And this despite the fact that they shared a similar reality with Kashmiri Muslims, whether in terms of livelihood issues, official apathy, or their experience of violence and insecurity in everyday life. It was for this reason that, while our main aim was to document the lived experiences of the displaced Pandit community in one of the camps in Jammu, we decided to initiate the study from the Valley instead where some Pandit families had chosen to stay back. This, we felt, would help us gain a more nuanced understanding of the personal as well as the social and grasp the political ramifications of the mass displacement as it occurred in the different lanes, by-lanes, neighbourhoods and localities of Kashmir. We were also keen to extend our research further to trace the starting point of the departure of those who left, to map their subsequent journeys, to understand how, even in neighbourhoods that had faced threats and intimidation, some people had chosen to stay back, and to document the different experiences of both as well as their interactions with their Muslim neighbours. We also tried to observe and document, for a deeper and more humane understanding, the remnants and landmarks of their departure: abandoned homes, fields and orchards. Who better than their long time neighbours – both Kashmiri Pandits and Muslims – to help us understand the impact of mass displacement and the many consequences both at the family (personal) and community (social) level?

The fieldwork lasted one year and six months – from March 2005 to September 2006, interrupted briefly because of the massive earthquake. Subsequently, we were able to make several repeat visits to Kashmir and to keep in touch with people we had interviewed. Thus we were able to follow up on developments in their lives. Keeping in mind the qualitative nature of the study we tried to keep the key sample size small, not exceeding 15 interviews each in two camps in Jammu. In Kashmir, we conducted 20 interviews with resident (non-migrant) Pandits in six districts where a number of them have continued to live. Another set of people we interviewed included professionals, academics, trade union workers and community volunteers, both Kashmiri Muslims and Pandits; men and women, in Jammu as well as in Kashmir. These interviews preceded the more intensive ones with Pandit families and were more in the nature of a consultation on the question of displacement and their perspective on it. This helped us gain clarity regarding some of the details of the experience of displacement from their homes and their arrival in camps in Jammu. In an environment where resentment and a sense of breached trust between both communities were still palpable after more than two decades of the event, this was an essential part of our research.

We used a semi-structured interview format with the camp residents in Jammu mainly because it provided more flexibility, and was conducted with a fairly open framework that allowed for focused, conversational, two-way communication. It was less intrusive and allowed the interviewee the scope to ask questions of the interviewer.[8] We did not use an interview format with the Pandit families who remained in Kashmir. Their narratives were based on a few simple questions such as why they had decided to stay back when the majority of their community had left, and so on. We also

asked them if they could recall the situation that had prevailed then
and whether they had been witness to the en-masse migration of
their own community. These simple questions led us to many other
aspects of the Kashmiri Pandit story as it unfolded in Kashmir as well
as in Jammu.

The interview format we used covered a range of themes such
as: (a) the socio-economic background both prior to and post their
displacement, (b) the migration profile in terms of the circumstances
that prevailed at the time of migration as well as details of their
journey, (c) the status of children/the younger generation in
relation to education and employment opportunities and their
future prospects, (d) gender roles and livelihood issues, e) political
perceptions regarding the conflict and militancy in J&K, including
the role of the state (f) their social interaction/relationship with
Kashmiri Muslims and the meaning and interpretation of azadi
and (g) government schemes and facilities regarding their living
conditions, relief measures, access to healthcare and the prospect of
their return and rehabilitation. While touching upon these issues,
our attempt was also to highlight, through people's narratives, aspects
of the dynamic relations between Kashmiri Muslims and Pandits,
which are often depicted as hostile or communal, particularly post
migration. The experience and voice of the resident Pandits is what
we now begin with as our journey was from the Pandit mohallas in
Kashmir to the camps in Jammu.

The Ones Who Did Not Go: Kashmiri Pandits in the Valley

At the time of our study, there were 6,667 Pandits living in Kashmir
but as we found, by 2011 their number had dwindled to 2,700–
3,400 – and remains more or less the same today (at the time of

writing).[9] According to Sanjay Tickoo, president of the Kashmiri Pandit Sangharsh Samiti (KPSS),

> ...the figures reveal that the Kashmiri Pandit population in the Valley is still draining out and obviously it is not for security reasons but clearly indicates that the state and central governments have failed in restoring their faith in the community and nothing positive has been done to stop this (migration) effectively. The dwindling population of KPs in Kashmir says a lot about the apathy they continue to face at the hands of successive governments.

Many resident Pandits we met in Kashmir reiterated Tickoo's point about government apathy and the complete lack of concern for their welfare as compared to that of the migrant Pandits. They believed that the government was discriminatory as it had done nothing for them while spending crores of rupees to provide various benefits to migrant Pandits, including financial assistance and reservation of educational seats for their children in different states.

It is noteworthy that while the experience of Kashmiri Pandits is always understood in terms of their displacement, the experience of those who decided to stay behind, though much closer to that of Kashmiri Muslims, remains on the margins or neglected. When we travelled one morning from Srinagar to village Chaudhrigund in Shopian to meet Omkarnath Thakur, a retired teacher personally known to two of our Kashmiri Muslim friends, we saw a row of abandoned homes on the way that were in a state of dilapidation and decay with a few doors still fastened with locks but with open windows. One could sense the hurried departure of the families who must have left, hoping to return home someday soon. Omkarnath welcomed us warmly, embracing his Muslim friends who he was meeting after many years and we could see how closely he identified with them as they began to talk animatedly in their own language,

Kashmiri. Once we settled down and told him the purpose of our visit, he shared many details of the time of migration but was visibly upset that like him, the other Pandits who stayed back did not seem to exist for the government. This is what he had to say:

> The government said it will give a job to all the Kashmiri Pandits who have stayed back, but we still haven't got jobs or any other benefit. So what is the use of also giving promises to people who have left when we ourselves who stayed back have got nothing? We stayed through such difficult times and have got nothing. No government official has ever visited us in all these years; there is no army or police to protect us. We have no reservations here, no scheme for education for our children. The way the Kashmiri Muslims are here, so are we. We share similar problems. I never expected the government to do anything, nor do I expect it to do anything in the future. I stayed back because I have ancestral land here that I did not want to leave behind. People who left have got better opportunities and done well for themselves. They are better off than us. I do feel that I made a mistake by not leaving. I went through difficult times here and what did I get? My sons' education suffered due to my decision to stay back. With better education they would have had a better future indeed.

Like him, the only regret many Pandits who had stayed back had was for the future of their children. They worried about how their educational and employment opportunities had been impacted because of the uncertain and violent situation in Kashmir, they were concerned at the collapse of the education system. 'The atmosphere was such that colleges would remain closed for days', recalled Omkarnath. 'And due to firing and blasts the village bridge had been blown up. How could our children travel then? Whoever went out had to face security checks and searches. Other Pandits living outside

Kashmir did not have to go through this and they have been lucky to receive good education, especially technical education.' Another reason attributed to the disruption in education was that large numbers of Pandit teachers had left and those who had stayed behind were not interested in teaching anymore. 'Kashmiri Pandit teachers are most sorely missed in schools', said a young man, Veerji Kaul, who lived in the same mohalla. As Sanjay Tickoo had pointed out to us earlier, 'the government should have tried to rehabilitate us first as we decided to stay back despite facing many hardships and lack of security. We have continued to stay here because of our Muslim friends and colleagues who provided us with a sense of safety. They in fact helped us survive through the worst periods of militancy. There existed mutual support and understanding between us.'

As we met more Kashmiri Pandits, we realized that it was important to also be attentive to the problems of those who had stayed on: homelessness, for example, dogged them too and they experienced not only fear, insecurity and a sense of loss, but also dispossession and homelessness as they moved from villages to towns or from their own homes to those of relatives or friends in search of safety and security. In fact, the government had approached Kashmiri Pandit Sangharsh Samiti (KPSS) to help move some of the Pandit families from rural to urban areas and according to Sanjay, 24 families were moved from Budgam to Srinagar and 63 families were locally displaced within Srinagar during different phases of militancy: 'Many of these families had to put up with other Pandit families or with relatives or had to rent houses in safer localities. These people who were locally displaced became the worst sufferers although hardly anybody talks about them. The government has done nothing for them after having promised to pay their rent and provide them with other relief measures but they have been forgotten and left to fend for themselves.' In 1998, after the massacre at Sangrampora in Budgam district where eight Kashmiri Pandits were killed, 23 families were relocated from remote villages of the district to Budgam town.

We met a few families from that time. At the time of our visit, 226 Pandits lived there and had been provided with CRPF security. Most of them had earlier owned land, orchards or both, these were now unattended and rotting because, as they said: 'The government has forgotten about us, and our land in the villages. We have been dumped here with hardly any facilities.' Four families lived in one double-storied house (two families on each floor) with one room for each family, and they shared a common living room and kitchen. Not all the families were from the same village. Budgam is the only district/town where the government had intervened to move Pandit families here for reasons of safety, and they were accommodated in houses that were earlier abandoned by the Pandits who had already migrated. As promised by the government, this was meant to be a temporary arrangement but families who lived there told us that it seemed to have become their permanent abode, where they now felt like they were in an extended family. The house was situated on the main road, and was flanked by a CRPF post with three soldiers on guard. We met and interviewed Nanaji, who had moved there with his family in 1998. He began by telling us that given the pathetic condition of their lives, he had stopped casting his vote in the elections: 'There is no point in it. Who or what would I vote for? None of us in this village votes any more. What does the government do that we must vote for them?' His neighbour, a middle-aged woman from the floor above, joined us when she heard that we had come from Srinagar to meet them. She and her family had also been moved there at the same time as their neighbours. She spoke little but did say that she missed her village and her relatives, many of whom had migrated to Jammu. She also missed her vegetable garden in the village and was unhappy that she now had to buy vegetables from the market. Nanaji shared many stories with us but pointed out how they remained outside the ambit of government benefits or facilities, despite many promises. In his words: 'My family came here in 1998 at the request of the government. We are from village Chitrudanganpura. Thirty eight other families from rural areas were shifted here that year. Apart from two families who returned to the village, the rest have continued to stay on. It was after the Wandhama killings of Pandits that the government decided to shift us here.' Nanaji's narrative made it amply clear that it was the Kashmiri Muslims who had helped the Pandits, not only as they left but also after they had arrived at the new location.

When we were leaving, our Muslim neighbours helped us pack and load things on trucks to get to Budgam. They were upset that we had decided to leave. They still insist that we return, but we are settled here now. We left our lands and houses in the village to come and stay here in houses left by the Pandits who had migrated earlier in 1990. The government told us we would be safer here and that employment would be provided for our families, also that we would get help with educational expenses for our children. When we moved, the government gave us a one-time amount of Rs. 2,000 for each child's education. What kind of education is possible with this amount? We had no problems in the village; it was only because of the government assurance that we left. But the government has forgotten us. They have done nothing for us. The promised employment never came. And now we cannot go back either because all our Pandit neighbours and friends have left. We cannot sell our land because prices have fallen so much. It was fertile land but has been rotting since there is no one to take care of it. Once I retire, we will have nothing to live on. I have a son and two daughters who are employable but if they do not get any jobs, we will have no option but to

leave Kashmir, like others. The policy of the government
is such that it is obvious they are trying to get the few
Pandits living here to also leave the valley. We are not
safe staying with India. *Suraj ke kareeb aane se jal jate
hain, hamara bhi wohi hua hai.* The closer we have got
to the sun (India), the more we have got singed. Did you
see the CRPF stationed downstairs for our safety? We
have managed to remain safe here only because of the
Muslims and not the CRPF. Muslims have protected us
but we have become security bunkers for the CRPF. The
CRPF cannot be attacked, unless we are.

Interestingly, his daughter said something, which echoed what
a few Shia Muslims in Srinagar had told us about the sympathetic
bond between them as a minority community in Kashmir and
the Kashmiri Pandits. Nita said that one of the reasons she felt
'comfortable and secure in Budgam was because it had a sizeable
Shia population, another minority like us.'

The Decision to Stay Back

Ganpatyar in Srinagar was a Pandit-dominated locality until 1990
when the majority of the families there decided to leave because they
were facing mounting militant violence. The narrow lanes in the
area are flanked by abandoned homes which were either dilapidated
or in a state of disrepair at the time of our visit. The temple, located
on the main road, with the river Jhelum on the one side, led into
the mohalla where some of the Pandit families continued to live. A
tailor in a shop across from the temple greeted us and told us how he,
a Muslim, was entrusted with the temple keys for more than forty
years. He told us that he opened the temple doors each morning for
all those years but everything changed after 1990. 'Even the fabric

and design of the clothes in my shop has changed,' he said, adding that the majority of his clients now were Muslim women; the Pandit women no longer came to get clothes stitched. He remembered well the hustle-bustle of the streets before the migration, but his greatest sadness was for the loss of the privilege of opening the temple door each morning.

Sanjay Tickoo accompanied us and introduced us to some families in the area. We first met Bhushan Lal and Lalitha who lived on the first floor of a small, one-room house opposite the Ganpatyar temple. Other than their one room, there was a tiny makeshift kitchen and an abandoned cattle-shed adjacent to the house, which served as a bathroom and toilet. The Hindu Welfare Society helped them to move here after their house down the lane was gutted in an accident in 1994. Their room was earlier part of the temple, and was used by the head priest to store many rare Kashmiri Pandit manuscripts and it doubled as a reference library. The room still had two small cupboards built into the wall with books and papers chaotically dumped in them. 'These are the only ones left from the ancient texts,' said Bhushan Lal, 'all the rest were robbed and sold during the peak of militancy when thefts had become common.' The broken locks on the cupboards and the cracked glass on the shelves had not been repaired or replaced, perhaps as a reminder of those times. The couple greeted us warmly. 'Our biggest *paap* (sin) was that we were born in India', said Bhushan Lal as we began to talk. 'People less educated, but politically connected are all in high positions in the government or at least have jobs unlike most Kashmiri Pandits and many Kashmiri Muslims who are educated yet frustrated because of unemployment and government apathy.' He recalled how relations between the two communities had become strained during the peak of militancy: 'Initially, at the peak of militancy the Hindus and Muslims did not talk to each other but our *humsayas* (neighbours) told us to stay at home for our own safety. It was very sudden.

One day we were friends and the next day they wouldn't even talk to us, perhaps for fear of being branded informers. Pakistan played a crucial role by pumping Kashmir with money and arms but those who gave their lives were not Pakistanis but Kashmiri Muslims. It was the Pandits and Muslims here who faced the consequences of army crackdowns and killings – over a lakh of *us* have died as a result. Our landscape is dotted with graveyards.' Lalitha vividly recalled the time when Pandits migrated and how her own family had almost left but stayed back because of circumstances beyond their control.

> I remember the day when all the Pandits left from here. Trucks came and people packed up what they could and left. I also packed a few belongings. I got my boys ready, made a little rice for the journey and decided to buy vegetables on the way. We had asked the truck to come here by 1:30 in the morning so that we could leave quietly in the dark. Suddenly that evening a curfew was declared because of which the truck never came and we stayed on. But we did not unpack till a year later by which time we began to reconcile ourselves with the fact that we were going to stay on here. Also, the people-to-people contact had improved. Some people who had left from this colony came back to stay here. And anyway, where could we go? We had heard stories of snakebites, health problems and the dismal conditions in the camps from our relatives in Jammu. They are old now and will never return here, but I often wonder how they lived in those conditions.
>
> My eldest son finished his engineering over three years ago and yet he has not found a job and has been sitting idle at home. If he doesn't get a job here, we will be forced to leave too. The Muslims are doing the same because their sons don't have employment either.

> We seem to share the same fate with Muslims but those
> who have moved out have done much better. I have
> three sons, but if I had even a single daughter I would
> have left from here under any circumstances. Militants
> would enter houses; demand food – it had to be good
> food – and having a daughter would have made it unsafe.

We heard this from many displaced Pandits. The safety of women was a strong reason that pushed them to leave, but we also met others in Kashmir such as Santosh Koul who told us that once she made the decision to stay back with her family, she had decided to live without fear and saw to it that her daughters went to college and to work. In a period marked by such insecurity, how did she manage to cope with the fear? 'My faith in a Muslim saint has kept us here. He lived in Dirvesh village and was someone I had come to trust greatly. When so many Pandits started migrating, I went to him for advice as I always did in times of trouble. He assured me that we should not leave and that nothing would happen to us. It was only this that stopped us from leaving. Once you have that faith, all fear disappears,' she said. She went on to say, 'I have a 24-year-old son and two daughters, one of whom had just got a job when militancy began. Those times were hard with her having to go to work despite the fear and risk. The other daughter was 19 and in college. Militants used the house next to ours for interrogation but we were never troubled because of this. But some militants did come home once asking for some food in 1991. I said, "Look- we don't have enough for ourselves, how can I give you any?" They didn't trouble me after that.' She also told us how, in 1990 every mosque would have a Kashmiri Pandit hit list, indicating the ones to be targeted: 'The Muslims would see this in the Masjid when they went to pray. They would come home and quietly send their children to inform the listed family to leave. They protected us this way.'

Among the many consequences, the decision to stay back also
led to resentment amongst the displaced Pandits, as we heard often
in Kashmir. One of them, Pyare Lal Pandit in Pulwama, had this
to say:

> Pandits in Jammu shouldn't be resentful because we
> stayed back. We didn't support militancy; we tried
> only to save our own lives just as they did so by leaving
> Kashmir. We often think about how there are so few of
> us left here now. We realize our community is decreasing
> in numbers. Our children might also leave if they don't
> find jobs here. We are not angry with the people who left
> either. Each did what they had to. Ninety five per cent
> of Kashmiri Pandits sold their land before migrating. A
> total of 20 Pandit families left from here. They left very
> secretively, some not even informing their own brothers.
> Everyone was scared that they might lose their lives and
> so they took their own families in trucks and escaped,
> while we decided to remain here.

His family had also packed their bags to leave, he said, but added:
'Our Muslim neighbours and friends convinced us to stay back.
They said everyone was facing the same fear and we would all share
the same fate.' He also recalled how his fields and orchards were
neglected as Muslim labourers stayed away for fear of being targeted:

> Those initial months were hard for us because none of our
> Muslim labourers came to work on the fields. Kashmiri
> Pandits never worked on their own fields, we always
> employed Muslims to do it for us. Thus we faced a lot
> of financial loss during those months but we knew that
> Muslims were afraid that we were *mukhbirs* (informers)
> because of which they kept a distance from us but once
> they realized that if anyone could be a mukhbir, it was
> a Muslim, they co-operated with us and started working

on our fields again. We have survived only because of the
Muslim support we received.

When we first met Sanjay Tickoo, he told us how peace-loving
Kashmiris were and how Kashmir had always had a syncretic culture
with a strong tradition of Sufism but 'once the guns entered, peace
was gone, there was violence and terrible fear everywhere.' He said
that as migration began in the nineties, 'Kashmiri Muslims helped
the Kashmiri Pandits to a great extent. In fact, they helped us
survive and we did the same for them when they faced the wrath
of the security forces; at times, their women slept in our homes for
safety and vice versa. No one will tell you this as such facts have
been hidden, mainly due to fear of reprisal.' When migration began,
'people had no plan or strategy, they simply packed and left while
many others did not even have time to pack, and left in the clothes
they wore.' But he said, 'We were lucky to have stayed back', adding
that 'it was not an easy decision; the Muslims had started to look at
us as informers or government agents and the Pandits who migrated
saw us as traitors.' In an interview to a magazine, he had credited his
mother for their decision to stay back. 'I thank the women of my
family and particularly my mother who gave her steadfast support to
our decision. If either she or my sister had shown even the slightest
weakness, we too would have fled, and would have been forced to
uproot ourselves.'[10] As we talked, he described to us how difficult
the situation was at the time, particularly for the Pandits who stayed
back as they could not move about freely for fear of being branded
mukhbirs: 'We did not go out much and did not even know who
our neighbours were. We had to maintain secrecy. We would see our
Pandit brothers on the road but not greet them in order to protect
our own identities; people would not visit each other for fear of
being seen as informers.' He smiled and pointed to the red tilak on
his forehead and said that it was unthinkable earlier to go out and

move around freely, wearing this marker of identity as boldly as he did now. Similarly for Lalitha whom we had met earlier:

> For two years, when militancy was at its peak we had to conceal our presence. We did not step out of our house and it was our Muslim neighbours who would bring us milk and other basic provisions. Two years later when I went out in my tikka and *dejhoor* to buy vegetables, the shopkeeper exclaimed, 'Mubarak, look a Hindu has come back from Jammu.' I told him that I had lived here for the last two years, only without their knowledge. I wouldn't even let my son cry at home; scared that someone might hear him. I would cover his face to muffle his voice. I can never forget that period.

Others we met also shared their memories of that time, not only in terms of what they had personally experienced but also their apprehensions about how the situation would impact the 'composite culture' of Kashmir. Among those who stayed, some saw it as a privilege that their economic conditions let them afford this choice. They believed that they had earned the respect of Muslims with their decision, and resolved to stay back and not give in to fear or panic. Vimla Dhar recalled how, during the peak of militancy, women were expected to abide by the dress code imposed by militants but she refused to do so and went out in her sari and tikka and that became not only a marker of her identity but also a symbol of her resistance. Neerja Mattoo shared her own experience about how difficult and risky it was in the early nineties for women to go out wearing saris or a tikka. They had to conceal their identity with the result that the new generation of Kashmiri Muslims grew up without even knowing who a Pandit was or how she looked. She narrated an incident that had touched her heart: 'I was walking on a street with a cousin and both of us were wearing saris. A child walking in front of us with his mother kept looking back at us curiously, asking her something.

When I inquired from the mother what the matter was, she said that her ten-year old son had never seen a Pandit woman before and was curious to know about us.' She added that the Pandits who stayed back believed that they still represented the composite culture of Kashmir even though an entire generation was growing up without any knowledge or experience of this culture, an irreparable casualty of the Pandit migration.

Many Pandits who decided to stay back faced this existential dilemma, along with a sense of being part of a fragmented community, with distance and bitterness growing between those who stayed and the ones who left. As Neerja Mattoo told us,

> with Pandits who left, there is now a clear divide; the longer they stay away, the greater is the bitterness and the troubling memory of conditions under which they left. That is all they remember of the Valley, the terrible circumstances that led to their migration. There is a difference in perception about those who stayed and those who left. Many Pandits who left are bitter towards those who stayed back. They feel that we have undermined their plight and their struggle for justice. Pandits who stayed back are accused of supporting the movement for azadi and thereby supporting the militants.

She raised an important question about whether the Pandits had been targeted on communal grounds or because they were significant players in the political process. She mentioned how she or her family had not perceived any threat to them on account of their religion until 1991 when militants tried to abduct her husband but his Muslim driver helped him escape.

> My husband's attempted abduction has a special significance for me because this was the first time a kidnap attempt by militants had failed and it was also

the first time that ordinary people, including Muslims
had openly expressed their sympathy with the victim.
When my husband was returning from the house where
he had taken refuge, the entire neighbourhood, many of
them Muslims, came out and safely escorted him home.
Ordinary people offered their apologies to us. That is
when my family took a firm decision to stay back.

For many Pandits, the decision to stay back had to do with
economic compulsions as well. In Srinagar, those who were
professionals, government employees or in business were tied to their
place of occupation. One elderly Pandit in a village in Shopian said,
'We have our land – that's why we are here. There was no support
at that time, but our grain is here, so we could not leave – *hamara
dana yahan hai, kaise jaate?*' He added, 'There was a lot of fear in the
beginning but we got used to the situation. Our Muslim neighbours
were very good, that is another reason why we stayed back. If they
weren't good, who would have remained here?' Stories about the
abysmal living conditions in the camps that travelled from Jammu
to Kashmir also contributed to the decision of some of the Pandits to
stay back. For some, the decision to stay was due to domestic issues
such as having aged parents at home or not being able to leave the
land or orchards unattended. Commitment to their place of birth and
conviction that they belonged here were also cited as reasons to stay.
One of the main reasons, according to Sanjay, was the 'emotional
attachment to our soil.' But did that mean that those who left did
not have such a commitment, or that they did not yearn to return?
The fact is that nearly all those who left – or even the ones who
stayed – believed that migration was a temporary phenomenon and
that they would return home once the situation became 'normal.'
Further, the government had assured them that their return would
be arranged as soon as militant violence was brought under control.
Almost everyone we met among the Pandits, both in Kashmir and

in Jammu, expressed this opinion categorically and this was one of the main reasons that many of them left without any possessions. We were told that many Pandits, as they left hurriedly, even gave their house keys to their Muslim neighbours, certain that they would return within a few weeks or months but at the time of our visit, sixteen years had gone by and the return had not happened.

Freedom Songs: The Turn to Militancy

Most Pandits that we spoke to believe that it was militancy that caused migration, and that the Muslims as a community were not responsible for it. 'In the first stage of migration, Kashmiri Muslims provided protection to Kashmiri Pandits but as the situation deteriorated rapidly they – out of sheer helplessness – asked the Pandits to leave before they were harmed,' said Rekha Chowdhry who we met at Jammu University. There was however a divergence of opinions regarding this between the Pandits who had stayed and those who were displaced. Stories of the support and sympathy that the Pandits received from Kashmiri Muslims and instances when local militants provided support and protection to Pandits, came up often in our conversations in Kashmir suggesting that such support also helped some of them in their decision to stay back. According to a retired headmaster of a school in Anantnag whom we met at his home, 'I gave duty somewhere close to the town during militancy. The place was full of militants, mostly belonging to Hizbul Mujahedeen. I found that some of the militants were nice people. The HM Commander would come and sit with us and urge us not to leave. Local people have in fact encouraged us to stay back. The security forces ended up harassing the Pandits more in fact. They would ask us, "Why haven't you gone yet?" Only some of them would appreciate the fact that we stayed back.'

When we first met Sanjay Tickoo, I was struck by his unusual statement that militancy was *not* communal in nature; it was perhaps the first time we were hearing this from a Kashmiri Pandit. A few days later, when we were in Mattan (Anantnag), we met a former member of a communist party – CPI-ML – who was currently with the Hindu Welfare Society, and who told us how he had invented an experiment to test the nature of the militant movement: 'I had decided that if I found it was communal and not political, I would leave immediately. To find out personally I started going to the temple every day, walking there with a tikka on my forehead. As I said, I was an M-L activist, an atheist who had never gone to a temple before but I needed to know if Muslims would trouble me or stop me. Fortunately, no one did. I therefore decided to stay on.' He added, in a lighter vein, that it was in fact militancy that turned him into a practising Hindu.

Similarly, we heard many more interesting comments that provided nuance to a story thus far seen as only black and white. When we met Balraj Puri in Jammu a few weeks later, he shared this anecdote with us:

> I was the first person to go to Kashmir and meet the Kashmiri Pandits at the peak of militancy although the government had requested that I do not go, but I went, defying the curfew. When they saw me approach, militants who had occupied all the mosques, announced on loud speakers, 'We were waiting for you, welcome.' I asked them if it was in their interest to have the Pandits leave Kashmir. Their response was an immediate 'no.' I spoke with many militants who said they would never harm the Pandits and that it would in fact weaken their own cause.

However, while the dominant Pandit narrative centered on their forced exile and victimhood at the hands of Kashmiri Muslims, many Kashmiri Muslims in the Valley believed that they had been demonized as a communal community responsible for Pandit migration. Ironically, many Kashmiri Muslims as well as resident Pandits considered the plight of those who left advantageous in terms of all the government benefits they had received such as ration cards, financial assistance, and an option to move on. Almost everyone mentioned how some of the Pandits in the camps had obtained fake ration cards or more than one ration card, and were registered in more than one camp even as they continued to receive financial assistance/salary from the government. A Pandit we met in Anantnag claimed that his own brother had procured more than one ration card saying: 'If we Pandits who are considered scholars can do this, imagine the plight of the poor Muslims who get nothing!'

While many Pandits felt betrayed that they had not been taken into confidence by their Muslim friends when they began the movement for azadi, there were others who felt that as committed Indians, this was not a movement they could own. Rekha Chowdhry explained to us how Kashmiri Muslim politics had remained exclusive because the Muslims believed that Kashmiri Pandits would never be part of the movement as they strongly identified with India; moreover, there was no place for them in Kashmiri Muslim politics mainly due to a class divide. This, she felt, had led to polarization between the two communities. Some others we interviewed spoke sympathetically of azadi until 'the movement gradually transformed with calls for *Nizam-e-Mustafa* (Islamic Rule)' which they perceived as a 'religious and Wahabi' assertion that challenged Kashmir's composite culture and was therefore difficult to support. Once such a call acquired importance, they felt that the movement took a fundamentalist direction and because of this, it lost its earlier popularity and urgency. Some Kashmiri Muslims blamed the government as well as displaced Pandits for giving a communal veneer to what were otherwise normal, trustful relationships between the two communities.

Interestingly, not many – either Pandits or Muslims – spoke of Kashmiriyat much except to say that the only way for it to revive and survive was through ordinary people's commitment to secular values. The communalization of the issue of migration was attributed to the government, political parties and organizations, and the media.

Many Pandits also shared stories of how militants prevented Pandit families in villages from migrating by providing protection to them directly 'from rooftops and neighbourhood lanes holding their guns.' This was perhaps one of the reasons that many Pandits – both in Kashmir and the camps – drew a distinction between individual militants and the Muslim community when they spoke about Kashmiri Muslims. For some of those we met in the villages, militants were familiar people and had identities – they were students, neighbours, friends – prior to becoming militants. Many believed that the bomb blasts, sectarian killings and violence had nothing to do with azadi and that unidentified armed groups were responsible for it. Rather than blame the Muslim community, they held 'indoctrination from outside' responsible for the targeted violence. According to some – both Muslims and Pandits – had the Pandits stayed back, perhaps it would have been easier to find a solution to the vexed problem of Kashmir.

Like a few other Pandits, Omkarnath Thakur, whom we had earlier met in his village shared this with us about militancy and militants:

> Every family in our village has a story to tell about the nineties. No one was left untouched. When militancy began here, we didn't even know what the term meant. Many Pandit families started to pack and leave. They feared for their lives. We also packed our bags and were about to leave when some of our Muslim neighbours came and said, 'Don't go, what will happen to us will happen to you, let us face this together.' We decided then

to stay back. Some of the local militants also supported us. But when the situation worsened, I went to the local Area Commander and told him that one Pandit had been killed in a neighbouring village following which, three Pandit families from our village had left. I told him I was afraid for the safety of my family and asked him what I should do. The Commander said, 'Leave if you want, but I think you will be safe if you stay.' The Commander happened to be my old student.

Recalling the nineties vividly when the majority of Pandits had already left due to militant violence and killings, he said,

During the early nineties, there were massive dharnas with slogans for azadi reverberating everywhere. All of us were very scared, especially women and children. One day, some people came to burn down our village, but the militants protected us. They had circled our village from the rooftops, you could see them standing there with guns. The army vans were also patrolling the villages, but the militants didn't let anyone enter our village for two days. There was later another procession when hundreds of people were out on the street shouting slogans. The army again tried to make an entry; we again went and met the Hizb commander and asked him what we should do. He assured me yet again that no harm would come to us in his area. However, as the situation got worse, with targeted killings and threats, the militants who had earlier protected us said that they were now helpless and the situation could not be controlled.

Many Pandits spoke positively about Muslims and relations with them despite the prevalent threats. Dr S N Dhar, whom we first visited in his clinic and later met at his home along with his wife Vimla, told us that although Kashmiri Pandits feared that they would be targeted, it was the selective killings that proved to be the last straw but he added, 'We decided to stay back because I had this deep and abiding faith that the Kashmiri Muslim is a Kashmiri after all and not a person with hatred or viciousness. I have always believed that a Kashmiri Muslim is a secular person.' He went on to say, 'Being Muslim is not the most significant aspect of his or her identity. The Muslims and Pandits here share core beliefs and values that are similar to both. Even now, people who work for me – many of them Muslims – would give up their lives for me. My patients, mostly Muslims, love and respect me; this is because of the great syncretic tradition this place has. I have been shot by militants three times and kidnapped and kept in captivity for 83 days but I still wanted to be here, live here.' According to Vimla, she was alone at home the day Dr Dhar was kidnapped: 'I gained strength from my husband's patients, most of them Muslims, who would come and sit with me each day waiting to hear some news of him and encouraging me not to lose hope. This went on for 83 days but his patients' support did not diminish as they stood by me. Afterwards our relatives urged us to leave Kashmir but we decided to stay.' She was also advised to shut down her school – which she had rebuilt after it was burnt down by militants in 1990 – as there were now only Muslim students left after Pandit migration. 'Why educate the Muslims? Let them suffer', she was told by many in her community, but she remained committed although, she said, 'in those days our car always had a full tank and was kept ready, in case we had to leave suddenly – but we stayed back only because of the faith we had in our people and our land.'

The Search for Home

Despite the conflicting, opposing narratives 'the return of the migrants' kept coming up as an inevitability, both for the Muslims and the Pandits – who spoke about it in emotional rather than in political terms, recalling the close links the two communities shared over years. After nearly three decades as a displaced community, the question of 'return' evoked doubt and cynicism among the Pandits who felt that the government had failed in its promise. They continued to be homeless and the situation in Kashmir remained unresolved. As Rekha Chowdhry pointed out to us, 'When most of the Pandits left in 1990, they were sure they would return in three months. They were made to believe that militancy would end by then and a peaceful environment would be created for their return. This explains why most of them had not sold their land and other property at the time of leaving.' Similarly, according to Santosh Koul, 'no one realized that migration would last this long. Those who left believed they would return soon when the situation returned to normal.' In Anantnag, there were 500 Pandit families before 1990 of which only three families were left at the time of our research. 'They are old and their children have already moved to Jammu; they are not going to return to Kashmir,' said one of the Pandits we met. Many also emphasised the fact that an entire generation had grown up without any sense of attachment to Kashmir, they saw their future elsewhere and had no yearning to return to a place they had only heard about from their parents and grandparents: 'My migrant friends are well adjusted in Jammu, Delhi and elsewhere. They are all qualified and doing well. What's the point of coming back here? The new generation of Kashmiri Pandits will never choose Kashmir. The Pandits from Jammu who visit Kashmir say, we come back here because of the attachment we have to this place but our kids will not come, they have no such attachment. Most young Muslims here have never even seen a Pandit.'

This was Roop Raina who lived in Hutumura, Anantnag. Everyone agreed, however, that the return of the displaced Pandits was necessary for Kashmir to regain its composite, syncretic culture

and identity. But it was important, they said, for the government
to first take care of the people who have stayed back. The advised
strategy was to not force the Pandits to return, but improve existing
conditions in the Valley so the Pandits would themselves make a
voluntary decision to return.

The main problem that the resident Pandits envisaged with
the government bringing a few Pandits into special secure areas
in Kashmir was of ghettoization, which they believed would lead
to threats for the Pandits who had continued to stay in the valley,
making them easier targets. They argued that the Pandits should
instead be rehabilitated in clusters with the Muslims for each other's
safety. A few families we met at Sheikhupora, where the government
had built a cluster of more than 200 flats for the returning Pandits,
echoed this and were not sure how long they could live in isolation
there, surrounded by high walls and with a BSF post guarding the
gates. According to some, there could be conflict over benefits and
resources between the Pandits who stayed and those who returned.
There was resentment among many displaced Kashmiri Pandits over
the fact that the jobs they held prior to migration had now been
taken over by the Muslims. People thus expected very few Pandits
to return. However, there was a general sense that relations between
the displaced Pandits and Kashmiri Muslims had improved over the
years with more Pandits coming back to the Valley, even though for
short periods of time. During one of our visits, the Pandit New Year
was being celebrated in the Valley after many years and Muslims
participated in substantial numbers. We were told that the Pandits
had more in common with the Kashmiri Muslims than with Hindus
elsewhere in the country. According to Girdhari Lal, a retired teacher
in Mattan:

> The reason I returned to Kashmir from Jammu in 1995
> was due to my Muslim students. They had become big
> doctors, professionals and came all the way to Jammu to

convince me to return. They assured me that I would be safe and that my safety was their personal responsibility. Moreover, the situation in Jammu is not good. The climate, food, doesn't suit us at all. You can manage there in winter. Kashmir is a land of saints and sages. There was initially a lot of tension between the Dogras in Jammu and the Pandits. From the beginning we have had separate schools, stores etc., for the Kashmiri Pandits here. There was never any integration of the migrants with the local population in Jammu.

The Shape of Exile

After many weeks spent with Kashmiri Pandits and Muslims in the Valley, it was time to visit the camps in Jammu to meet the displaced Pandits. I was going there with the realization that the narratives I had heard so far and the situation as it obtained then was much more complex than I had thought. Despite sharing a similar situation, in many ways, the narrative was not a uniform one, reflecting divergent and at time, ambivalent views on migration, militancy, azadi and the social relations between the two communities. I was told more than once by many of the people I had met during fieldwork in Kashmir regarding the anger and bitterness that marked the lives of the displaced Pandits residing in the camps of Jammu. No one mentioned that it was a natural response to a traumatic and calamitous change that had occurred in their lives, individually and as a community. I was also told that I would perhaps be met with hostility and resentment inside the camps. I had already heard and read about the abysmal living conditions there and as I began to visit and meet people, it became apparent that it required a rare kind of courage and resilience for the displaced to live in such conditions.

Even basic facilities such as healthcare, sanitation, water and power supply meant to be provided free of cost, had to be fought for by a proud community that had lived a privileged life earlier. What was also apparent was the utter failure of the government in this regard as it had done nothing regarding its promise of 'honourable return and rehabilitation' of the displaced community even after thirty years. It was during the summer months that we visited the camps and the searing heat reminded us of the cool and pleasant climate in the Valley. We realized that adjusting to this changed climatic conditions was one of the hardest challenges that the displaced Pandits faced.

Muthi camp is located at a distance of 7 kilometres from Jammu city. The camp is made of one-room-tenements (ORT) measuring 10' × 10.' It is divided into two 'phases' – Phase I and II – each with five blocks. Each block has around 100 families. There are 12 toilets and 12 bathrooms (6 each for men and women) in each block. In Phase II, four families live under one dome-shaped roof covered with a thick layer of tar, with one room (12' × 12') for each family. Four families share one toilet and bathroom. According to the then Relief Commissioner, Mohinder Singh, Muthi Phase I has 499 families and Muthi Phase II has 619 families, totalling 1118 families. The camps were congested with narrow lanes that held the one-room-tenements set close together, along with a few shops that sold basic necessities. The (tin) toilets and bathrooms were in the middle of each block, wet and crowded at most times, with a few women waiting their turn.

According to the camp commandant, Muthi II has eight blocks with F Block being the largest. The camp has a total of 123 domes with each dome containing four one-room houses:

> It is also the most congested of all camps. JD camp, where migrants lived in tents in the initial period was located close to Muthi II and I, which were constructed simultaneously. Many families from the JD camp shifted

here. The migrants stayed in JD tents for two years when they first arrived from Kashmir but there were several cases of death due to snakebites and heatstroke. It was to help people out of this situation and ease their hardship that the Muthi camps were constructed. All camp residents get the same relief of a maximum Rs. 3,000 (Rs 750 per person), 9 kilos of rice, 2 kilos of atta and 1 kilo of sugar per person.

When we began our fieldwork in the camps in the summer of 2006, Pyare Mohan's family in Phase I was the first one we visited in Muthi. The taxi driver who brought us from Jammu knew him and suggested that we meet them first and with his help, visit others. Their one-room-tenement faced the main road. The small veranda had been covered with a tin roof and converted into a medical shop. A teacher by profession prior to displacement, Pyare Lal decided to set up this shop as a means of survival for the family. A tiny portion behind the shop served as a kitchen where Vimla, his wife also bathed instead of using the public bathroom. A curtained door led into the small room where the family lived with their two teenaged sons. There was just enough space in the room for a bed, a television set, and a few trunks, with clothes lining the walls along with a neon-lit poster of a Hindu saint who Vimla said was her guru. As we explained the purpose of our visit to Pyare Mohan, his young sons came in and joined us, followed, soon after, by his father-in-law. Vimla also joined us although she was clearly upset and resentful that many such visits and interviews later, nothing positive or concrete had happened and she wondered aloud if any purpose would be served by talking to us. She was agitated as she began to tell us about the circumstances the led to their sudden displacement. In a voice charged with anger and resentment, she narrated her own experience breathlessly saying that there was not even enough time for her to change her clothes, leave alone pack anything to bring with them.

She left the house with her two sons in the clothes she was wearing, she said. The passage of 17 years had not dimmed her memory of 'that moment of utter confusion, fear and grief.' Her husband, however, appeared calm, detached and spoke more coherently even though they had shared the same 'fate' but as happens in such situations, their specific experience at the time of fleeing and the articulation of it was significantly different. Subsequently, as we made many more visits and always stopped by to meet her and the family she began to welcome us warmly; her camp-home became our refuge during fieldwork where we took shelter from the scorching summer heat, shared food with them along with snippets and stories of the day, before returning to Jammu. One late evening, in a touching gesture, she pulled out a couple of chairs saying, 'let's sit in our drawing room today for tea' and there we were, sitting on the pavement, facing the main road in front of her house where she had placed the chairs. She laughed and said that the traffic noise or smoke did not bother her any more as she had become used to it, along with much else.

As we learnt during the course of our fieldwork, this wasn't Vimla's story alone; many other women had similar experiences of displacement, of a difficult adjustment and the constant yearning to return. Camp life was hard but many residents felt that while the community was earlier scattered, camp life had brought them closer since they now lived as neighbours. 'My neighbours have helped me on so many occasions. Though we are from different villages, we all live like one family now,' said Rekha, Vimla's neighbour.

Despite the similarity in circumstances leading to migration, each person's experience was unique and all had their own particular ways of keeping alive the memory of 'that fateful night.' The suddenness and secrecy of their departures meant that they could not say goodbye to their friends and relatives. Many divided families later found their members at different camps, sometimes in the long registration lines. According to Vimla Raina, 'I didn't know where my other relatives

were until one day we all met at Gita Bhavan while standing in lines
to be registered and get our ration cards. I turned around and looked
behind me and suddenly found my father- in- law. Then, in another
corner I saw my aunt. I felt so relieved. Many of us shared the same
experience of lost-and-found relatives.'

Nearly everyone we met vividly remembered the charged and
volatile atmosphere when they had to leave. Processions chanting
slogans of azadi filled every street while mosques blared slogans
and speeches. The slogan that stayed in their minds was one that
promised that Kashmir would be turned into Pakistan, and Pandit
women would be kept back, without their men. There were many
accounts of how people felt that women's honour was at stake. Ashok
Pandit, a zamindar from Kupwara, told us that it wasn't only the
threatening slogans that made them leave but when the army, meant
for their protection, started being targeted and killed by militants
they decided it was time to go. They were very anxious for their
women's safety: 'We knew that the Muslims could do nothing when
the goondas came. Izzat ka sawal tha. Ma thi, beti thi, behan thi.
It was a matter of honour for us. I had my mother, my daughter,
and my sister to protect.' According to Rekha Chowdhry, 'Kashmiri
Pandit families are close-knit, and stories of violations, even a single
one, spread easily. Sharda Dhar's death for example became a big
issue and created panic among the Pandits and led to rumors that
the names of the victims would be called out in mosques before they
were killed, and that Muslim men were claiming to keep the Pandit
women without their men. Feelings were no doubt exaggerated at
that time.'

According to a survey report by the J&K Centre for Minority
Studies (2006), only 1.04 per cent of the Pandits in camps cited
kidnapping or the rape of women as a reason for migration whereas
for majority of them, it was insecurity that led them to flee. Many
Kashmiri Pandits in camps said that blaming the then governor

Jagmohan for their displacement was the easier way out. 'Who would agree to leave their house, property, memories on someone else's suggestion? It was the killings, the fear and insecurity that made us leave.' A doctor in Muthi II said, 'Jagmohan didn't help us to leave but he didn't stop us either.' According to another, 'The government allowed us to go to Jammu. If it had told us all to come to one place in Kashmir that was safer, we would have done so and stayed on but they said nothing, which is why we assumed Jammu was safer and went there.' Babli Raina told us that 'the police had arranged trucks for us to leave. We paid for them and 10-12 families left together.' Many said they left because of the targeted killings of fellow Pandits. As one family left, others followed, as 'it didn't make sense to be the only Pandit family to stay on.' People spoke about direct and indirect threats and the final decision to leave being made after they'd seen so many – family, friends, people known to them – who'd experienced violence. The overwhelming sense was one of fear and uncertainty; there were rumours that militants were seeking out able-bodied men. Everyone believed that militancy had led to huge social trauma and extreme fear and insecurity, which made living everyday life a formidable task.

Vimla's story, below, echoes the experiences of many other women:

> We left in January 1990 because we feared for our lives. I had Rs. 3,000 at home and I had gone to buy our monthly stock of groceries. Suddenly, curfew was declared and I had to come home. The situation was really tense. I had my two small sons and an unmarried sister living with us. I was most worried for her *izzat*. I put the television on high volume to drown out the noise. I did not want to know what was happening out on the streets. We didn't want to hear those frightening sounds and threatening slogans. We had just built a

second floor in our house. It had a glass front. I covered it with black cloth. We hardly ate for over seven days as none of us could step out and we didn't even want kitchen smoke to come out of our house for fear that it would alert people to the fact that we were still living there. All the looting and processions scared us terribly.

Her husband added, 'There were instances when Muslim men entered our homes to escape from army atrocities and said to our women, tell them we are your husbands. Which Hindu man will tolerate such talk? The Muslims always wanted us to leave. It was a nexus between them and the government.' Vimla came in at this point:

> We decided to flee when our neighbours came to warn me that a group of 30-40 men had come looking for my husband. 'Log tab tak bhadak bhi gaye the' – people were so charged up by then. How do you reason with men holding guns? We left early morning in a bus. Only one bus left that morning from the tourist centre. We left our house to get to the tourist centre through inside lanes, leaving separately from different routes so that the entire family wouldn't be caught. We had to maintain utmost secrecy. All I had with me was the money I carried that morning to buy groceries and the clothes I wore but we managed to escape, hoping to return soon.

Vimla also spoke about how vulnerable the children felt days before they left. Her son Sandeep, now 22, recalled: 'My brother and I were playing cricket. The Muslim kids suddenly turned to me and said, hey Pandit, tell your father to get your insurance. We are warning you.' Sandeep was only eight years old then but remembered the warning vividly.

For most families, the main reason for leaving without any belongings was primarily because migration was believed to be temporary. Everyone we spoke to narrated how he or she never imagined they would still be living in camps or in Jammu. As Vimla pointed out, 'Now it is sixteen years since all this happened, but whenever I talk about it, the memories return as though it was only yesterday. In my spare time I watch TV serials and sometimes I cry along with the women in the serial as it lightens my heart. We left expecting to return after a few days. We still think about going back, especially when summer comes. We cannot tolerate this heat. But tell me, which one of us will go back there to die? We will go back only when conditions improve. We need to have safety. If the government remains this weak, it will never happen. *Yeh dheeli sarkar kuch nahi kar sakti* – this weak government cannot do anything.'

Her husband lamented that they had 'become vote banks for each political party; when they need us, they do something for us. Many of us had jobs in Kashmir, but there is no place for us to continue working in Jammu. Here we are discriminated as migrants and can hardly find any jobs.' According to Rekha Chowdhry, 'the most underprivileged Kashmiri Pandits are the ones living in relief camps. These are the people who become fodder for communal politics. Situations have sometimes been created to facilitate their continued stay in camps. It also serves the Indian government well to say the situation in Kashmir has not improved.' While we were still talking to Pyare Mohan and his wife, the vice president of the Pandit Vistapit Sangathan walked in and having gauged the strain of our conversation, interrupted us and said angrily that,

> in 1989 when the processions took place, azadi looked
> so close. The Kashmiri Pandits didn't want azadi
> because they were with Hindustan. *Mussalman khate
> hai India ka, par geet gate hai Pakistan ka! Yeh kaise ho
> sakta hai* -the Muslims live off the fat of this land but
> sing praises of Pakistan. How is this possible? During
> that time, local shops where we had regularly shopped

stopped supplying milk and other things to Pandits. The Kashmiri Muslims never intended to involve Pandits in their movement for azadi. They considered all outsiders *kafir* (non-believers). Instead of talking with our leaders, they killed them. If they really wanted azadi, why did they not talk to our leaders instead of killing them? Why did they have to destroy our temples and schools? What did we have to do with it?

The resentment in the camps against the government as well as Muslims was obvious and as mentioned by some, it was the vested political interest groups that were responsible for it. 'We have become fodder for local politics' was a refrain. There were many young Panun supporters in the camps who aggressively pointed out that there was probably a nexus between the present government in Kashmir and the Muslims there. 'Together they made sure that Kashmiri Pandits left', said one of them. Many camp residents believed that the government and political outfits such as Panun Kashmir exploited their victimhood by communalising and polarising relations between the two communities. Resentful of the Indian government, one Kashmiri Pandit said, 'This government is Hindu in name only. Hindus live in India but they mean nothing. It is the Muslims who rule India. The government is gaining from our displacement, not the other way round.' We sensed the extent of resentment and anger when we visited Muthi Phase II. While we waited for the camp commandant to introduce us to some of the camp residents, we were joined by a small group of men who were also waiting outside his office. Soon, others arrived. They were all curious about our work and keen to know the purpose of our visit. They also wanted to share their views so that these were included in our 'report.' The men began by expressing their anger and irritation that there had been so many so-called 'concerned people' who had come to interview them but no one had done anything concrete for them. 'Nothing has changed in our situation,' they said. The conversation that started casually soon grew into a loud and angry outburst, as they seemed to be competing with each other loudly to share their views with us. The nature of our work in Kashmir with Kashmiri Muslims and Kashmiri Pandits seemed to further upset them and each of them reacted strongly: *'Hindustan ko bomb se uda dena chahiye kyunki Hindu ki raksha nahi hoti hai is mulk mein. Mussalman ke pas sub kutch hai. Unhon ne hamein bandooq ke zor par bhaga diya. Unko marne do wahan par.* (India should be blown up because we Hindus are not protected here. Muslims have everything. They forced us out with the power of the gun. Let them die there).' One of them also talked about how Islamic fundamentalism was on the rise all over the world and how it was always a Muslim who spread terror: *'Islamic fundamentalism har jagah phail gaya hai, poori duniya mein. Jis ne bhi kand kiya woh Mussalman hi raha.'* Another had this to say: *'Tasveer ke do roop hote hain. Jehan gulistan tha ab wahan khabristan hai'* (There are two sides to a picture. Where there was a garden earlier, there is a graveyard now.) They all cursed the Kashmiri Muslims 'who led the azadi movement for their own personal gain. They are dishonest people. No earthquake hit Kashmir, all the damage was in PoK, but they still managed to get aid from the government. The Muslims have their own government, it belongs to them. Militants kill a soldier from the Indian army, but still receive help and other benefits while we who live and die for India get nothing.' They cursed the Indian government for constructing buildings in Mumbai and Kashmir for Haj pilgrimage for Muslims.

> What is being done for us Kashmiri Pandits? What about our children and their future? Where do we go and stay in Kashmir if we wish to? A hundred kanals (approximately 12.5 acres) of land have been used in Bemina to construct the building to facilitate those going

on the Haj. Don't the Hindus go to Kheer Bhavani and Amarnath for pilgrimage? Why does the government not construct buildings for us? The Haj committee even offers free food and a ten-day stay for the pilgrims. The truth is that the Indian government is scared of the Muslims. We gave our lives for India, but the army that is being killed by the Muslims is building roads etc., for the same Muslims who kill them. The army has given us nothing. We do *jai jai kaar* for the army, but what for? Even their Sadbhavana scheme has nothing for us, it is all meant only for the Muslims.

Most people we spoke to were completely unwilling to listen to any accounts of the problems Kashmiri Muslims were facing in Kashmir. They cut us short angrily when we tried to talk about this: 'the Muslims have got what they deserve. Their suffering is of their own making. If their family members are disappearing or dying, it is their own fault. Please do not talk to us about their problems or suffering.' They were equally unwilling to understand the situation of Kashmiri Pandits: 'Kashmiri Pandits still living in Kashmir are not Pandits anymore; they have become like Kashmiri Muslims now. They will do as the Muslims say.' According to one of them,

the Moulvis (Muslim clergy) has guided the Mohammedans poorly. They made them believe that all non-Muslims were evil. It is these teachers who need to be killed. But the Mohammedan ideology is slowly changing; Pakistan is now ready to talk with us. The Muslim ideology here still needs to change. Both Hindus and Muslims have the same blood but still we are divided. The Pandits have also made many mistakes. We were also misguided before we left, as the Muslims were. We all need to meet and clear the air. We need to understand each other as brothers.

As we were leaving, one of them asked us about our religious identities, our organization in Delhi, the director's religious identity and having learnt that he was Muslim, said, 'Next time you must come back with more Hindus in your team so that they can see the deplorable conditions in which fellow Hindus are living in the migrant camps. It is their duty to spread the word around.'

The government's relief measures for the displaced both within the camps and outside have helped them to survive and sustain everyday living, but also seem to have exacerbated their sense of victimhood. The state had failed to create better living conditions for the displaced and had simultaneously rendered many of them unfit to work. According to Ved Bhasin, 'Several displaced Pandits have more than a single income (many still receive their basic salary from the government jobs they left, and have private jobs in Jammu or elsewhere). They are known to possess more than one ration card. Pandits are given reservations in jobs in different states across India and the government has a separate budget to take care of their needs. Such treatment can at times make whole populations unfit to work.'

While this was one reality, Pandits in camps lamented that everything they had cherished from their past was gone, including their land which had been taken over and their houses ruined. Most importantly, as Kumar Wanchoo in Srinagar had pointed out to us, 'While providing relief on humanitarian and compassionate grounds to the migrant Pandits, the government has succeeded in destroying their self-respect and dignity, turning a self-reliant community into one dependent on aid.' He also shared with us the plight of those Pandits who got posted back in Kashmir and now found the office routine too stressful, as they had remained idle for all these years, while receiving their salary regularly. This was one of the main reasons that many men in the camps felt disempowered and lacking in the more positive and constructive role they had earlier played in the family and society. They were now 'at the mercy of the government dole.' Ramesh Bharti, who took care of a family of ten, including an ailing father, regretted living on the dole – 'I feel humiliated to live on the dole. I feel ashamed that we have to eat what is given to us in ration. A person like me who once had enough wealth cannot live this kind of life but I am forced to.' He also added that as a husband, he felt ashamed and helpless because of a lack of resources and facilities and he saw how hard women in the family had to work: 'Our women have to carry water containers on their heads and by the time they reach home, their clothes are wet. It's a matter of shame for us, and our women because the men standing around can see their wet bodies.'

When we met Indu Killam, lecturer at the government migrant college, one of the things she had said as we began to talk has stayed with me all these years, perhaps because of its pathos and poignancy; 'I start each morning by reading the obituaries in the newspaper (*Daily Excelsior*) to see if any more amongst us has died.' She lived in her own house but we met her at her college in Jammu. Among the many experiences she shared with us, she also recounted how her husband had suffered due to the fact that he received the salary while remaining idle:

> He was employed as an engineer in Kashmir. After he moved here, he has been receiving his salary cheque every month even though he remains without any work. This has weakened him as a person. We have lost our dignity because of this way of life. Initially he suffered a lot, he was humiliated to receive his salary without putting in any work. But what choice did we have? We had left everything behind when we migrated.' Her parents too had to move to Jammu but 'they never got over the sorrow of leaving Kashmir. My father suffered more as it was against his pride to go and collect Rs. 2,000 every month from the relief commissioner. He was a

land-owning person and it hurt his ego so much that he
managed to find a way to have the cheque delivered to
his home each month.'

Sheila Kaul, a 40 year old woman (she appeared much older
because of what she described as 'stressful living') spoke about how
her husband had suffered and died after moving to the camp because
he could not bear the shame of not being able to provide for his
family any more. He was ruined by the fact that his orchards in
Kashmir were encroached upon and sold: 'Our self-esteem does not
allow us to sell vegetables or do other odd jobs; we are an intelligent,
educated community.'

The Kashmiri Pandits had a strong sense of pride in their
culture, their levels of education and their social status. We were
told repeatedly: 'We Pandits are a proud community – proud of our
past, our education, our culture, and our contribution to society.'
However, there were also complaints about the vitiated atmosphere
in the camps: *Jis imandari se prem aur mohabat se rehte the Kashmir
mein, yahan nahi hai.'* (There was a kind of honesty and caring in our
relationships in Kashmir, it's not the same thing here.); *'Koi hamdard
nahi raha.'* (No one really cares for you); 'Our social relations with
each other have also changed under these circumstances.' Their
hardships notwithstanding, displaced Pandits were determined to
give their children a good education so that they could move out
of the situation the parents were in. As some of them told us, it
was not until their arrival in Jammu that they began to learn the
value of education and also began reading newspapers. Indu Killam
articulated for us what many others had also expressed,

> The Pandits moved to Jammu and elsewhere with their
> reputation of being scholarly. Hence, most of them
> chose to move into one small room in the camps, rather
> than rent a place, so that they could afford to pay for

their children's education, which no Pandit family would compromise on, not even in the camps. They would sit in their one room on the floor, with a chowki for their children to study at. Due to our reputation as good teachers, we still have many young people coming from Srinagar in their holidays to be tutored by us. Even the newspaper-reading culture among the local people in Jammu started only after we Pandits migrated here.

Life in Jammu

People described their first few days in Jammu with mixed feelings of despair, anger and disgust. Prior to finding accommodation in camps, men, women, children had to live in very difficult conditions in temporary tents in the wasteland for more than a year. As Vimla described to us, 'staying in those tents in the heat was unbearable. Because we were out in the wild, many suffered snakebites; we remained anxious for our children. There was no privacy at all with all of us sharing one tent with no toilets or bathrooms. The tents were not strong enough to withstand rain, wind or the cold. We also stood in long lines for hours for rations. We suffered a lot.' According to Ashok Pandit:

> The night we arrived in Jammu, we stayed in a *tabela* or *astabal* (stable). Four or five families stayed in that one shed for two months. Like the other migrants from Kashmir, we later registered our names at the Gita Bhavan and got a tent in Nagrota. We spent Rs 500 per family to get a ration card then. After staying in Nagrota for four or five years in a 12' x 12' tent, the government made these quarters (Muthi II) where we now live. A lottery was drawn and we were allotted this place.

We met T N Khosa, President of the Kashmiri Pandit Samaj (KPS), 'a 100 year old organization and the only elected one in Jammu.' We had heard that it had facilitated the migrants' arrival in Jammu. In his words:

> Starting 19 January 1990 began the exodus of Kashmiri Pandits to Jammu as well as our introduction to the economics of the situation as it obtained then. The Pandits, a well-off community in Kashmir suddenly required basic material support in the form of rations, blankets etc. We received calls from hundreds of affected people requiring urgent help. The Pandits have moved out of Kashmir since then at different periods of time. There are now about 24,000–26,000 Pandits in the camps. Many families who had young girls with them did not go to the camps and tents. It was people from Jammu who opened their doors for such families. I tell my friends repeatedly that the Kashmiris would never have done such a thing. Local people here moved their cattle out, emptied rooms and made space for the Pandits.

Pyare Lal had told us how thankful he and his family were to people of Jammu for their support and friendship, but he was interrupted by another Pandit who said that they did not need to be grateful as they were state subjects and had the right to live in Jammu.

T N Khosa's remark that families with young girls avoided coming to camps reminded us of what the camp commandant in Phase II had told us about how some Kashmiri Pandits living outside the camps wanted to also move into the camps. 'These are mostly people who had moved out of the camps because they had daughters and they felt the camps were not safe for them. Now that their daughters are married, they want to move back. There are 3,000 such families who wish to move back to the camps. Most of them are presently in rented accommodation, which they cannot afford any more. The government refuses to give money to cover their rent and there is no place in the camps for them.'

All camp residents complained about their living conditions: 'The surroundings are dirty and the people are dreadful, even the wind here is different. Our houses here are in a pathetic condition. The walls are so thin that we can hear what is happening in the next house. The roof also leaks and during the rains we become like Gujjars—like them, we also have to pick up all our belongings and move to a corner. Some rooms don't even have a window and the roof is so low that in the summer it becomes unbearable,' said Rekha. The camp commandant told us that Phase II had many more problems than any other camp mainly because of the dome shaped houses here: 'The building material used is not environment friendly and the domes, layered with tar, trap the heat. These were meant to be temporary shelters, it was generally believed that the migrants would be there only for a few months but now it's been more than sixteen years…the wear and tear is visible everywhere. The houses are hot in summer and leaky when it rains. The government did sanction small amounts for repair but they weren't enough to cover all the houses. The people here face a lot of stress and hardship.' He went on to add that 'until five years ago the camp did not have even a drop of water. We had to manage with water tankers that came once a day. The pipes had been laid but there was no connection for years. Even now there is one water tap for a cluster of four domes [20 houses].' He said that earlier there were near riot situations as women scrambled to fill water but then they evolved a method that worked for all of them. The water was available twice a day for two hours or less.

In both the camps people complained about having to arrange for water and electricity illegally. Despite the fact that pipes had been laid and taps installed, they were useless as there was no supply. Water tankers were common for drinking water until the camp residents illegally managed a water pipe connection in each block. In Phase II residents got water every alternate day with six or seven houses having to share one tap. We saw women bent over an underground water pipe. Lifting heavy water containers has created back and shoulder problems for many women. There is also the ever-present risk of drain water getting mixed with drinking water because of faulty pipes – many people were said to have contracted jaundice from drinking contaminated water (other forms of waterborne infections were also common), and women were forced to take on the additional task of boiling water to make it potable.

Resistance and the State

'If it was a fight for azadi, why were the Pandits not asked to help? We had the power of the pen instead of the gun.' Several Kashmiri Pandits believed Pakistan was responsible for communalising the Kashmir issue because 'until Pakistan entered the scene, all Kashmiris lived harmoniously like different flowers in a garden.' Some Pandits identified with the Indian army and saw it as an extension of themselves. 'They are Indian Hindus like us. Does Pakistan feed all those Muslims in Kashmir?' asked Vimla.

There was a great deal of anger and resentment against Pakistan. Many camp residents were of the view that Pakistan had suppressed Kashmiris on the their side to keep them from protesting while fomenting trouble this side of the border. They had heard that conditions on the other side were far worse than on the Indian side. Another said, 'The problem in Kashmir is not a Hindu-Muslim one. The Muslims want their azadi, but many of them also told us not to leave. I don't know what they want azadi from: they are free to do their namaz the way they want and live their life the way they wish to.' Many suggested that India cut ties with Pakistan because they believed Pakistan was responsible for all the violence in Kashmir: 'Kashmir is a political issue and not a communal one. How can it be communal when we all lived happily together there? The pervasive hate and terror are Pakistan's doing.' According to another camp resident, 'It was Muslims who started it. We have become homeless for *their* azadi. They didn't get azadi then and they will not get it now. Many Muslims also died because of azadi; I feel bad for them too. We are living in jails here and look at the way people live in Kashmir. To us life there represents freedom. What they have is what I would call azadi. Why should the Hindus be harmed and why should azadi be for a few at the cost of others?'

One of the Panun supporters, Amarchand Pandit, said, 'We do not believe in azadi. The Muslims want Pakistan but we want India. Also, which azadi movement is this where so many people are killed, including many Muslims who opposed the movement? The problem is a political one. They wanted to rid Kashmir of any community other than Muslims.'

The belief that militancy had been sponsored and funded by forces outside of India was widely held. 'They didn't think of the consequences. They started killing their own neighbours because of militancy. And they are suffering now. The Muslims are not safe either. They are now neither with the militants nor with us. Those militants ruined both Pandit and Muslim lives. The Kashmiri Muslims have nothing either, they are also a deprived lot. They were illiterate and had fewer opportunities than the Pandits. The Muslims got jealous due to this. The Pandits also had land and property, unlike the Muslims. 'Kashmir wants the benefit of Indian money and the Indian army but Pakistan's name', said Ashok Pandit, adding that the government should have given the Pandits enough security in Kashmir so that they would not have left. 'The government could have stopped us; there was after all only one highway for us to leave. Government *hi sab museebaton ki jad hai* (The government is the root of all our problems.) One cannot simply blame the Muslims. Everything is hostage to political power, even our lives.' Many blamed leaders such as Syed Ali Shah Geelani and Yaseen Malik for inciting Muslims to take up guns against the Pandits. A young woman called Ruchi said, 'Muslims want to stay separate and azad from India. We wouldn't have been a part of it [the movement], even if they had tried to include us. We want to be a part of India.' Another woman, Pooja, said she did not know much about militancy, as she was only a few years old when her family migrated. All she knew was that 'the Mohammedans and Pandits did a lot for each other but the Muslims were incited. My father had only Mohammedan friends earlier. They are very nice people. Some of them still visit my father.'

According to some, azadi was meant to remove all social evils in Kashmir: 'The talk of azadi and about a Kashmir with Pundit women without their men started later. We felt unsafe for our women because of which we left. After all we all have to die and I didn't care if I died there or here, but our izzat was more important.'

Memories of Loss

The memory of January 1990 was vivid for most people. They felt that the Muslims wanted to create a society where Pandits would either be subservient to them or leave. 'This was their revenge for our dominance in Kashmir for so many years,' said one. For those who were older things were not so extreme, bonds of friendship between the two communities had meant that neither felt threatened by the other. But for the new generation it was different. Amarchand Patil, a 72-year old man from Anantnag, said, 'The younger generation made it clear to us that they wanted us to go.' Ayesha, a Muslim

widow who fled Kashmir in 1991 recalled how it was snowing when
she left.

> Militants had killed my husband. He was matric pass
> and a daily wage worker in the government irrigation
> department. The militants came one night, told me
> they were suspicious of my husband and took him away
> for questioning. My brother was in the same room and
> taken away as well. My brother-in-law saw their dead
> bodies two days later in front of a relative's house. I
> was left with my three small children. How could I live
> there? I too left for Jammu.

She and her mother-in-law left Srinagar and went straight to a
Pandit neighbour's house in Jammu and stayed on his open terrace
for a month. They left Kashmir in a truck one night with no money
or belongings. A Sikh friend of her father-in-law then offered her a
room. To survive, she worked at a construction site, doing odd jobs:

> I would never have imagined doing this – *mazdoori* –
> in Kashmir. I loaded sand for a year at a construction
> site. The employer would give me Rs. 100-200 a day to
> not make me feel like I was getting just mazdoori. He
> could see my plight. He would even buy clothes for my
> children. Those days I made several trips to Nagrota to
> get a ration card made. My children would trudge with
> me the whole day, tired and hungry.

Ayesha also mentioned that her brother-in-law left Kashmir soon
after her husband's death out of fear that he would be targeted next.
She added, 'He is now a butcher here, selling meat in a small shop in
this camp. Before this there were no butchers in our family.'

Manna Devi, a widow with two teenaged daughters recalled:

> We came here in the summer of 1990. A Pandit had
> been killed in Kheer Bhavani because of which we left.

We thought we would be next, as we lived close by. My
husband's grandparents and few of us left together. Of
my two daughters, one was a year old and the other
only about 10 days old. I was still weak after delivery
but had no choice. There were huge processions, which
were frightening and leaving was the only option. All
of us left in a truck. We did not carry anything because
we thought we would return soon when the situation
improved. We had our own house, which my uncle later
sold off.

According to Ranjana from Kupwara,

We left in April 1990 because there were many killings
and Kashmiri Pandits being a minority, we were scared
that even we would be killed. We heard from others that
some Pandits in Kupwara had been killed. The radio and
newspapers gave similar information. There were also
slogans like 'Pakistan Zindabad' and 'Indian Dogs Go
Back.' Six other families left with us that day. We took a
truck and only a few belongings because we thought we
were leaving only for a few months. If the government
had stopped us then, it would have been a different
situation. We wouldn't have had to bear this trauma.
The government should have given us security there in
Kashmir. They could have stopped us, there was after all
only one highway for us to leave.

A Sikh woman, Rama, described the day her youngest son was
born as 'a jihad that took place in my house that night. It was 31st
December 1990. Some men barged into my house demanding that
my husband leave his job and that we leave our home. They also
warned my husband to watch out for us – his wife and children. All
our friends advised my husband to leave immediately.' However,
it was a Muslim man who helped her when she decided to leave:

'A Muslim man helped us leave. He said, you have helped so many people from our community; the least I can do is to help you in your time of need.'

The processions and killings in 1990 created fear among families about 'having to protect the izzat of our daughters.' The fear and threat of getting sexually abused was so great that a group of women told us that they had decided to hold live electric wires and kill themselves to protect their 'honour' rather than surrender to the militants.

Suman left with her sister in March 1990. She said, 'My parents wanted to send the girls out first. They went and stayed with their aunt in Jammu.' She spoke about the situation in the valley at the time: 'The situation was terrible. One couldn't even wear a tikka on one's forehead and go out. I was in 8th grade then. There were other slogans like *"hame chahiye azadi, panditayen ke saath"* (we want azadi but with Pandit women).' Usha Kaul and her family heard loud noises at midnight on the 20th of January. She was alone at home with her son that night and was terribly scared by the large processions she saw. She said, 'I didn't even know the meaning of azadi. I hadn't heard the term before. I decided to leave with other families.'

Shouldering Multiple Burdens

For women, the survival of the family in the harsh camp conditions was a daily challenge even as they mustered enough courage to make everyday living more bearable. Many spoke of how the lack of privacy, congestion and the changed climatic conditions added to the stress of daily existence and how it had taken a toll on their physical and mental health as well as their family life. While we saw many men loitering outside, playing cards or sitting around in the shade, the women were mostly at home, or out shopping for groceries. When we remarked to the women on the men's absence from the home, they explained that they went out so that women and children could have some privacy and space. They added, 'Even during summer when we need shelter from the heat, it was difficult for all family members to stay inside. That is why we have so many cases of sunstroke.'

For women who had lost their husbands, life in the camp was much harder. Bringing up children alone was the hardest. Several women complained of general anxiety, persistent headache or body ache as well as kidney problems or palpitations. None of them wanted to put up their late husbands' photographs 'so that the children don't feel sad all the time.' Manna Devi had to struggle to bring up her children after moving into the camp. In the process she fell ill and needed a surgery; her brother-in-law helped by raising money from different Pandit organizations in Jammu. She still finds it difficult to work but her two teenaged daughters help her. Many women said they would not marry their daughters to a man living in Kashmir: 'After all, we came all the way here for our daughters' safety and now if they went to live there, it would not make any sense.'

Nearly all the married women in the camps said the one thing that had been lost after moving into the camps was intimacy with their husbands. The complete lack of privacy in the small tenements ensured this. In Muthi Phase II, a woman put it poignantly: 'When our children go out, which is rare, we try and stay back. We tell each other that this is our Eid. That is the only time we feel like husband and wife.' Many women felt embarrassed to even hang their night-clothes or undergarments out to dry, as the clotheslines were so public. To change sanitary napkins was an ordeal for most as they had to use public toilets. Many women waited for the cover of darkness to be able to do so. As Rekha said, 'We women have to wait for the night to relieve ourselves.'

T N Khosa of Kashmiri Pandit Samaj told us that 'there were now a lot more cases of divorce, which is a new phenomenon for this community. I think there are about 350 cases registered in the court. For a small population of 26,000, this is a formidable number. Inter-family relations have broken down. This probably has to do with living in small rooms, and with the lack of space and privacy.' Indu Killam agreed but also added that 'one of the problems regarding migrant women is that the rate of divorce is high. There are 350 cases pending in the local courts. This is because of the lack of patience and to an extent it is also the result of women's mobility and exposure to a different culture.'

The only leisure activity women enjoyed was to watch television serials. 'I watch the serials and cry. It eases my burden', said Manna Devi, echoing Vimla's words. Women and girls had restricted mobility. Renu Bhatt, a single woman said, 'My son is free to stay outside after his tuitions are over, but my daughter has to stay home. How can she go out? I need to be doubly careful as they don't have a father anymore.'

Another group of women who faced hardships were those who are seen as non-state-subjects (people who were not original residents of J&K according to the 1937 Act). In their case, the government had, without warning, stopped supplying rations to them. They were told to go back to their states. But for some women, this was easier said than done. Rama, a Sikh woman from Amritsar, who lost her husband in the first few years at the camp, had no family except some distant relatives in Punjab. Her only brother was in Amritsar but not in a position to help her. 'We may not be state-subjects but are we not human beings too? Why have they raked up this issue after all these years? Our condition is worse than those recently affected by the earthquake. There are also rumours that non-state-subjects would also have to give up their one-room-tenements. Where does that leave me?'

In Muthi I there were 100 non-state subjects of whom 30 had managed to get the required documents to stay on in the camps. Rama spoke about another woman she knew who was also a non-state subject who had lost her husband and had three daughters to look after: 'Wouldn't those girls, out of *majboori*, take the wrong path for survival? We need to protect our women, but what can one do when there is no money and no support of any kind?'

We came across a few cases of Dogra women married to Pandits in the camps. Sunita Nag married a Pandit man who lived in Jammu, in the camp. Her family had met her husband when he was posted in Kathua where he rented a house from her sister. Sunita had heard about the camps but had never seen one until she got married and moved there. The trend of mixed marriages, she said, was not that uncommon anymore. 'There are many women like me who are locals but have got married to Pandits, especially women from Doda district who have married Kashmiri Pandits and moved here. Now the Kashmiri Pandits cannot marry only Pandits as they've left Kashmir and are scattered everywhere.' She was happy to have picked up the Kashmiri Pandit way of life: 'I have even learnt to speak Kashmiri and cook Kashmiri food.'

Children and Youth

Many Pandits sold their houses and land in Kashmir so that they would have enough money to educate their children. 'The schools in Jammu are nothing compared to Srinagar where people like Mahesh Bhatt, Anupam Kher and other famous people studied. Had my children studied there, they would have become doctors, teachers, anything they wanted', said Vimla Raina. Children who left Kashmir when they were older found it harder to adjust to the 'terrible life in the camps.'

'Migration altered our economic status', said Renu Bhatt. 'There was such a drastic change. As women we had much less to spend on the family and yet we took care of the children so that they would not feel deprived or sad, it was difficult but somehow we managed. Kashmir is known for its hospitality and even after migration we still tried to do as much as possible. The Muslim neighbours in Kashmir were helpful. They even helped us at the time of leaving.'

Children of widowed women suffered much more. Rama Devi, whose husband died suddenly at a young age after moving to the camp in Jammu, said that her sons were good at studies but had to give up education to earn money. Since Rama is a non-state subject and the government cut off her allowance suddenly without warning, they suffered even greater setbacks. She said she consoled her children who barely got one meal a day by telling them that things would change, that the dark night they were living through would one day be over. This sense of hope among Kashmiris – at least those who had seen better days – and the desire to be able to help others was common. Rama told us, with tears in her eyes, 'My husband had never seen a beggar's life. He was used to being the generous one. We were the happy ones; the sad and downtrodden would come to us for help. We suddenly became the unfortunate ones and he couldn't cope with this humiliation.'

Rekha said her daughter Preeti, now 18, 'hasn't learnt to play any games or anything new. She used to be thin but sitting at home all the time she had now put on weight. I can't let her go out because of the number of boys sitting idle and roaming around outside.' Another mother said, 'Our children have learnt to suppress their desires and needs, they know we cannot give them anything.' But there were women who went out as well. Nineteen-year old Puja, who found employment in a private company, said she had to take care of her family. 'My father has no sons, I have to show him I can earn and be his son.' She has often heard her parents talking about their sense of insecurity and fear that they might be pushed out of camps too 'like we were pushed out of Kashmir.'

Single parents had almost given up on educating their children because they couldn't afford it and single women, usually uneducated, said they could not even go out and find work to earn some extra money. Almost every child in the camp attended tuitions because parents felt that the atmosphere in camps was not conducive to studying. People like Rajendra Kumar, a mechanic in a local shop said, 'I gave up on my studies one or two years after migration because I didn't see the point of studying. The educated also remain unemployed here. I lost my childhood in Jammu. From being a schoolboy in Kashmir, I had to suddenly become a man and be responsible for my family. I was tense about everything – tense about studies, about my family, going out, everything. I couldn't go out also because of the changed climate; the heat was unbearable.'

Distressed Bodies, Distressed Minds

The shock and strain of the move to Jammu resulted in the deaths of a number of people. The harsh weather too contributed to this. According to the camp commandant of Phase II,

> Ninety per cent of the population here suffers from hypertension, as people are frustrated, jobless and stressed. When I came into this camp five years ago, I was appalled to see men sitting by the roadside playing cards, gambling the whole day. I stopped all this by renovating the Gita Bhavan and starting pujas there. This was an alternative for the people to spend their time in a better way. I want to now try and put up a library here so young people may also benefit rather than loiter around. Social interaction is necessary to divert people's attention from useless activities.

A doctor at the Primary Health Centre at Muthi II mentioned that until three years ago the health centre in Muthi I had functioned out of a tent. According to him, the problems Pandits in the camp were facing were new: many had first generation diabetes, hypertension and several skin diseases. Depression was also common and patients were being referred to the psychiatric hospital in Amphala. Both women and men suffer from similar problems, particularly stress related. Doctors were of the view that many of the health problems were probably caused because people had not changed their food habits and in the changed climate in which they now were, the food they ate was not suitable. While older people largely suffered from high blood pressure, high sugar and hypertension, the young had more stress related problems, addiction to tablets and general anxiety. Women faced hygiene related problems because of a lack of proper toilet facilities. Despite limited medical facilities, very few used the government Primary Health Centre in the camp as 'doctors take no interest in us; they have no equipment or medicines either.' Doctors also spoke about the exceptionally high cases of sunstrokes reported in the first few years of migration as well as about the heat and the poor living conditions that often led to psychological problems. The lack of an adequate number of public toilets, and the resultant crowding, had also led to increased gastrointestinal problems.

According to Dr Sushil Razdan, a senior psychiatrist in Jammu, 'Obesity, stress diabetes, arthritis are problems that have seen an increase among the Pandits because of a change in their lifestyle. Girls and women are more affected by stress. Men have fewer ailments: because they work in offices and are heads of families, their attention is focused elsewhere.'

Renu Bhatt's family fled from Sogam, Kupwara, in April 1990. They were tired of the daily processions, threats and stone pelting. But since they left Kashmir, she said, 'I have only seen problems. My husband fell critically ill after coming to the camp and died subsequently. This camp is so full of infections, no one here is used to the summer heat either. He was so well in Kashmir, where he didn't even complain of a headache mainly because the air and water were so different there.'

While we were talking with the doctor a middle-aged woman came into the clinic and complained that her husband had been watching television non-stop for the past four days: 'He used to be employed in Kashmir but hasn't found work for even a single day in the camp.' The doctor said that one in 100 migrants suffered from psychological problems: 'Young people too have become aggressive, they get into frequent fights because so many of them are unemployed and idle. Drug abuse is quite rampant among them.' Another doctor told us that the medicines at the Primary Health Centre were of such poor quality that people needed much higher doses: 'They come back to us complaining of the same problem, despite medication. When we advise them to buy medicines from outside, they get upset because all the ministers who come here say we are giving you free health care and medicines. Why should they have to buy medicines then?' The health clinics we visited were mostly bare, with minimum facilities – no refrigerators to keep medicines and hardly any laboratory equipment. The camp had no place for the critically ill. For instance, Ramesh Bharti had to take a loan of Rs 50,000 for his father's treatment and he had no idea how he would repay this, given that he was jobless. The constant worry and stress had negatively impacted his health too.

Several people we met seemed much older than their actual age. A 40-year old woman told us, 'I'm forty years old but some people refer to me as auntie and others call me grandmother.'

Another problem was that doctors were constantly moved around, so they could not build long-term relationships with their patients. As one of them told us, 'we are like footballs, posted anywhere, anytime.' There was an overload of doctors posted in each camp but only one small room was provided for them and this did not have any facility for water. Muthi Phase I had 50 doctors and there were 48 in Phase II. Of the 48, 14 were women. One of them told us how they had to adjust their timings: 'How can 48 of us be expected to work here the entire day in one room? It is like mental torture. We have to do some adjustments every day so that not all of us are here at the same time.'

The Impossibility of Return

'What is there now to return to in Kashmir? We have nothing left there anymore. We will go back if the government gives us guns for our safety', said a fire department official, for whom the safety of his two young daughters was his biggest concern. 'The government should give us jobs and consult us before making those shelters where we will never stay. The central government seems to function with its eyes closed', said another. Many saw duplicity in the government's rehabilitation policy of constructing new tenements in Jammu while at the same time encouraging the Pandits to return.

According to T N Khosa:

> We are part and parcel of India and have been for hundreds of years. Where will you throw us? I am against the separate housing being constructed for Pandits in Kashmir. We will be looked at with suspicion. We must be given the security to go back to our own homes. We do not want to go back and make enemies there which is what this flawed housing policy of the government will lead to. We were never consulted regarding this and already over 200 flats have been constructed. We have the right to live in Kashmir, among our own people. We want peace, normalcy and jobs in Kashmir

as prerequisites for us to return to our homes. But I wonder how the local Muslims will react to our return? They now run all the Pandit businesses and agencies in the Valley. Hence pockets of economic interests have developed there. There are dozens of banks where Kashmiri Pandits used to work; these have also been taken over by the Muslims. We were teachers, doctors; patwaris, and Muslims have also taken all this over and therefore might not want us to return.

A Panun activist believed that azadi was of advantage for Pandits 'because if Kashmiri Muslims get their demand for an azad Kashmir, we can also legitimately push for the same solution for ourselves, a separate homeland within Kashmir for Kashmiri Pandits. This will make us feel safer and more secure. We are all like living corpses here; we want a decision, a resolution to this problem.'

A widowed Muslim woman, Ayesha who lived in Muthi camp, had gone to Kashmir at the death of a relative but the fear wouldn't leave her: 'It was a traumatic experience. I would hear all kinds of sounds. I kept imagining someone was coming to attack us. I just couldn't forget the situation in which we had to flee nor could I imagine returning there.' Militants had killed her husband in 1990, suspecting him to be an informer. For her, finding accommodation in the camp was a difficult task. She met many 'influential people' to get a room there. But once she went and settled there she wondered, 'What will I do in the midst of Pandits with no Muslims around?' But she added, 'Soon everyone had become close. To me, my Pandit neighbours have been more than my relatives.'

Several Pandits said they would go back to Kashmir if Muslims who caused their exodus called them back: 'If the common man in Kashmir asked us publicly to return, we would go back, but if the government tells us to go, we won't because we don't trust the government enough. It is the people we trust. Why can't the

Muslims come out in large processions as they did for azadi and ask us to return?'

One of the solutions suggested for improving the situation in Kashmir was to remove Article 370 (a constitutional provision that provides autonomy to the state of Jammu and Kashmir, similarly as Article 371A does in Nagaland). Another suggestion put forward was that the government help each of the families to go back to their district headquarters in Kashmir as well as create links with the district officers to help them get jobs: 'This would encourage us to return.' Others wanted the kind of azadi in Kashmir they had earlier enjoyed: 'I used to travel in the bus with Mohammedans and felt safe. If anyone dared to so much as scratch a Pandit, the Muslims would immediately step forward to help.'

According to another, 'What is the point in making houses in Kashmir for us to return? We spent half our lives there, the other half here on the road. Should we now go back to Kashmir to die? Our children don't even know where our houses and property are. What will our children or we do there?' People also felt government policies that touched on the lives of migrants were confusing. Santosh Kumar said, 'Why are they constructing houses in Jammu as well as in Kashmir? I personally believe that it is not a good idea to arrange for Hindus to stay separately in Kashmir. This kind of segregation will tear the social fabric of Kashmiri society.'

Many Pandits in camps told us that they had recently managed to sell their lands and orchards, giving up hope of ever returning, deciding instead to improve their lives in Jammu. However, some had positive stories to share about their short visits to Kashmir. The camp commandant of Muthi II who returned to Rafiabad, Baramulla where his parents still owned land said that the local Muslims were taking care of it and recalled the warmth with which he was received and welcomed: 'Over two thousand people came to greet me when they heard I had arrived. The Muslims there are still taking care of my parents' land. The ethos of the village has hardly changed. They are very sincere people. Because I didn't have enough time during my visit there, they took my kids to show them our ancestral land. My parents live in Rafiabad because most of our apple orchards are there. They trust the Muslim families there.'

Vimla also went back to her village and had returned only a few days before we met with her.

> I went back to my village this year after 15 years for my nephew's thread ceremony. The environment in the village is still so nice. Our Muslim neighbours greeted us so warmly and said that they remembered us in our absence. They spent so much time at home with us. In fact, we spent most of our time with each other. Our Muslim neighbours knew how big the ceremony was but insisted that we must not call the police for protection. They said, 'no one will harm you.' The police arrived on their own for security reasons since we had returned after so many years. I had such a good time with over a thousand families gathered together. They kept telling us to leave the camp and return to our village. The Muslim children had never seen so many Pundits in one place earlier. They wanted to stay at our house, refusing to even go to school that day.. When I visited Srinagar though, I did not feel the same warmth as in the village. Those people in the city still seem to be jealous of us. No one said anything to us, but we felt uncomfortable there.

However, the fear of losing one's identity if they returned to Kashmir was something of a deterrent for some. Suman's husband was posted in Kashmir because of which they had an opportunity to go back and visit their old house. 'Everything had changed.' She said her husband managed to get a posting to Jammu because staying in Kashmir would mean losing one's identity. 'We couldn't all move there to Kupwara because we had no one there any more who was ours. Also, if we moved to Kashmir, we would have to live like the Muslims; say salaam, cover our heads, wear full sleeve kurtas and not wear a bindi.' Sunita told us about her family's visit to Kashmir: 'My husband went there twice sporting a beard. You need to look like the Muslims. My sister-in-law just went to stay in Mattan a few months ago. She told me she had to wear a full sleeve suit with no tikka.' They felt they belonged neither here nor there – neither fully integrated in Jammu nor ready to go back to Kashmir. Some Pandits spoke about 'the flavour' of Kashmir: *Pandit ab azan ke baghair nahin reh sakte.* The Pandits who have migrated here cannot live without hearing the Muslim's call for prayer. But we can wear a tikka in Jammu without fear.'

The Kashmiri Muslim leaders' plea for Pandits to return was also seen with suspicion by several people. 'If they were not responsible for ousting us, why do they feel responsible for getting us back? It should be the people of Kashmir who threw us out who should discuss our return. If they can come out on the streets to demand azadi, why can't they do so to demand our return?' asked Raina, adding, 'Why didn't they protect us in the nineties so that we wouldn't have to leave? We smeared a black mark on our foreheads and left Kashmir, didn't know whether we would live or die.' The fear of having to 'leave again' was mentioned by many as the situation in Kashmir had not improved and returning was therefore not an option. 'We don't think about going back because at least we have managed to get a life here. Imagine if we went back and had to leave again and start afresh?' a young woman wondered.

In describing their longing for Kashmir a group of men in Phase II said, 'The peace that we had there it's impossible to find elsewhere. Here, we're fighting with death every day, when you go to sleep at night, you don't know if you will wake up in the morning.'

But, they went on to say, return seemed impossible to them as the situation in Kashmir was far from normal.

❋   ❋   ❋

The nearly three-decade old political conflict in Jammu and Kashmir has led to tragic and at times dramatic consequences. The tragedy of 95 per cent of the Pandit community having had to flee their homes amidst fear, trauma and insecurity has to be seen as part of the larger tragedy of Kashmir.

Although the selective killings and the subsequent migration and displacement were an outcome of the specific political developments that marked the period prior to migration, they were perceived and projected in the media as a consequence of a communal, Hindu-Muslim conflict. However, we found that the communal propaganda and the concerted efforts of certain right-wing organisations such as Panun Kashmir to divide and polarize communities had largely failed on the ground as many of our interviews revealed.

That the majority of the Kashmiri Pandit community remains displaced and scattered even after three decades despite government plans and proposals for their honourable return and rehabilitation mainly reflects the failure and duplicity of the central and state governments and their administration. The construction of buildings simultaneously in Jammu and Kashmir for their accommodation while imploring the Pandits to return to Kashmir has sent confusing signals to the community in the camps as well as in Kashmir where segregated housing for the Pandits has raised doubts about their safety in the minds of the displaced, living in the camps. Hardly anybody we met was willing to return and live in such segregated areas. The government's economic packages and benefits for the migrant Pandits have also led to resentment amongst other migrants such as Muslims as well as among the non-migrant, resident Pandits in Kashmir who have been denied similar 'preferential' treatment.

According to the Press Information Bureau, Government of India, Ministry of Home Affairs (May 2015), the government announced a comprehensive package amounting to Rs 1,618.40 crore in the year 2008 for the return and rehabilitation of the Kashmiri migrants, which provides for many facilities for them such as financial assistance for purchase, construction and repair of houses, construction of transit accommodation, continuation of cash relief, scholarships to students, employment/self-employment, assistance to the agriculturists and horticulturists and waiver of interest on unpaid loans etc. The Prime Minister's Package of 2008 is being implemented by the Government of Jammu & Kashmir. So far, state government jobs have been provided to 1,553 migrant youths and one family has availed the benefit of Rs 7.5 lakh for house construction. Also, 469 transit accommodations have been constructed in the Kashmir Valley and these have been allotted to the newly appointed migrant employees under the package.

Kashmiri Pandit Sangharsh Samiti (KPSS) welcomed the Rs 1600 crore package and other incentives announced by the Prime Minister during his visit in April 2008 towards ensuring the return of the migrants but were upset at his turning a blind eye to the plight of those families from the community that stayed back: 'The Valley based Kashmiri Pandits only feel betrayed by the successive central governments which have ignored their suffering even though it is they who kept a ray of hope alive at the peak of militancy in the state.'[11] Under the PM's package, each family staying in Jammu will get Rs 7.5 lakh for renovating their houses in the Valley, with a job for one family member. The Hindu Welfare Society (now KPSS) in a press statement termed the PM's package a 'total injustice' with one of the members, Motilal Bhat stating that they 'deserved the package first as we have been demanding. Is our sin that we did not migrate to Jammu?' The continuing government dole and benefits had also resulted in aid dependency among a community known for its social and economic supremacy and independence. While government employees felt redundant and useless as they received their salaries without any work, other men felt emasculated, as they were not able to fulfil their responsibilities towards their families as they had earlier done. Women in the camps faced specific challenges on a daily basis as they tried to bring a semblance of normalcy to their uprooted lives.

The question remains that despite the generous government offers, why are the migrant, displaced Pandits reluctant or not willing to return? Has the government failed to ensure a secure environment for them to return, a demand that most of them have repeatedly made? And if the situation was safe and normal, where was the need for segregated housing for the Pandits, with surveillance and armed security for those willing to return?

As pointed out to us both in Kashmir and in Jammu, an entire new generation has grown up feeling alienated from the land of their own parents and grandparents, almost unaware of the historical and emotional roots that have existed and flourished between the two communities – an immeasurable loss as expressed by many of them whom we met.

Balraj Puri wrote in 1993 that 'suffering ought to unite those who suffered, not divide them against each other.' The suffering of Kashmiri Pandits and Kashmiri Muslims appears to have done what he feared, adding a competitive edge to the division, which is further exacerbated by the government's own intransigence and incompetence.

NOTES

1. The fieldwork and research for this chapter was jointly done with Juhi Tyagi, then a research associate at Aman.

2. Dabla, Bashir Ahmed. 2004. *The Sociological Dimensions and Implications of Migration in JK.* Srinagar: Department of Sociology and Social Work, University of Kashmir.

3. Bhasin, Ved. (Editor, *Kashmir Times*). April 6, 2006. Jammu.

4. Ibid. Dabla, Bashir Ahmed.

5. Mayilvanan M. 13 Feb 2003. 'Kashmiri Pandits: The Forgotten Community of Kashmir Conflict.' IPCS: Institute of Peace and Conflict Studies, New Delhi.

6. Bhasin, Anuradha. 2004. 'Auditing The Mainstream Media: The Case of Jammu & Kashmir' in Samir Kumar Das (Ed.) *Three Case Studies: Media Coverage on Forced Displacement in Contemporary India.* Kolkata: Calcutta Research Group.

7. Miles, Mathew B; Huberman, A Michael. 1994. *Qualitative Data Analysis: A Methods Sourcebook.* New Delhi: Sage Publications.

8. Case, D'Arcy Davis. 1990. *The Community's Toolbox: The Ideas, Methods and Tools for Participatory Assessment, Monitoring and Evaluation in Community Forestry.* Rome: Food and Agriculture Organisation of the United Nations.

9. A survey conducted by Kashmiri Pandit Sangharsh Samiti (KPSS) in 2008/9 revealed that there were 75,303 Pandit families residing in Kashmir as of 1st January 1990 but due to gradual migration, the number had reduced to 808 families comprising 3445 individuals by March 2008. The majority of the Pandits – 90-94 per cent – had migrated by mid 1990.

10. *Tehelka Magazine.* Vol 5, Issue 31. August 9, 2008. Delhi.

11. *Asian Age.* 29 April 2008. New Delhi.

chapter two

In the Absence of Their Men

THE PHENOMENON OF ENFORCED DISAPPEARANCES

> '*Mei cha dagh lalnawaan*' – I am cradling this pain – as
> a mother.
> I have been fighting for 27 years. Fight with me in
> whatever way you can. Kashmir is beautiful, but it is full
> of pain and grief. With this pain and grief in our hearts,
> we fight for justice.[1]

This is Parveena Ahangar, an aging mother, whose 16-year old,
school-going son was picked up by three officers of the Indian
National Security Guard in the early hours of 18 August 1990 from
outside her home in Batmaloo, Srinagar. He had returned late the
previous evening after studying at his uncle's home some distance
away. It was a daily routine for him to put in a few extra hours
of study so he could do well in school. He shared his name, Javid,
with another young man in the mohalla who was suspected to be
a militant and for whom the National Security Guard (NSG) was
searching. That morning, Javid heard a commotion outside his

house and stepped out to see what was happening. The sight of the
NSG officers and their Rakshak Gypsy jeep terrified him and he
scaled the nearest wall and ran. The NSG officers gave chase and
caught him a short distance away from his home, ripped his clothes
to check if he was carrying any weapons, beat him mercilessly and
then bundled him into the Gypsy and drove away. Home was not
the right place for Javid to be that night. The neighbours were
threatened and told to stay away and in his home, Parveena and
other family members were in deep sleep; his screams do not seem to
have penetrated the walls, built thick and solid to keep out the cold.
The incident happened at 3 in the morning as Parveena remembers.
It was only a few hours later, before dawn, that she was informed
by neighbours about what had transpired in the night and how her
son had screamed for Parveena to save him. Those who were present
when he was being taken away told Parveena that he kept shouting
(in Kashmiri), 'Save me my mother, save me my mother.'

Parveena was aware that such incidents happened all over
Kashmir but that her own son had met the same fate was something
she could not bring herself to believe. She ran out of the house in
search of him, hoping to find him hiding somewhere nearby but her
frantic efforts proved futile. Javid was nowhere to be found. He had
vanished. Twenty-seven years later, he is still nowhere to be found.
He has become one of the thousands of men, unofficially estimated
to be 8,000, in Kashmir who the custodians of law have 'disappeared',
a victim of the phenomenon that has come to be known as enforced
disappearances. Parveena continues to search for him relentlessly and
is also engaged in a legal battle with the government regarding his
whereabouts. 'Has the earth devoured my son or the sky gobbled
him up?' has been her query to the state authorities. She is not alone
in this. There are thousands of other women – mothers, wives,
daughters, sisters - of the disappeared men who have been searching
for them, some have approached the courts of law, after exhausting

all other means of locating their men. Wives of the missing men are
referred to as 'half-widows', neither wives nor widows since the fate
of the husbands is unknown – they could be alive or dead. Tragically,
this in-between status restricts their access to any legal recourse or
remedies. The Association of the Parents of the Disappeared Persons
(APDP) estimates that there are at least 1,500-2,000 half-widows
in Kashmir. Parveena has been instrumental in bringing together
such families and organising them for a collective struggle against
enforced disappearances.

❈   ❈   ❈

I first met Parveena in Srinagar ten years after she had lost her son. I
had just started my fieldwork in the early summer months of 2000
and when I tried to contact her, I was told that she was one of the
most interviewed women in Kashmir, with her life story and struggle
well documented in texts and videos. Everyone I met in Kashmir
mentioned her: they described her variously as an iron lady, a brave
mother, a mighty fighter, and a crusader for justice, spearheading
a unique struggle to find not only her own missing son but all the
other men who had met with a similar fate. Even though she was the
most interviewed woman in Kashmir, I felt I had to meet her because
she, in a way, epitomized the transformative journey of ordinary
Kashmiri women who challenged the heavily militarized state on
enforced disappearances and other brutal acts of state violence and
violations. I was also interested to know what Parveena thought of
militancy and the movement for azadi – which had led the state
to use its military might and repressive mechanisms against its own
people – and whether she had participated in any azadi processions
or protests. I knew her elder sister who was also a known and popular
woman in Kashmir, although for different reasons. She was known
to have worked for destitute women; particularly widows, in the
initial years of militancy but became one of the most politically active

and prominent women leaders in Tehreek-e-azadi through her close association with JKLF, the Jammu and Kashmir Liberation Front. We talked briefly about her sister's story. I was meeting Parveena at her APDP office at Amira Kadal that afternoon, and she greeted me with a warm embrace. We were meeting to specifically talk about her missing son and how his loss had changed her life along with that of her family.

The first time I went to see Parveena, the driver of the auto rickshaw I hired knew her address and recited it to me even as I began to explain where I wanted to go. 'Everyone knows her,' he told me. Over a period of time, as we met at her home, with other family members, at her mother's house where her sister and brother also lived, our friendship grew. I joined her in some street protests, and we also travelled together to different districts to meet other families of the disappeared. Little by little, I learnt her story.

Parveena told me that she had been married at an early age – twelve or thirteen – and within a few years she had become a mother of five children. She lived at home, did not go out much and generally led a peaceful life, caring for her children and the house.

> I do not know why people here picked up the gun. *Hum toh ghar baithe the – kya maloom kyun aisa hua* (We were people who stayed home, who knows how or why [militancy] happened. My sons never touched a gun. But see what happened? There's no justice anywhere. The Divisional Commissioner himself said there was no easy solution to this militancy problem. In fact, it will increase, he had said. The forces are brutal. In villages, they violate women's honour – our *ismat*. Such cases are not always reported as parents fear for the reputation of their daughters. They do not want to say that their daughter has been raped. There are cases where both mothers and daughters have become victims

of such brutality. Young men are full of anger. They feel
outraged. That is why they picked up the gun. Although
we use our own money/resources to fight our legal cases,
the government felt it necessary to verify why we had
formed this association. I told them I have nothing to do
with the Hurriyat or the Mujahedeen.

Before we turn to the story of how Parveena, along with Parvez
Imroz formed the Association for the Parents of the Disappeared
Persons (APDP) for the families of the disappeared, we need
to understand the phenomenon of enforced disappearances as
it unfolded in Kashmir, as well as the implications – both at the
personal and political levels – for people whose family members have
disappeared.

What does it really mean for these women, their families, the
community and the society they live in when their men are forced
to disappear thus? How and where did the phenomenon of enforced
disappearances originate? It is important to trace this practice as it
provides a historical glimpse into the phenomenon that has been
adopted by various countries around the world as a tool for violent
repression against their own people. The practice is not unique to
Kashmir but the systematic way in which it has been used in Kashmir
by the state authorities has destroyed innumerable individual lives as
well as those of their families, causing irreparable damage to both.
The 'invention' of this practice is credited to Hitler's 1941 Night
and Fog decree under which prisoners in occupied territories who
were suspected of endangering the country's security were seized,
secretly transported to Germany where they disappeared without
a trace, with no information ever given about their whereabouts
or fate.[2] The phenomenon reappeared as a systematic policy of
state repression during the late 1960s and early 1970s in Latin
America, starting first in Guatemala and Brazil. The term 'enforced
disappearance' was first used by Latin American NGOs and is

a translation of the Spanish expression 'desaparicion forzada.' Since then, the practice of enforced disappearance has become a universal phenomenon. Over the past 20 years, the United Nations Group on Enforced or Involuntary Disappearances (set up in 1980 as the first so-called 'thematic mechanism' of the UN Human Rights Commission UNHRC) has transmitted some 50,000 individual cases of disappearances to the governments of almost 90 countries in all regions of the world. Only about 10 per cent of these cases could be clarified through the efforts of the working group. India has attracted the attention of this working group as one of the countries with the highest number of unclarified cases of enforced or involuntary disappearances.[3]

The state's counter insurgency agencies employ many different methods to nab suspected militants and in the case of enforced disappearances, while men become direct victims of this violent method of abduction/arrest/disappearance, women and other family members not only suffer the social and economic consequences but are also psychologically terrorised and de-humanised. Enforced disappearance is a deliberate act used by the state and its agencies to intimidate and punish not only the individual victim but also his family and the community – a collective punishment. The UN has termed this practice 'a crime against humanity.'

In December 2006, the UN General Assembly adopted the International Convention for the Protection of All Persons from Enforced Disappearances (ED). It was for the first time that an international treaty required states to incorporate the crime of ED into domestic legislation and to prosecute and punish the perpetrators of such crimes. The Convention outlaws secret detentions and requires that states hold all detainees in officially recognised places, maintain up-to-date registers and detailed records of all detainees, allow them to communicate with their families and counsel and give access to competent authorities. The Convention also establishes the right of families to know the fate and whereabouts of relatives who have been detained.[4] However, India has not ratified this Convention and in Kashmir, successive governments have refused to set up a commission of enquiry for a time-bound investigation into all cases of enforced disappearances despite repeated demands from the families as well as civil society.

In Kashmir, the phenomenon is as old as militancy (1989). As every Kashmiri man is a suspect in the eyes of the state and the Indian Security Forces, a large number of innocent men, mostly civilians, have become victims of enforced disappearances. It is well known that a majority of them are from socially and economically underprivileged sections of society. In their search for militants, the Security Forces have not even spared school-going children (as in the case of Parveena's son), as the age of the missing ranges from ten to seventy years, according to APDP records. The relatives of these victims, after having exhausted all other means, have filed hundreds of *habeas corpus* petitions in the courts, following Parveena Ahangar's first petition in the Srinagar High Court in 1991. She told me that her son had just passed his matriculation exam and had already bought some books for college.

> He used to be very scared with all that was happening outside. I was told that the National Security guards who had taken him away were very big officers and that they would never be brought to book or punished. In 1994 the Srinagar High Court sent an affidavit to CBI to look into the case. They told me this. I had given names of all the three officers responsible for my son's disappearance. The police team returned with two of them. I was told one officer was seriously ill. The other two were not brought to court even though a date for hearing had been fixed.
>
> My file was also sent to the union home ministry in Delhi for grant of sanction to prosecute the two officers.

It has been two years now [this was in 2000-1] but there is still no sanction. The case was sent to CJM (Chief Judicial Magistrate) court. I went there to fight the case. There was a lady judge there who told me not to ever give up the case. She said I had worked very hard. She told me to go back to the High Court. Then last year [in May 1999] I again filed the case in the High Court. Last month's report declared that this case was unfit– even after investigation, inquiry and testimonies. There are five or six hundred such cases there, mine is the first one. I am not going to give up my search. So what if ten years have passed? I will fight till I am alive. I cannot forget my son even for a moment.

For a year after that fateful night when she lost her son, Parveena knocked on many doors, starting with the local police station, to file a missing person's report, and to register an FIR (First Information Report). She later went to the NSG (National Security Group) headquarters where she was told that her son was undergoing treatment in the army hospital in Badami Bagh but when she went there and obtained an entry pass, she did not find him anywhere in the hospital and the authorities were clueless about his whereabouts. They did not know anything about him, she was told. Another visit to the headquarters confirmed her worst fears when the authorities there simply denied that he had ever been in their custody. She visited many other police stations; control rooms, interrogation centres, hospitals and different jails in Kashmir as well as in Jammu but found no trace of her son anywhere. She then started travelling to different parts of the country, mainly visiting the jails, as it is a routine practice in JK to transport/lodge an arrested Kashmiri in jails in other states in India, thereby making it difficult for the families to travel to different parts of the country to meet their loved ones. How tortuous and insurmountable the administrative and legal procedures are for the families of the disappeared, both in terms of investigation

and delivery of justice is brought out clearly in the following account
of Parveena's own case.

From the Divisional Commissioner, Srinagar, to the President of
India, Parveena approached every official but to no avail. In December
1990 she made a presentation to the President, the Prime Minister,
and the Home Minister of India requesting them to direct the state
administration to disclose her son's whereabouts. Even though the
PM directed the concerned SHO to investigate the matter, nothing
came of it. Further, after receiving her *habeas corpus* petition in 1990,
the Srinagar High Court appointed the Additional Sessions judge
Srinagar as the enquiring officer. The judge examined a number of
witnesses during the investigation. One of them told the judge that
he had seen Javid in the custody of an NSG officer (name given) near
Grand Palace hotel on the night of August 17/18 as the witness was
himself undergoing interrogation in the Joint Interrogation Centre
(JIC), located adjacent to the hotel. The enquiry officer submitted
the report before the Srinagar HC in 1992 with the observation
that the officer mentioned above had arrested Javid. The case, along
with the findings of the enquiry officer was sent to the Union Home
Ministry for grant of sanction to prosecute the NSG officer. The
sanction was refused.[5]

❊   ❊   ❊

At the time of Javid's abduction, Parveena also had three other sons
and a four-year-old daughter at home whom she left in the care of
her husband as she embarked on what turned out to be an endless
search. She gave up wearing her burqa as the search intensified. She
gave it up for her son, she once told a young woman interviewer that
she had to appear in court, visit jails and interrogation centres and it
was not possible for her to do all this in a burqa.

My first interview with Parveena took place at the APDP office
at Amira Kadal in April 2000. She told me how she had given

innumerable interviews about her missing son and how his sudden
disappearance had turned her world upside down. 'Are you a mother
too?', she had asked me, as we began to talk. I told her about my
two daughters, one of whom happened to share the same name as
Parveena's daughter. She was delighted and embraced me saying that
I was like her younger sister then – although I knew that she was the
younger one. '*Meri umar toh ujad hi gayi*', she said in response to my
question regarding her age. 'I have lived with so much grief and stress
that I feel old', she said, adding that she suffered from constant pain
in her chest and that her health had deteriorated steadily.

> I do not keep well any more. I live on medicines. *Mein
> tension ki dawai khati hoon* - I take medicines for stress
> relief. *Main tho gham se pagal ho gayi thi - jab ladka
> ghayab ho gaya, bus tab mein pagal ho gayi* - I was crazy
> with grief when my son was lost, I really went crazy then.
> The first few months I had gone so crazy that I would
> throw stones at anyone who entered the house. I went
> to a local peer baba to seek solace and sanity. Then all
> these young boys from the neighbourhood would come
> to console me, saying we are your sons and we will do
> whatever Javid did for you. We will help you find your
> missing son. Their sympathy and affection gave me
> strength and restored me somewhat. Other women also
> came to me to say that their sons too were missing. It
> gave me hope that my son might be alive. I had heard
> that some mothers were offered a lakh of rupees as
> compensation but I refused to accept it and registered
> a case instead. Once, an *afsar* (officer) said to me, 'We
> will give you ten lakh rupees.' I told him, 'Give me my
> son's dead body instead. *Mujhe bhi tassalli hogi ki mera
> beta mar gaya hai* – it will satisfy me to know that my son
> is dead. My son was innocent. He never even touched a
> gun. Why should I accept money as a compensation for

him?' I started crying and he said, 'You are still crying
after ten years? You cry a lot.' There were five or six other
women with me who were also looking for their missing
sons. I told them that they could take the money if they
wanted because I knew how impoverished these women
were. But they also refused. I felt I shouldn't have come
to meet the divisional commissioner. *Jidhar bhi jate hain
dhakka hi khate hain. Koi nahin sunta hamari baat* –
wherever we go, we get pushed around, nobody listens
to us. I asked the officer, 'What is the use of casting
our vote?' I have submitted a list of missing persons. 'It
is a very grave situation for us', I told him, 'Please do
something. At least tell me whether my son is alive or
dead.' But nothing happened. I have seen pictures of
militants on TV. If my son is also a militant, why don't
they display his picture like they do of the others?

I went to Hindustan also. I met some members of
parliament in Delhi, human rights activists also. In the
High Court there was the Army/SHO/DSP/Police on
the one side and I on the other side, alone. They asked
me, sister what do you want? I said I want my son. They
told me to take ten lakh rupees and leave them out of
this, close the case. I told them *mein aurat hoon. Mujhe
paisa de kar chup karna chahte ho*—I am a woman. Don't
try to silence me with the money. I live in a *toota-phoota*
(dilapidated) house. I am ready to even sell that house
to continue to fight this case, I told him. Afterwards
many families followed my example and joined the
Association. They saw that I was not afraid. Why should
I be? I am fighting for truth. Nobody can harm me. But
this loss and grief have taken a toll on my health. I have
been taking tablets, morning and evening, for all these
years. *Neend nahin lagti. Darwaza khatkataya toh lagtha
hai mera beta aaya hai. Kaise neend ayegi*? I am not able

to sleep. Every time I hear the door open, I think my son
has returned. How can I sleep then? Sometimes I just
fall asleep at odd times in the day. *Bahut yaad ati hai bete
ki. Raat aur din. Main bhool hi nahin sakti.* I remember
him all the time. Day and night I think of him. I just
cannot forget.

Parveena broke down many times during our conversation.
Every now and again there were long spells of silence; I could not
find words to comfort her, words that were adequate or meaningful
enough, given the enormity of her sorrow and I felt a deep sense of
helplessness. She wanted to know whether I, as a mother, understood
the pain and anguish she was sharing with me. I was terrified at the
very thought of something like this, I told her, adding that I would
have perhaps picked up a gun to avenge my child's disappearance,
that I too would have gone crazy with rage and grief not knowing
whether my child was alive or dead. She looked at me calmly and said
that picking up a gun would have been an easier option. The path
she had chosen was a long and arduous one: she and others like her
were standing together to demand answers from those in authority,
to hold the military state accountable, to find justice where none
seemed to exist, to build a circle of solidarity and bring together other
women and families like her in pursuit of their missing children, in
pursuit of justice that would bring closure to their grief, which was
both difficult and challenging. It was a mother's resolve, she said,
that gave birth to APDP.

> We decided to come together and organize ourselves, the
> families of the disappeared. We are now more than 400
> members from different districts and villages – women
> and men both. It is mostly the fathers of missing sons
> who come forward to do the casework in the courts—
> mothers do not always come to the court but they come
> out on the streets to protest. I myself never used to go

out of my house before this happened. I would only
work inside the house not outside but since my son
vanished, so has my fear.

As is evident from her life trajectory, along the way Parveena also
lost the fear to cross the threshold of her home, the fear of the outside
world, fear of the police or the military, and the fear of the unknown.

> I will not sit at peace until I find him, till justice is done.
> In the Court they tell me, we have not seen a mother
> like you. I have worked so hard, not just to locate my
> own son but all the missing sons in my land. I have
> suffered a lot as a woman, as a mother. I have suffered a
> lot for my son. Some people laugh that I have become
> a leader. They don't know how my home and family
> life is disrupted: my husband's health has deteriorated,
> and my children don't have me around as I am hardly at
> home. But my demand is simple. I ask the state—if my
> son is dead, hand over his body to me. If he is alive, tell
> me, where is he? It is not a private matter concerning my
> son alone; it is a public matter concerning 8,000 missing
> men and their families.

Parveena's life, like that of hundreds of other Kashmiri women
who have lost a son, husband, a brother, a father, has been
dramatically transformed from that of an ordinary home-maker to
an active campaigner and fighter for justice and it is their collective
grief that fuels their activism. Certain words such as peace, justice,
normalcy, safety, security that have become part of daily political
discourse in Kashmir have acquired new meanings for these women
as they negotiate their daily lives in the very absence of these: the
violence of an enforced disappearance fundamentally alters the
relations of trust and safety that the family once enjoyed within and
outside the four walls of their homes. 'I am not afraid', she told me
more than once as we talked.

Only once I felt very afraid, not for my own safety but
for Parvez Saheb because one mother, an active member
of APDP, one of whose sons was missing for nearly ten
years and another had been killed, was shot dead by the
Army. I think this was done to intimidate and silence us.
Her name was Haleema. This happened in 1997. That
was the only time I stayed in the house for three days. I
was also scared that they would take my other son away.
I stayed home and kept an eye on him. I had to protect
my family.

As Parveena crossed the threshold of her home, in panic and grief
in the first instance and then gradually with resolve and confidence,
the boundaries between the private and the public began to blur. As
the privacy of the home was brutally intruded upon by a ruthless
state apparatus, it also (paradoxically) provided her and other women
like her an opening, a space to raise issues of mutual concern, to
meet and devise new strategies for collective struggle, to share their
experience of the prevailing political violence in its myriad forms and
to understand the specific consequences, for their everyday lives, of
the enforced disappearances of their men. In this, each woman's grief
found a new meaning and an articulation, a mutual recognition, and
an echo of hope from the others. One woman's assertion that 'there
will be no peace until I know his whereabouts, whether he is dead or
alive,' laid the foundation for shared solidarity and became the basis
of a collective quest for justice and accountability. It became one of
the many concrete ways in which to cope with this grave tragedy
as it simultaneously led to their politicization and radicalization.
For women like Parveena who resist, negotiate, and protest, their
activism marks a significant passage from victimhood to a sense of
agency. It is interesting to note, however, that during one of our
conversations about how women have had to take on new and
challenging roles that defied their victimhood and foregrounded

their agency, Parveena emphasized that she preferred to be known as a 'victim' as it held more meaning, more value for her in terms of being a mother of a disappeared son – that she as a woman/ mother victim had gained moral legitimacy to lead APDP more than anybody else: 'I know the pain and suffering of losing a son to these dark forces of enforced disappearance and I am therefore able to not only understand but empathise with other families who have met a similar fate.' Isn't it true that only a victim can feel the pain and suffering of another, she once asked me. She also made it a point to deny that her work was in any way political in nature, despite the fact that it was due to the violent political upheaval in the state that even her home had been targeted by the forces and had become a political space where she held regular meetings with other women to work out strategies of protest. She once mentioned how the women would earlier meet outside but since it was inconvenient, Parveena invited them to her own house. Those who came from outside the city or from a distance would stay the night with her, along with their small children. The women talked, cooked and ate together and also comforted each other. According to a young woman reporter, Parveena had mentioned that though the meetings were held at her house initially many of the women felt that they had to step out and be visible. That was how their monthly public protests had begun.

The Search for Justice

The Association for the Parents of the Disappeared Persons was formed in 1994 as the number of women looking for their missing sons/husbands continued to increase. It is one of the core members of the Asian Federation against Involuntary Disappearance (AFAD), which is based in the Philippines. The APDP has more than 500 families of disappeared persons from across the districts of Jammu and Kashmir as members. Its guiding principle, as stated in the APDP brochure is: 'We shall never allow the past to be forgotten and we shall never allow this crime to happen to our future generations. The justice we seek lies not in forgetting the past but in remembering those who should never be forgotten.'

It was during one of Parveena's visits to the high court in Srinagar that she met Parvez Imroz, a lawyer who was also looking into the increasing number of cases of the disappeared.

> For more than a year after my son was picked up, I was in a state of delirium. Later I began to visit homes to find out if they had experienced a similar fate, if any man in the family had become a victim of disappearance. I prepared a list of 120 such cases. I went to the court and filed a petition. Many other families began to do so. In the court I met one advocate, Parvez Sahib (Parvez Imroz), who offered legal advice and support. Since a growing number of families were now visiting the courts, we decided to form an association. We used to give a call in the newspapers. That is how many parents contacted us. Amnesty also sent appeals to parents to contact us. The numbers began to increase. It was not an individual, lonely struggle any more, as more and more families joined us. There was also a notice in the newspaper from the Divisional Commissioner asking parents of the missing sons to come and meet him. I went to see him. He said he was aware of the brutality of the Task Force that is why he had issued the notice. He told me that since I had spent so many years fighting I should try and organise all the other women whose sons/ husbands were missing. He said, form an association – call a meeting of such people otherwise your ten years will have been wasted. He told me, *Hindustan in logon ke liye 25 crore rupiya rakha hai* - India has kept 25 crore rupees for these people.

According to Parvez Imroz: 'The relatives of the arrestee exhaust all the extra judicial remedies to locate their dear ones. First, the law-enforcing officials are approached to know the whereabouts. They are assured that the detenues will be released shortly. After a few more visits, the helpless relatives are politely told that they did not arrest the detenues at all. The relatives, in a desperate state, approach the other security officials for help. They move applications to the civil authorities....some of them approach politicians of different parties who seem to be equally helpless. The police officials invariably hesitate to file an FIR against the security forces. These activities cost a lot of money. They [the relatives] travel to different interrogation centres in the state and outside the state. At first they are hesitant to seek a judicial remedy, as they feel it may endanger the lives of the detenues. Finally, with the passage of time, having exhausted all the channels, dejected, desperate relatives take recourse to the law.' Many families are known to have sold or mortgaged land and/or any other valuables while others have incurred heavy debts to meet the legal costs.

For women, the sudden loss of their loved ones often meant the loss of livelihood as well. Most families became destitute as a result. The spectre of an uncertain future followed them in the search for their men.

The transition in social status from a wife to a half-widow, not knowing whether the husband is dead or alive, was experienced by women as emotional violence and a social catastrophe. Family life, including the children's education, employment, and health was deeply affected and disrupted. The new reality was harsh on women and brought with it both new challenges and new roles. Prolonged armed conflict meant continuing trauma and grief and, in the absence of the dead bodies of their men, no closure.

The issue of women's well-being assumes greater significance in this context: not only is it challenged on a daily basis but there is a continuing and enhanced sense of vulnerability and insecurity for them. At the same time, the throwing open of 'unexpected' spaces can also be very confusing. The emotional, social and economic disruption that this causes has a direct bearing on women's lives as the very survival of their families is at stake. As the whereabouts of the disappeared men are not known and their bodies remain untraced, their wives and children are not entitled to any official relief and rehabilitation (except for a one-time ex-gratia payment that comes with a rider that once payment is received, no case shall be filed against the ED) that is available to other widows and orphans under the state's militancy victim scheme. As Parvez Imroz describes it:

> The enforced disappearance of the earning member of the family threatens its very existence. The half widows are sometimes deserted by their in-laws along with their children or forced to remarry against their will. They become a burden on their parents and this economic dependence affects the education and the future of their children. Besides the economic instability, the relatives suffer from constant agony…. They cease to have a normal existence. With the passage of time they suffer from different physiological and psychological disorders, including PTSD.

Education, employment opportunities and access to health services are among the major casualties that also bear directly on women. Many of them are reported to have become first generation workers in the absence of their men.

According to the records of the Association of the Parents of Disappeared Persons (APDP), there are approximately 8,000 victims of enforced disappearances (this figure relates to the time of writing), affecting more than 200,000 family members. The official figure for the 'disappeared', according to a statement on the floor of the legislative assembly by the former chief minister of J&K was stated to be 3,189 (2003), later altered to 1.093 (2005) and in February 2007, according to the then chief minister G M Azad, the number of disappeared stood at 700. The inaccuracy of these official figures reflects the government's confusion as well as its apathy, indifference, and ineptitude.

As I learnt over the years, the question of enforced disappearances was quite closely linked to that of fake encounters and the discovery of mass graves in Kashmir. In 2007, five cases of fake encounters had surfaced and the bodies of the victims were exhumed after intense public outrage against these civilian killings. It was found in all the cases that the faces of the victims had been disfigured to hide their identities and to escape scrutiny. Weapons had been placed on their bodies and then they were photographed, which made it possible to label these innocent civilians as Pakistani militants. As the Kashmir Solidarity Committee in Delhi (2006) wrote in its leaflet to protest against these fake encounter killings:

> These killings are not aberrations as officially stated but part of a system in which the security forces enjoy impunity under the AFSPA as well as [being] rewarded, awarded and promoted under the 'catch and kill' policy operating in J&K. These cold-blooded killings are conscious acts and not accidents or collateral damage where arms are planted on ordinary civilians to make the encounters appear genuine.

The families of the victims of enforced disappearance now feared that their loved ones might have met a similar fate. Even as protests over these fake encounters continued, reports started coming in of the discovery of unknown, unmarked mass graves in Kashmir.

In 2009, a human rights group in Kashmir – IPTK - International People's Tribunal for Human Rights and Justice in Indian-administered Kashmir– released a report entitled 'Buried Evidence' that had details of 2,700 unmarked graves in Kashmir, containing more than 2,943 bodies across five villages in Bandipora, Baramulla and Kupwara districts in Kashmir, based on detailed investigation and research that the team undertook between November 2006–2009. The report was submitted to the state and central governments but was first dismissed with the claim that the bodies were of militants (foreign) who had been killed in action and buried. The protests and demands for investigation mounted after the State Human Rights Commission's (SHRC) own report was released, that found 2,156 unidentified bodies in 38 sites in the region. The report recommended that the government undertake a thorough investigation to determine whose bodies were in the mass graves. Could some of these be the bodies of the disappeared men, wondered many, including families of the disappeared men? The government claimed that DNA tests could be conducted but soon abandoned the idea, given the large numbers of individuals and families that would have to be required to undergo forensic tests in several districts in the state. It also created a divided opinion among the organisers and members of the APDP as many people found that the argument that the mass graves contained bodies of the disappeared gave the government the advantage while rendering the APDP's struggle weak or even futile. Many refused to believe that their missing men were dead and buried and would never return, with Parveena categorically voicing their collective concern and anguish. During one of the protest meetings following the discovery of mass graves, she told a news reporter, 'Our children are not dead. We believe that they are alive and it is the government of India that is responsible for their safety.' She demanded an impartial commission of inquiry to look into the enforced disappearances, and at the recently surfaced reports about unmarked graves. This was important so that the members of her association could deal with the lack of knowing that had virtually paralysed their lives. Parveena felt that those who claimed that some of the disappeared youth may be buried in the nameless graves were trying to sabotage her struggle and that their claim was aimed at diluting APDP's political stand and creating confusion among its members. 'We would have accepted this expose, if it had come on the lines of the Ganderbal fake encounter where bodies were exhumed and later DNA tests were conducted which authenticated their [the victims'] identity as civilians. But we cannot say who the persons buried in those graves are,' she told the news reporter.[6]

Life After Loss

At one of our meetings Parveena told me that although her elder son was a graduate, he had remained unemployed: 'Wherever he goes for a job, he is told that I should first close this case before he can find a job. I told him not to go to any of these people. He has been asked to give it in writing that I will close this case if he were to be given a job.'

In other families too, the sudden hardship and grief altered all other aspects of their lives. Women who were earlier not required to go out to earn had to do so now, adding to the numbers of female-headed households. There were families where, after the disappearance, not a single earning male member was left which meant women had to take on multiple roles and also carry the hardship it entailed. Zaheeruddin explained to me that the problem was compounded because, according to Muslim Personal Law, if the disappeared person could not be traced dead or alive, the heirs could not inherit his property for seven years, after which they were required to move the Court to have the disappeared person declared dead. The judicial process would take another two years to complete, which in effect meant that the heirs had to wait for nine years before they could inherit whatever property there was. Moreover, the wife of the disappeared person had to similarly wait for seven years and then seek judicial intervention to have her missing husband declared dead. She was required (legally) to wait for nine years before she could exercise the option to remarry. Since the government does not officially recognize disappearances, women and families have to face many other challenges such as applying for ration cards, transfer of land title etc. If the disappeared is a public servant, his disappearance is treated as 'wilfully absent', leading to termination of service and benefits. Even to access government relief (such as ex-gratia and employment on compassionate grounds) proves difficult as it is contingent upon the family being able to provide a death certificate and proof that the disappeared person was not involved in militancy. How is it possible to provide either a death certificate or No Objection Certificate (NOC) when the disappearance itself is not acknowledged?[7]

There are instances where families, reluctant to keep their half widowed daughters-in-law, have taken the step of throwing them out along with their children. The fortunate among the women were able to return to their natal families but others were forced to remain at the mercy of their relatives and neighbours. Young half widows were sometimes coerced into marrying their husband's brothers; refusal often resulted in the threat of separation from their children. Parveena described how a young half widow suffered on this count:

> My heart goes out to this young woman whose husband has been missing since the day the military picked him up. She has four small children whom she has to look after. She has nothing. We all try to help her. The children are forced to go begging. Her in-laws have disowned another woman, with two small children, after her husband went missing. We tried to convince her to remarry but she refused, as she believes that her husband will return one day. She earns a small daily wage by working on the charkha at home.

In such cases women had to file petitions in the local court for custody of their children. In this regard, young half widows seek moral and emotional sustenance from their older counterparts like Parveena who advise them to bear the suffering with fortitude, for the sake of their children's well-being.

Children who grow up in the forced absence of their fathers and brothers are, tragically, known as half orphans. Too young to comprehend the gravity of the situation, they sense and absorb the grief around them. Year after year, mothers console their children and find ways to explain the absence of the fathers – generally the story is that fathers have travelled out on work and will soon return. Many of the children also accompany other family members to participate in public meetings and protest demonstrations that are organised by APDP every month. They can be seen holding placards that ask, 'Where is my father?' and 'Am I really an orphan?' In a meeting to commemorate the International Day of the Disappeared in Srinagar (2004), an eight-year old girl's response to a query regarding her problem was straightforward, '*Mere bhi abba gum ho gaye hain. Ammi unhe dhoondti hai*' – My father is also missing. My mother is searching for him.

All day long, children sit patiently and listen to stories of how a particular disappearance took place, how it affected other family members, how they coped and the continuing, valiant search for their loved ones by the family. Many of the children have grown up without any memory of their fathers. They have learned to internalize and live with the language of absence and grief that they hear around them such that, when they speak of their absent fathers, they often do so by borrowing the idiom of the adults. Unlike the adults, though, they do not cry that easily.

Parveena's own daughter Saima was barely four at the time of her brother's disappearance and she does not have any distinct memories of him although she has grown up hearing many stories about him, the oft-repeated one being that of his disappearance. Once, when I was with Parveena at her home and sitting with her under warm blankets, Saima, a teenager then, snuggled with us, chatting and laughing. She was in school then and determined to join college for further studies. I asked her what she would like to do once she was done with college and prompt came her reply: 'Carry forward my mother's work and struggle.' She added, 'I will continue the search for my brother and will not let my mother's hard work go to waste.' She had already started going to the APDP office whenever she could and planned that once she had completed her graduation she would go there every day of the week. She had told me how concerned she was at her mother's deteriorating health and wished that Parveena would rest a little. Now a young mother, Saima tries to distribute her time between the APDP office and her home, looking after her little son. Parveena once told a reporter that she had prepared her daughter to take on the struggle – 'mere peeche meri beti ko mein ne tayyar kiya hai is ladai ke liye.' She recently told me over the phone that it is now three generations at the APDP office as her grandson accompanies her and Saima on certain days.

I also visited many other families of the disappeared and met women whose future meant nothing more to them except the ardent hope that the 'the father of the children will return.' There were others who had given birth to a child after the disappearance of the father. One such young woman described her situation thus:

> I am 18 years old. I was married at the age of 14. I have two children. This little one in my lap was born after my husband was taken away. His friend who visited us often wanted my husband to become a militant but he always refused. His friend was an *ikhwan* (informer). He is the one who came with the Army one day and pointed out my husband to them. He was arrested in front of me. I pleaded with them but they dragged him away. I have

not seen him since then. I constantly worry about him
and my young children. How will they grow up without
their father? I feel scared. Now they have grandparents
but after them, what will be our fate? I am so young,
what can I do? I have to educate my children. There are
many young women like me but their situation is worse
as their in-laws have abandoned them. I live only for
my children's sake; otherwise there is no meaning left
in my life.

In our meetings, the women implored us to help them in their
quest for justice, they wanted their long wait to bear fruit and their
loved ones to be returned to them: 'If not alive then at least their
dead bodies should be handed over to us so that we may bury our
grief along with their bodies.'

According to Parvez Imroz, 'the relatives of the disappeared are
initially hesitant to seek judicial remedy for fear that it may endanger
the life of the detainee. At the same time, the police are hesitant to
register a First Information Report (FIR) against the Security Forces
for fear of reprisals. It is a problem-ridden battle from the start. The
state gives an ex-gratia payment of Rs 100,000 to the half widows
but it is then required that they close the legal case and accept that
the disappeared person is dead. While the majority of them have
refused to do so, some have had to do it due to destitution and under
family pressure.'

Of the 1,417 cases documented by APDP in the initial years, it
was found that most disappearances had occurred in the rural areas
where women enjoyed less economic and social independence. This
rendered them economically dependent, most often on their in-
laws, with their property and custody rights undermined, and also
left them open to economic exploitation and extortion by those in
positions of power for any information on their disappeared loved
ones. It is alleged by some that even government officials at times

make direct demands of money in exchange for any information regarding the disappeared person.

The list of the 1,417 cases was submitted to the J&K government in 2011 but there was not even an acknowledgment that it had been received. Government indifference and apathy is compounded by the difficulties and obstacles of taking recourse to the legal route: here procedures are convoluted, long-drawn out and daunting. Only about 5 per cent of the women who are half widows choose the legal option and those who do so often lay themselves open to intimidation, harassment, coercion and blackmail at the hands of the perpetrators. Sometimes, to pursue their cases, they need to meet with the police or with government officials, and this makes them even more vulnerable, for now they are suspected of being informers.[8]

In addition, the majority of the women are uneducated, and have little awareness of legal procedures or of their rights. To address this lack, APDP and Aman prepared a basic booklet to help families understand the steps to be taken post a disappearance, and how to seek legal redress. The idea was that this booklet would be shared/read out/discussed in meetings at the district level where many families gathered. It was distributed widely among the families in different districts. However, the loss of faith in the judiciary is a much more widespread problem than just among the families of the disappeared. I travelled with Parveena to Handwara and other districts to distribute/discuss the booklet and meet the families of the missing men; every time scores of men and women would arrive within minutes of our arrival to meet her, seek her support, advice, and help. Even though we were stopped frequently at check-posts and told to get out of the vehicle and walk while the vehicle was being searched, it was interesting yet ironic to see how respectfully the J&K police officers would greet Parveena and express their sympathy to her.

On any given day large numbers of men, women and children could be seen in the premises of the district magistrate's court where they would come either to file or follow the *habeas corpus* petitions they had put in about their disappeared relatives. According to APDP records, there were more than two hundred such cases languishing in the High Court, without a single conviction having taken place even in cases where family members had witnessed the arrests and identified the guilty officers. Under AFSPA, the perpetrators were indemnified against prosecution without prior approval of the home ministry/central government – and such approval has never been sanctioned.

❖   ❖   ❖

Faceless Victims

Enforced disappearances render their victims faceless. But women in the family, as they shared details and descriptions of their disappeared men, as they displayed their old photographs, lent them a certain persona. Everyone I met had a plastic bag tucked away in the house, which they pulled out to share the newspaper cuttings and photographs that it contained. These plastic bags were a precious possession for the women for they contained not only memories but also proof of the existence of the disappeared person. The dusty bags, with folders containing faded photographs, indicated the passage of time. In Parveena's house it was poignant when she asserted with pride, looking at the framed photograph of Javid on the window sill, that her missing son must now be a young man: '*mera beta ab jawan ho gaya hoga*', she had said, holding the photograph and imagining her missing son. For her, he was no more a school-going boy. She believed that a young man would return home one day in place of the little boy she had lost.

For a glimpse into the lives of the disappeared and their families,[9] we undertook a survey (2002–2003) and visited nearly sixty families in three districts of Kashmir to try and construct a profile of the disappeared as well as that of the family through in-depth interviews and informal conversations. We were keen to understand the predicament of the families and the many implications of their loss, and more specifically, to resurrect the disappeared. Our questions related to the socio-economic background of the disappeared person, to his age, his level of education, whether or not he was employed, was he the sole earner in the family, and so on.

We picked a random sample from the APDP list of the disappeared in consultation with Parveena and Parvez Imroz. It took more than five months for us to conduct the interviews because of the high security environment and the constant surveillance that accompanied us. In fact, our young colleague from Srinagar – Sohail Shehri - who helped in conducting the interviews was detained by the army and interrogated on three different occasions, forcing us to be more clandestine in our efforts to reach the families. Many of them were anxious that the army might visit them to find out what information they had shared. It was the fear of the army backlash that prevented them from filing FIRs at the police station or, if they had managed to file one, pursuing their cases over time. In Handwara, an active member of APDP – a young half-widow with three children - was shot dead by unidentified gunmen in her own house. This is where APDP had held many of the meetings that I also attended, where people from other districts would come in an effort to bring the grieving families together. While her killing created fear and panic, it also triggered anger and rage among the people. They continued to demand justice for her and her three children and for her missing husband. Nothing came of it though, as far as the government was concerned - no investigation, no punishment, and no compensation for the family of the victim.

We met and interviewed whoever was available at home to talk about the disappeared member of the family and while it was by and large women (wife/sister/mother) who spoke with us, in some families, there were also men (father/brother/son) who did so. What we found through our survey was revealing and also confirmed what the records of the APDP suggested. The age range of the disappeared victims varied between 9-70 years. The majority of those who had been picked up were illiterate (23) but the highest numbers of the victims were students (14). The occupational profile of the disappeared showed that the majority of them were engaged in small business/petty trade (11). There were five government employees and five others who were teachers at government run schools. As enforced disappearances were based on suspicion or used as deliberate acts of intimidation, even government employees and teachers were not beyond the pale. When we looked at the economic status of families we found that, after the disappearance, the majority of families survived on a meagre monthly income of Rs 500 or less. On the issue of the large number of cases filed in courts, our survey found that 56 out of 65 families had registered a case and 47 of these were filed in the Srinagar High Court. Nine families had not filed a case as they had accepted the one-time ex-gratia payment of Rs 100,000, mainly because of destitution and ill health.

❀   ❀   ❀

The emotional upheaval and uncertainty caused by the disappearances also impacted people's health, in many cases leading to long-term health problems, particularly mental health issues as the families of the victims were traumatized by the sudden loss of their loved ones. In addition, there was no closure on their grief – the constant hope that they were alive was matched by the fear that they may be dead. It is noteworthy that whenever Parveena shares details of her son's disappearance and recalls the traumatic moment in her life, whether at home with visitors or in public meetings, she is overcome with symptoms that are akin to PTSD. Her narrative is often accompanied by intense sobbing, palpitations, cold sweat and high blood pressure. The passage of time has not healed the deep psychological wound that she nurses, nor has the continued medication helped. In her case, Dr Mushtaq Marghoob, a senior psychiatrist at the government psychiatric hospital, told me, 'The search for her son is the only concrete meaning left in Parveena's life and allows her to cope with her grief. The day she stops the search, her life may be endangered.' Among the many workshops we (Aman) did on 'trauma' with different groups of affected people, there were two we organized with a group of women from the families of the disappeared at a houseboat on the Dal Lake. Except for one woman in a group of nine, none of them had ever been on a houseboat earlier and expressed how peaceful and calm they felt in these surroundings. During the course of the workshop, when different colour pens were offered to them to draw out the specific events and markers in their lives, they all giggled and laughed as they had no memory of ever doing such an exercise but as they slowly and hesitantly began to draw, they used all the vibrant colours to indicate marriage, childbirth, school admissions etc. However, to mark the disappearance of their loved ones, all of them used only black to fill the page to express how dark their lives had become since then and many of them broke down and sobbed while also trying to console each other.

Parveena repeated what she has often said, that she is waiting to see her son as a young man now, refusing to even consider the possibility that he may not be alive anymore. *'Jab mein sunoongi ke mera beta mara hua hai mein kya kar sakti hoon? Mein phir zinda nahin rahoongi. Lekin lagtha hai woh ek din zaroor ayega. Mein intezar karoongi. Aaj das sal ho gaye. Mere pair bhi gal gaye – aankh ki roshni bhi chali gayi. Lekin mein dhoonthi rahoongi'* - If I were to hear that my son has died, what will I do? I will not be able to live anymore. But I do believe that he will return one day. I will wait. My legs have no strength anymore. The vision in my eyes is bleak. But search I will, until I find him.

The issue of enforced disappearance is interlinked with that of women's rights, their privacy and their health. Mental health, which has been severely impacted in Kashmir, as well as the question of women's well being, must be understood in the context of the conflict, the ongoing attendant violence, and specific violent acts such as enforced disappearance. The trauma it generates afflicts the individual (victim) as well as the social group (family) it targets. The intense trauma shatters whatever meaning the world held for them. Paradoxically, it also radicalises many who build a culture of resistance and struggle, as in the case of APDP. For women, the traumatic manner in which mediation occurs between the private to the public sphere also colours their perception of the self and the world. The story of Parveena Ahangar and women from other families of the disappeared epitomises the larger reality of the unresolved conflict and violence that has touched each life and breached the social harmony of the community, altering women's lives and their perception of the world, both as victims as well as agents. The quest for justice and accountability, safety, and security has become the essence and hallmark of women's existence as they try to protect the remaining men in the family with a 'heightened sense of urgency.'

The state's enforcement of coercive laws and its indiscriminate suspicion of ordinary people, in effect means that the people are constantly under surveillance, confronted with the threat of abuse, detention, and even death. The AFSPA, with its sweeping mandate to raid, search, detain, or kill, has undermined fundamental rights while creating lawlessness in society. Every individual or a family has an experience of violence and loss to narrate.

As far as legal recourse is concerned, people have lost faith in the judiciary as it hardly delivers justice. In the rare instance where prosecution does take place against personnel of the security forces, conviction does not. Hundreds of cases of disappearances, filed by the affected families, continue to remain unaddressed in the Srinagar High Court because the union home ministry refuses to grant sanction for prosecution of the guilty. However, the state's tactic of intimidating and punishing ordinary civilians in order to force them to submit and to break their will to fight has had the opposite effect as clearly seen in the case of the APDP. The women's resistance and protests, the campaign mounted by human rights activists and their consistent demand for the state to come clean about the whereabouts of the disappeared, has brought the issue into the national and international realms. Parveena and APDP have gained in strength, worldwide solidarity and prominence through this unique struggle and campaign that began in the 1990s, nearly thirty years ago.

※　※　※

While the Indian government refuses to acknowledge enforced disappearances, including her son's, Parveena and Parvez Imroz who co-founded APDP in 1994 were recently conferred the prestigious Rafto Award in November 2017 at Bergen, Norway in recognition of their pioneering work/campaign against this inhuman practice. To conclude, I would like to reproduce excerpts from Parveena's speech on the occasion:

> In the beginning, I searched for my son everywhere. I went mad with grief. But then I began to see others who were also searching for their loved ones, their sons, their husbands, their brothers, their fathers. Along with the family members of the victims of enforced disappearance, Parvez Imroz, and I co-founded APDP....the women

and men who are part of the APDP come to Srinagar
from many parts of Kashmir, on the 10th of every
month. We sit in Pratap Park, in Srinagar, to protest,
to keep our memories alive. The process has been going
on for decades now, but the arrogance of the Indian
state is unchanged. We share our tears and our grief at
the absence of our loved ones. We demand that India
ratify the protocol against enforced disappearances. We
demand that India let us know where our loved ones are
or what has happened to them. We demand justice. We
usually say, *'yeh tamasha nahi hai, yeh matam sahi hai'* -
this is not a spectacle, our mourning is for real.

My struggle began with searching for my son. I was
illiterate and a woman living in a militarized zone. I had
not stepped far from my house. The search for my son
has led me far and wide. It has led me to others who
were also searching for their children, their husbands,
their fathers, their brothers. I now travel with APDP
members across Kashmir not only in search for the
enforced disappeared, but to listen to, document, and
witness stories of family members killed in extra-judicial
encounters, torture, and rape. I know that this is also a
struggle for many mothers like myself around the world.
Some of these mothers include the Mudur de Plaza
de Mayo from Argentina, mothers in the Philippines,
mothers in Sri-Lanka. I accept this award in the name
of all these mothers as I accept it for the families and
mothers of Kashmir. I am known as the 'iron lady' of
Kashmir. And I say to you all – that all these mothers are
iron ladies – we have been fighting for our children – and
we will fight from beyond the grave. One of our APDP
members, Mughal Masi, died after 20 years of waiting
for her son. But we carry on her struggle. We carry on
this struggle by sitting in Pratap Park Srinagar every

month, letting everyone know that our memories of our children or husbands, or fathers or brothers being taken away will not be erased. For us, our family members who have been taken away are our life. Our memories are the wounds of injustice. Our memories are our resistance. This daily resistance is our life.

❊   ❊   ❊

NOTES

1. Ahangar, Parveena. 2017. Excerpt from a lecture given at The Rafto Conference. Bergen, Norway.

2. Enforced disappearance consists of a kidnapping, carried out by agents of the State or organized groups of individuals who act with State support or tolerance, in which the victim 'disappears'. Authorities neither accept responsibility for the dead, nor account for the whereabouts of the victim. Petitions of habeas corpus, or other legal mechanisms designated to safeguard the liberty and integrity of citizens remain ineffective. Enforced Disappearance constitutes a grave threat to the right to life and violates fundamental human rights:

   The Right to Liberty and the Security of the Person

   The Right to Recognize as a person before law

   The Right to legal Defence

   The Right not to be subjected to Torture

   The objective of enforced disappearance is not simply the victim's capture and subsequent maltreatment, which often occurs in the absence of legal guarantees. It creates a state of uncertainty and terror both in the family of the victim and in the society as a whole. Uncertainty exists because people do not know what to do or where to turn. Terror is caused by the unknown yet undoubtedly terrible fate of the victim, and the realization that anyone can be subjected

to enforced disappearance and any motive may be used to justify the
disappearance.

See more at: http://apdpkashmir.com/enforced-disappearances/

3. Roy, Laifungham Debrata. 2002. 'Enforced Disappearance', Manipur
   Online, March.

4. Zahir-ud-Din. 2001. *Did They Vanish in Thin Air? A Book on Enforced
   Disappearance in Kashmir*. Volume 1. Revised Ed. Srinagar: Owaisi
   Publications.

5. Imroz, Parvez. 'Enforced or Involuntary Disappearance in Kashmir.'
   Combat Law, Oct-Nov 02 Vol. I Issue 4.

6. Ibid.

7. *Kashmir Times*. 10 April 2010. Srinagar.

8. Association of Parents of Disappeared Persons. July 2011. *Half Widow,
   Half Wife? Responding to Gender Violence in Kashmir*. Srinagar.

9. Ibid.

10. Sohail Shehri, a student at Kashmir University then, helped me greatly
    in conducting the survey and in collecting information from families
    of the Disappeared in different districts, despite the risk he faced from
    the army/paramilitary during the period.

chapter three

The Other Face of Azadi

THE PRESENCE OF WOMEN IN THE MOVEMENT

It was the call of azadi that first brought us out of our homes. All of us – women, men, the young and the aged – came out from villages and towns in support of it. My mother also rallied around this call. In the beginning of the *Tehreek-e Azadi* people came out voluntarily in support of the militants. People even invited them home for meals and also donated money for the cause. They were treated as though they were gods. The spirited, fervent slogans and the people's enthusiastic response made it seem as though our victory was only a few days away. Then days turned into months and years…*yehan se nara toh wahan se goli* (a slogan from here and a bullet from there). To contain this upsurge, army atrocities on people increased leading to untold suffering and injustice.[1]

It is well known that when militancy began in Kashmir, women participated in large numbers. They came out onto the streets with their men, raising slogans for azadi, they played a constructive and strategic role in the movement, supporting their men wholeheartedly in the *Tehreek-e-Azadi*, providing moral and logistical support to militant outfits. Many women I met during my fieldwork recalled how that moment was charged with a sense of imminent change

and a better future for all. At the time, women did not worry if their
men were late returning home. If a man died in the conflict, he was
considered a martyr, and grief at his loss was accompanied with a
sense of pride. Both men and women described in vivid detail the
excitement of participating in large processions; they talked of how
slogans and songs for azadi rent the air from village to town and
how inclusive and widespread the processions were. The demand for
azadi cut across class, gender and occupation as everyone came out
on the streets with women being both visible and articulate. While
this was clear to me as a researcher, I was also interested in something
that was less known, and that was the experiences of women who
were related to militants and what that meant for their safety, and
the security of their families. I wanted to document this reality, to
pay particular attention to women whose husbands, brothers, fathers
had crossed over for arms training. Their long absences – some of
them never returned – left their families vulnerable to violence at the
hands of security forces. Women I met and interacted with believed
that their contribution to the movement also lay in the fact that
they took on all kinds of responsibilities, both within and outside
their homes. They managed and sustained the survival of their
families, took care of their children's education, and looked after
aged or ailing parents while at the same time drawing strength and
sustenance from them. In many homes where mothers gave birth
to children after the father crossed over, women devised ways to
keep alive the absent father's memory for the child as he/she grew
up. No wonder then that during interviews and conversations with
women in their homes, many teenaged children also recalled details
of what had transpired at home and how courageous women in the
family had been, particularly when women broke down or there
were spells of silence. The children had grown up on stories of their
father's bravery, stories of azadi and with the dream of receiving and
welcoming their Mujahid father home one day. However, as many
women pointed out, they or their homes were not particularly safe

even after the men returned. As a woman in a village in Kupwara pointed out to me, the security forces had picked up and tortured her husband twenty-seven times even after he had given up arms and returned home. There were times when his battered body would be left outside the door and 'nursing him back to stand on his own feet was a severe challenge for us.' 'Our homes are not safe even after the men have disarmed and returned home', she said. The women and their homes were marked forever in the eyes of state agencies as those who had harboured and supported militants; in their own eyes, however, the women believed that they were the backbone of the azadi movement.

Azadi is my dream too, said a middle-aged woman to me once as I met her one afternoon, along with many other women and men who had come out to protest against a raid by the security forces on one of their homes. The raiders had ransacked their home, abused and threatened the residents, particularly the women and had threatened further raids. Women led high-risk and dangerous lives, both inside and outside their homes, due to the sheer fact of being related to a militant. Men who had crossed over, picked up the gun, returned and fought many battles, also remembered how women had played a major role during the period. As one of them said:

> Women were so proud of us as Mujahids. They'd compose songs and sing them in our praise to welcome us as we passed through any village or town. It was like a festive occasion. It was meant to welcome and encourage us. We felt as though we carried a burden of responsibility but azadi was their dream too. They were prepared to take any risk for our safety. If any of us got arrested, they'd be the first ones to come out of their homes and protest until our whereabouts were confirmed. They were fearless.

Women in the family echoed him: 'We women always supported the Mujahids and even if we were abused or beaten up, we would not disclose where a Mujahid or his associates were. This was our way of participating in the movement.' Despite the harassment and torture by the security forces, women welcomed militants in their homes, whether they were alone or in groups. They offered them food and shelter. Some of them even managed to keep ammunition hidden in the house to hand over to militants, often at grave risk to their own safety. So enthusiastic and committed were the women that militants had no need of entering any house forcibly. They commanded respect and even adulation, and entire families would prepare a feast for them and wait for them to come and eat. Each house was ready to welcome them and it was a matter of prestige for the residents that a Mujahid had visited them. Anjum Zamarud Habib of Muslim Khawateen Markaz (MKM) recalled that period:

> When militancy began, many of the militants found a hideout in our house in Anantnag that was very large. One portion of it belonged to my uncle who had shifted elsewhere; that is where the militants would come and stay. Some of them were my own close relatives. Due to this, the J&K police and later, the Indian Army and the BSF raided our house frequently. It was a new beginning in Kashmir where our young men had picked up the gun and soon they became local heroes; they were welcomed everywhere and many people would come to see them personally and that is how there was always a long queue of people who came to our house simply to get a glimpse of an armed militant and to see their guns. This was the time when many young women would approach me and express their desire to work along with the militants for azadi. We played a role in strengthening and taking forward the sentiment for azadi by enrolling new members and by being politically engaged in the movement.

A former militant narrated an interesting and layered story of how he was once hiding at a friend's house when the army had surrounded the entire area in search of a group of militants. His friend had got married only a few days ago and in a bid to provide him protection, he asked him to lie down next to his own wife as though *he* were her husband. The militant got into bed but stayed in *sajda* all through the night beside her, hoping to be forgiven by her but 'to my surprise, she did not even utter a word of protest. This is how far women could go to support and protect us', he said with a tinge of pride in his voice.

A young woman recalled how she had found her husband missing from home one morning when his parents told her that he had gone to Jammu for some work although he had taken their blessings before leaving. She later learnt that he had in fact gone away across the border, leaving her and their three-month-old son behind. 'I cried for days as I did not know what to do but his own parents had blessed him and later helped and supported me through his absence. I was not anxious or worried that he may not be able to return at all because '*hum aurtein is tehreek ki jaddh hain, mein unhein kabhi nahi rokti'* (we women are the roots of this movement, I would have never stopped him from leaving). In many homes that were raided to nab the militants, the soldiers would beat up family members and scatter everything around in the house, not sparing the women who were also beaten up as they refused to disclose their men's whereabouts. Due to the many crackdowns in villages and towns, there was a time when villages and homes were emptied of men; they had run away for their own safety. In fact, it was women themselves, 'our mothers, wives and sisters who would exhort us to leave rather than be caught and tortured by the security forces', said one former militant as he shared his memories of the time when militancy was at its peak. In homes where women often broke down while narrating incidents of violence, their young children would try and fill in the details, as though they had been witness to that particular situation although they had not even been born at the time. But they had heard the stories over and over from neighbours, their grandparents and others. A teenaged girl told me how proud she felt of her mother – despite all the suffering she had endured, she told me, her mother supported her father determinedly in the cause of azadi. Two young boys I met felt differently though: one wanted to pick up the gun to avenge the humiliation and suffering that his family had undergone at the hands of the security forces while the other had taken it upon himself to grow a beard, master the Quran and spend time in the local mosque to be able to understand the injustice that his family had experienced and to find a way to counter that. He added that it was not he alone who felt this way, there were many young men he met in the neighbourhood mosque who nursed such feelings. In fact, the scores of youth who poured out on the streets across Kashmir in 2016 when Burhan Wani, a young and popular militant commander of Hizb-ul-Mujahedeen, was killed by the security forces, and who had nothing more than stones in their hands to confront and engage in battle with the security forces, reflect this reality. They belong to a new generation of young people in Kashmir that has grown up with violence; they have witnessed the brutality, often experienced it, they have had to live with injustice and humiliation as part of their everyday lives. As Anjum Zamarud pointed out:

> Our younger generation would earlier refer to themselves as social activists working for the protection of human rights but today, they openly state that they belong to the Resistance and are part of the Resistance Movement in Kashmir. This change is worth noting. They are fearless now and more involved in the *tehreek* as they have seen the manner in which our women have been on the streets protesting against injustice and how so many of our men have been martyred.

Hundreds of men were killed and thousands jailed under the draconian Public Safety Act and they have remained in prisons even after more than a year. Many suffered grievous injuries as pellets were showered on them, blinding large numbers and injuring as many as 13,000 youth. According to a Kashmiri journalist, a paramilitary officer he had met in Anantnag told him that he had not seen this level of anger among protesters in his six years of duty on the ground: 'I have seen the 2010 uprising (but) these are not the same people. Young children carrying stones are ready to face bullets. They come [out] in thousands. How many can we kill at once? We cannot stop them.' A young protester that the journalist met told him that 'one of the impacts of this uprising was the transition of the movement to a new generation and that this movement was goal-centric rather than leader-centric.'

This was the time when women, young and old, also thronged the streets against the killings, demanding justice and shouting azadi slogans. These protests included women whose young sons had been killed by the security forces and who exhorted other women to come out and join the processions. In August 2010 the BBC profiled a protesting mother whose 14-year-old son, Wamiq, was killed when a tear gas shell fired by the local police exploded on his head. The mother, Firdausi, told the correspondent that she had decided to hit the streets after her son was 'murdered.' 'Why should I not pick up a stone? I am doing this in honour of my martyred son. I am doing this for azadi from subjugation and oppression.'

'A Glorious Page of our Resistance History'

Women played a definitive, constructive role all the way through militancy but their participation and their contribution to the movement remained unacknowledged and more or less in the background, while their sacrifices and suffering were not only acknowledged but also extolled. What Yaseen Malik said on the occasion of International Women's Day in 2017 comes to mind as an example of the way in which women were typecast as passive, as those who sacrificed and suffered in silence. In his words:

> Kashmiri women have suffered more than anybody else during the last many decades, as she [sic] had to bear the onslaught of oppression more than the men. She suffered as a mother when her son got martyred or disappeared in custody, she suffered as a wife when her husband became a target and she suffered as a woman when her chastity was attacked by the Indian soldiers. The sacrifices rendered by Kashmiri women are a glorious page of our resistance history.[2]

In the initial phase of my fieldwork I found that while both men and women recalled the politically charged, tumultuous times, in public memory, women were conspicuous by their absence in the political narratives or when public debates or discussions were held on the different aspects of the azadi movement. It was difficult for me to imagine that the militants would have managed to do what they did without the active support of women who played multiple roles in support of militancy/azadi. The sense of assertion and empowerment that people experienced during this period also touched women who felt emboldened to challenge the 'occupation of our land', because they had themselves grown through that period. How far had this political assertion, this public participation translated within homes for the women is a question that is still debated.

It is often argued that since Kashmiri women have played a supportive role in militancy rather than being active combatants in the movement, their contribution therefore was less significant. It is possible that the azadi movement in Kashmir may not have been as radically transformative for women as, say, women's involvement as combatants in the LTTE in Sri Lanka or in the Maoist movement in India. These movements were more radical in nature and women participated at every level, organisational and political, with no difference in importance between men and women combatants and the work they carried out. The difference is that Kashmiri women's experience in militancy did not receive the kind of acknowledgement and recognition that it deserved, at least until 2008-2009 when their participation became a benchmark and their assertion in the movement became more prominent. It was the Shopian incident of the rape and murder of two women by the army in 2009 that once again galvanised the women into action and that spark lit fires that spread far and wide in Kashmir. The protests were no longer confined only to the specific experiences of the two women – they also brought into focus other rapes that had taken place elsewhere in Kashmir, turning the spotlight onto the widespread use of sexual violence, abuse and harassment as a counter-insurgency strategy by state forces. It was perhaps for the first time that women's concerns and their contribution began to find expression in the media in a sharper and more challenging manner and it was this political recognition and expression that defined the period from 2008 onwards. This period was also interesting because the protests took new forms and new expressions through poetry, music, literature as well as debates and discussions – the earlier phases of militancy did not see these kinds of cultural articulations. The years following 2008 saw other changes: once again, after the period of the 1990s, people took to the streets to protest. Women were prominent and numerous in these protests. This was also the time that, unlike in the nineties, militants began to expand their activities and decided to wage a peaceful, unarmed resistance. They also declared they would withdraw from civilian areas to avoid civilian casualties. They realised that the fact that people were now supporting the movement meant it had become a mass movement, a people's movement, and they needed to ensure that people could participate without fear of violence. The years following 2008 were important for all of these reasons. For the first time, people's anger found expression in creative ways and both men and women acknowledged each others' contribution. They went together to police stations to file cases, they visited survivors, spoke out against injustice and many refused to remain confined to their homes. Women fought this battle, and they survived.[3]

In Kashmir, it was the specific nature of militancy and the phases it went through – armed/unarmed/stone-pelting – that determined the extent of women's participation and the kinds of roles they played. Women have always been there in support of the movement but once the guns were out, they were not expected to pick up arms but to extend their support in other ways; this was their socially ascribed role. Asiya Andrabi of Dukhtaran-e-Millat told me in an interview at her home in 2012 that when militancy began, a group of senior militant commanders, among those who had started the movement, approached her and told her about the movement and that they were going to introduce the gun in Kashmir.

> They asked for my opinion and also asked me to let my women's cadre join the movement. I told them that we would provide them moral support for the movement, for the gun and the jihad; that all the men from our families should also join them but as far as women's contribution was concerned, I said you will not take women directly into the (armed) movement. I told them that if women also picked up the gun and joined jihad, then the entire system would be destabilized, homes would be destroyed, as we are the ones who look after your homes when you leave. But if we women were also to join you, then what would remain of our homes, who would look after the children? I therefore requested them

not to include women in their struggle but also assured
them of our moral support.

Over a period of time, women's presence in the movement
meant that the cry for azadi became closely linked with the demand
for justice and accountability. As state repression and brutalisation
became rampant, women led protests and devised ways to protect
the men in their families and communities; they played a pivotal
role in getting men released from the jails into which they had been
routinely thrown. The question of enforced disappearances also took
centre stage in the early nineties and the formation of the Association
of Parents of Disappeared Persons (APDP) helped galvanise women
to come out in search of their men and to demand their whereabouts
from state agencies responsible for their disappearances. It was
Parveena Ahangar – whose school-going son was picked up in 1990
and became a victim of enforced disappearance – who led this struggle
and mobilised other women and men from the families that had
suffered a similar fate. This was a turning point not only in her own
life but also for the movement for azadi that now had to take up this
issue in a systematic manner. The 1990s also witnessed the emergence
of two women's organisations – Muslim Khawateen Markaz (MKM)
and Dukhtaran-e-Millat (DM) – the first led by Anjum Zamarud
Habib and Baktawar, and the other by Asiya Andrabi – which were
instrumental in encouraging women to come out of their homes on
to the streets and to provide a mass base for the movement. It is
interesting how these women's personal life trajectories radicalised/
politicised them and pushed them beyond the boundaries of their
homes into the larger politics of azadi. In this, they were fully part
of the cataclysmic upheaval Kashmiri society was undergoing at the
time. Professor Dabla from Kashmir University was of the view that
Kashmiri women at the time were among the most politicised women
in the subcontinent, as was evident from their public engagement in
the larger politics of Kashmir. According to him, Kashmiri women

were compelled to come out and protest because of the injustice and repression: 'They have seen their children, husbands and fathers being killed and routinely humiliated by the security forces.'

It is therefore women's own life experiences and understanding that determined their participation in the azadi movement and in militancy. Their everyday experience contributed to the nature of their involvement. While women did not pick up the gun – except in 1947 against the Pakistani tribal invaders – they worked at every level of the movement; they facilitated and actively supported the armed militants in many different ways – as couriers for arms and ammunition and messages, in maintaining communication networks, providing food and shelter, finding safe passage for militants to move from one place to another, taking the injured men to hospitals, facilitating their escape during raids and crackdowns, and as many women would narrate, withholding information from security forces regarding the whereabouts of militants, despite physical abuse, harassment and threats. During the peak years of militancy, MKM organised nursing courses for women to enable them to provide basic medical care to the injured and wounded, mainly militants. The organisation also held blood donation camps. A few of the women leaders helped recruit cadres for militant outfits from student organisations at the colleges and universities where women students were also politically active. Another significant way in which women contributed to the movement was to act as protective shields for the men by marching in the front rows of azadi processions. 'We had to be out on the streets also for our men's safety,' said one of them. Interestingly, many women I spoke with used the word *jazba* (passion) for their involvement in the movement and to describe their emotional commitment to azadi. In fact, as militancy began and the men with guns were being celebrated as heroes, many young women, according to Asiya Andrabi, also expressed their desire to pick up the gun and join the ranks of the militants but she dissuaded them from doing so. In her view, their main responsibility, in the absence of their Mujahid men, was to look after the family and the home.

> Militancy may cost us our lives but we did not include women in it as it could have led to many problems; I told them that they may not be able to understand the import of what I was saying but would realize it in the long run. However, they understood my point and agreed that this was not the right thing for them to do. I had to face a lot of difficulty in controlling my women cadres because they too were swept with the wave of pro-azadi sentiment that was swaying the Valley with slogans of 'Rawalpindi, Rawalpindi' resonating in the air. The women were ready to join the armed movement but I told them that we were fighting for Allah's *deen* and we must understand that we as women had some limitations. Allah had opened the field of work for both men and women but it was different for both and we should stay and work in what is our own prescribed field.

She later learnt that despite her advice, a few young women did cross the border for arms training but 'they did not return as they decided to get married and settle there.' It is interesting that contrary to her advice to other women, Asiya could hardly stay at home herself through her political life and she spent many years in jail and in the underground.

It was clear to me that Muslim Khawateen Markaz (MKM) and Dukhtaran-e-Millat were the only two women's organisations that have been working at the grassroots level and that infused a certain political grounding to the women and provided a mass base to the movement. As Anjum Zamarud Habib explained to me,

> It is women who made it possible for the ideology of the movement to be accepted at the grassroots level

because women had more acceptance there. Our women are no different when it comes to political movement or struggle for a better political change in our society; they do possess the capability and capacity to undertake, participate and sustain this kind of a political struggle because they are intelligent and perceptive. We have played a defining role in strengthening and taking forward the *jazba* for azadi by enrolling members and by being politically engaged in the movement at the grassroots.

Women's contribution in the movement remained unacknowledged for a long time: it was a time of tremendous social upheaval; fear and violence, and the heavy presence of the state had become a constant in people's lives. Inside homes, the absence of men meant that gender relations were being transformed, often in unpredictable ways. It became difficult for people to make sense of what was going on around them. Paradoxically, it was also this moment that led to a much sharper political understanding among the new generation of men and women, and today in Kashmir, there is greater appreciation of women's contribution to the movement, as well as a recognition that women have been the backbone of the movement and they have also provided care, logistics, and sustenance. However, an important and persistent question underlies the political discourse in Kashmir, and is one that is common to similar situations across the world: should issues of women's rights and their empowerment be raised at all in the face of the larger 'movement for self-determination'? It is axiomatic that while a conflict of this nature throws open unexpected spaces for women to negotiate, it does so at the cost of their own rights as women. Issues of dowry, divorce, desertion, custody of children, domestic violence and other legal rights are brushed aside, as the movement captures the popular imagination and for women, the 'business of search and survival' becomes paramount. According to a senior woman political activist and teacher at Kashmir University, 'women's issues, if prioritised, distract from the movement, so it would be better if they were addressed and resolved once freedom has been secured.' What further compounds the problem for women in Kashmir is that while militancy is the outcome of the state's brutal repression, it carries a patriarchal, Islamic streak despite the purely political nature of the conflict; in this situation women's concerns and their rights become a casualty. Despite women's visible presence in the public realm, the political movement tries to push what it considers reformist ideas into the background. This is what Anjum had to say in this regard,

> When militancy began, the entire community rose up to support the cause of azadi, of political change, and given the charged environment, it seemed as though there was no place anymore to raise issues related to women, whether about dowry, violence or their education and employment opportunities. The community was engaged in a greater struggle and women were part of it. The majority of Pandit women had left the Valley due to militancy and moreover, the purpose for which I, along with Bakhtawar had set up the Women's Welfare Association (WWA) in the mid-eighties was now defunct as the movement took centre-stage. The purpose of the movement was now seen as far bigger and greater in meaning and significance compared to our struggle as women. I have seen that any big movement or struggle that takes place for a fundamental change in society, does not give enough space or importance to women or to issues that are specific to them. Women were overshadowed as the movement gained momentum. It was an armed struggle that had begun and many of our young men had guns in their hands now; women-related problems or issues had no meaning then or

even now. We women had made a significant beginning
through Women's Welfare Association but all of it was
scattered due to militancy. It was around this time that
many militant organizations sprung up. There were no
women's organizations left but I still believed that there
had to be one that addressed issues specifically related
to women. Among the many militant organizations
that came into being, there was not a single one that
addressed women's issues and I felt it strongly.

What one also learns on the ground, however, is that people need
to be cognizant of how important it is for both men and women
to work in solidarity with each other for it is only then that their
struggle will gain strength and become more inclusive. In Kashmir,
there was a general sense, because of women's visibility, that the
space had largely been won over by them, and that they enjoyed
the support and solidarity of many more men than they had ever
done previously, whether in the streets, the courts of law or other
public spaces. However, the women specific issues still remained
outside the parameters of the movement rather than being addressed
and resolved within it. This was particularly unfortunate as women
leaders such as Andrabi and Anjum have continued to provide a
political expression to the movement through their work and their
organisations. Throughout the movement, Kashmiri women were not
mere victims but also agents, who made conscious political choices
and decisions, including devising different strategies to confront the
security forces and other state agencies while supporting their men in
the cause of azadi. Anjum commented thus on her own commitment
to the movement and women's participation in it:

> Yes, I believe in azadi and I was and continue to be
> very much a part of it. It is not possible when such a
> big movement starts anywhere that women can remain
> mere bystanders rather than be active participants in it.

It would be a grave injustice to the cause and towards these young men who had now armed themselves for the cause of Kashmir, if women did not support them. After all, they had picked up the gun only after their peaceful protests did not bear any result. We women had to support them.

However, it is also well known – even within the movement – that militants did breach the trust that people had reposed in them and this had serious repercussions for women. How and why did this happen, given the popular support that militancy otherwise enjoyed?

Hope and Disillusionment

In the nearly three decades of its existence, the nature of militancy has changed, as has its relationship with social and political realities on the ground. These changes have also affected both the cause militancy had espoused and those who actively, wholeheartedly supported it. After the initial phase when JKLF and Hizb-ul-Mujahedeen reigned supreme, many other militant groups and formations began to mushroom in a bid to expand their social base. This inevitably led to splits and internecine battles among the different groups that sought both political and ideological supremacy. All sorts of conflicting loyalties now began to find articulation. This period also witnessed the rise of the *Ikhwanis* – renegades and surrendered militants who joined the state agencies in counter-insurgency operations against the militants – and the 'unidentified gunmen' whose repressive and brutal tactics were similar to those that were employed by the security forces against them. As Anjum pointed out,

The most unfortunate aspect of this process was that our own militants tortured many women on mere

suspicion of them being 'informers.' There were men
with guns and we believed that they were all militants
but the extent of infiltration was such that even some
rowdy, characterless men had also picked up a gun and
it was difficult to differentiate between them. It became
clearer gradually that many of them were Indian agents
or *mukhbirs* (informers) but by then many of our women
had been tortured and killed by militants. Islam or
Humanity does not permit that women should be killed
and it is truly unfortunate that this happened despite
the fact that women sacrificed so much to support them
and be part of the Tehreek, which would never have
succeeded without the role that women have played in it.
Militants were targeting ordinary men and women who
they suspected to be mukhbirs, including many from the
Pandit community.

When militancy began, militants had a certain
perception about women; they did not take them
seriously or I'd say, they in fact looked down upon
them. They also had this indiscriminate suspicion of
women being informers. Women became angry and
disillusioned that they were treated like this despite the
fact that, as they said 'we fed them, we washed their
clothes, we even supplied guns to them sometimes.'
It is tragic that despite the support and sustenance the
women provided and the faith they reposed in them,
militants betrayed the women: those they targeted were
sexually abused, tortured, or killed.

This was the period (1990-1995) when women suffered
grievously in every way. It was not just the physical violence that
they were subjected to but there was an intrusion into the privacy
of their family lives and homes that caused not only disillusionment
among women but also a sense of deep betrayal. In political terms,

this betrayal meant a profound violation of the trust and faith that women had reposed in the men who had picked up the gun for the cause of azadi. As one of the aging men who had earlier been a 'warrior' himself explained,

> One of the reasons for women's disillusionment with militants was that during this period when different elements joined or infiltrated the ranks of the militants, many violations also began to take place, including sexual violence. The black shawl, the bandana, and the gun had become fascinating symbols of power for the young men, some of whom could be seen wrapped in black shawls outside women's colleges to impress the women but they mocked them. The songs of praise that women had earlier sung for the militants to welcome them, resonated with a different kind of verse and meaning now. For instance, earlier if they sang 'Mujahid Bhaiyo, hum aap per waare jaayein, aap aage badho hum aapke saath hain (our fighter brothers, we are proud of you, march forward, we are with you) – the altered line would be (roughly translated from Kashmiri), 'we, your Mujahid brothers have come to caress/touch your breasts.'

Many families who had earlier given shelter to militants began to worry for the safety of their women when militants knocked at their doors. A young student who often accompanied me in the field narrated this incident, which he said remained etched in his memory:

> I was alone at home with my younger sister when there was a loud knock at the door late one night. When I opened the door, I was shocked to see five tall men wrapped in black shawls holding guns in their hands, their faces covered. As they entered, I immediately thought of my sister and felt terrified thinking of what

they could do to her. I quietly went upstairs and locked
her inside a room telling her not to make any sound.
They asked me if there was anybody else at home and
I lied to them, praying for my sister's safety. They
had come seeking food and shelter, which I provided,
keeping awake and vigilant the whole night as my sister
was locked upstairs. It filled me with terror. I cannot
ever forget that night.

The earlier stories that contained vivid memories of the resounding
public adulation and support that militants received both from their
families and the community as courageous, brave and powerful
warriors now had a counter-narrative that spoke of how militants
took advantage of the very families that provided them with moral
and logistical support. A senior journalist I met in Srinagar echoed
what many others had expressed:

The biggest mistake we made was to believe and treat
the militants as *farishtey* (angels). We held them in such
great esteem that we let our women interact with them
or serve them food whenever they came to our homes for
shelter. It was a normal practice for young women of the
house to carry food and water for the militants and even
make their beds. This is the level of trust that ordinary
families had reposed in militants but they misused it
terribly at times.

While the men and women have continued to challenge the
security forces as the main perpetrators of the crimes committed
against them, a question that needs to be asked is: have they been
similarly able to challenge the militants as perpetrators of violence
against them? Until recently, people preferred to remain silent on
this question. It was as though talking about militants as perpetrators
would be tantamount to betraying the larger cause of azadi or
robbing the movement of its credibility. The sense of loyalty to

the movement and the need to preserve its reputation had hushed this unpleasant aspect of reality into silence. However, for women, an added reason to remain silent was the actual threat of reprisals and more violence than they were already facing. This prevented them from openly confronting the militants or coming out onto the streets to protest against them. 'What about the two women's organisations?', I asked Anjum. She explained that when women could not come out to protest, she and her organisation often took the responsibility of confronting the militants whenever she learnt of any such incident, because she believed that women owned the movement as much as the militants did.

> There was a case in Rainawari during the early phase of militancy; I got to know that a few militants had called five women to a house. I contacted Behenji (Bakhtawar) and we went there and saw these dangerous faces of the militants. We knew what they had in mind. They told us to check the women's purses but we found nothing in them. We somehow managed to rescue the women but imagine if an ordinary woman had gone there instead of me and Behenji, it might not have been possible to rescue the women; the militants knew that we were part of the Tehreek.

However, because these women leaders were identified with the movement and the Hurriyat, ordinary women also felt angry at them for their inability to stop militants from targeting women. In Anjum's words:

> It was also a challenge for us in MKM, which is part of the Tehreek; women victims/survivors would be very upset with us because we had failed to prevent such incidents where militants who were fighting for a cause and were part of Tehreek were targeting unarmed, innocent women. They would say, why don't you stop

them rather than come to us or why should we come
to you?

She said that it was mainly due to security reasons that
women could not come out on to the streets to protest
against what militants were doing.

But we used to meet the militants secretly for security
reasons and confronted them both at the individual
and organisational levels. We had to do so because it
is also our movement, our Tehreek, it is the women's
movement too because they are the ones who have lost
their loved ones in the process. If we do not speak on
behalf of women or in their favour, then we will not
be doing the right thing for the movement either. I'd
have done injustice to womanhood if I had ignored such
grave incidents of violence involving women. I told the
militants that they should restrict themselves to the cause
they had taken up and leave social problems to other
organisations such as ours. Or, if militants believed that
some women had committed a wrong, then they should
ask us to intervene in the matter or contact their parents
for help. I felt very moved and upset that the situation
had come to such a pass that our own women were not
safe any more. It is in public knowledge how militants
had also specifically targeted Kashmiri Pandit women as
informers, and carried out sexual assaults, torture, and
killings. Anantnag district was the one where most of the
sexual offences and violence against women took place;
the perpetrators were gunmen and I cannot say clearly
whether they were our own Mujahids, due to the kind
of infiltration of the ranks that had taken place. Ours
is a conservative, patriarchal society and such incidents
led to a lot of resentment among ordinary people. We
haven't offered all these sacrifices to be told by a gunman
or a militant that our way of dressing is not appropriate

or that the way we walk is not proper. Militants' own sisters and mothers have often supported them and suffered greatly due to this but is this how women were treated then? How could militants use the guns against their own women? It was not easy to procure guns or ammunition and now it was being wasted by its utter misuse. It was against humanity to train their guns on innocent women.

It is a fact that the killing of many prominent Kashmiri Pandit men as well as some Muslims on suspicion of being informers, brought disrepute to the militants and also to the movement. Bakhtawar, who had spent many eventful years of her life in the azadi movement felt despondent and angry that the militants had not lived up to the moral standards that the movement demanded from them.

Times have changed. It is not the same atmosphere where people's aspirations are voiced openly. Today, some of these militants have become sahibs and leaders. But we have not changed. They are not doing anything to alleviate people's suffering despite having received their support. I remember a time when women even sold their jewellery to raise funds for them. If they had been able to do something concrete for people's benefit, the situation would have been different today. No wonder that people do not welcome them in their homes anymore. The fervour that we had witnessed earlier is gone, it's missing now.

Despite this serious breach in the movement, recent times have shown how ordinary people – men, women, children, and the aged – have thronged the streets in towns and villages, pelting stones and engaging in fierce and fearless battles against the armed security forces. The slogans for azadi are as fervent, and the demand for justice as well as an end to state violence is still loud and strong. People's resistance to the military occupation of their land increases in equal measure to the repression and violence that the state unleashes on them. Entire neighbourhoods continue to defy the security apparatus at encounter sites to find safe passage for armed militants, often at the risk of their own lives. Men and women continue to come out in large numbers to attend a militant's funeral and thereby express their solidarity and commitment to the movement. The intense and widespread protests that took place in 2016 following the killing of Burhan Wani by the security forces, were the first such, according to some journalists, since 1990. Thousands of people poured out onto the streets all over Kashmir. The participation of youth and women in such large numbers has shown that the movement is alive to its history and carries a strong memory of the violence earlier generations of Kashmiris have faced. Indeed, one of the things that characterises this ongoing movement is the generational link between the past and the present for Kashmiris who have gone through a long process marked by violence, loss and the destruction of lives.

Women's Initiatives

In this section, I look closely at the lives of three women leaders and the personal and political trajectories that brought them to centre-stage in the Tehreek-e-Azadi. I quote quite extensively from their interviews so that their story is told in their own voice. Apart from the scores of women who gained visibility in the public realm, militancy and the movement for azadi also led to the emergence of women political leaders who played and continue to play a pivotal role in the movement and who have helped shape women's political aspirations and articulations within the movement. In fact, it is interesting that it was the 'social work' that these women initially undertook that led to the emergence of the two women's organisations preceding militancy. The four women leaders – Parveena, Bakhtawar, Anjum, and Asiya – I met and interacted with closely shared fascinating stories of how they came into public life and the kind of social and political churning that was taking place around them at the time within and outside their homes. While Parveena was forced by a violent incident to cross the threshold of her home and enter the public realm, the other three women entered public life because they were driven by a common desire to do something to alleviate the suffering of fellow women and take up issues that concerned them. Bakhtawar and Anjum came together in the mid-eighties to set up the Women's Welfare Association (WWA) with a mandate to reach out to women to 'alleviate their suffering'; Asiya, who founded the Dukhtaran-e-Millat, was driven by 'the desire to bring a revolution in the lives of Muslim women.' Parveena came out as a witness to grave violence and injustice, as a mother whose son had been abducted and disappeared by one of the state agencies and, as Urvashi Butalia described, she used 'motherhood as a way of access, a badge of courage' to leave home and enter a world that was hitherto unknown to her.[4] 'The outside world did not matter to me', she had once told me, her home and family life kept her busy and content until the day she lost her son to oblivion. She too believed in the cause of azadi but told me that she did not participate in the azadi processions or shout slogans that rent the air at the time. She garnered all her energies and strategies towards finding her son while reaching out to other women and families who had experienced a similar fate. It was a mother's resolve for justice, according to her, that helped her establish the APDP. Despite the political context within which enforced disappearances took place and even though she confronted the state authorities against this practice and demanded accountability, Parveena did not see herself as a political being or her struggle as part of a political process. She continues to proclaim and see herself and her role in the public realm as primarily that of a mother and a victim but perhaps unknown to her, she has 'turned what is seen as traditional and disempowering (motherhood/ victimhood) on its head and used the supposed weakness as a strategy of resistance and mobilisation. In her case it shows how thin the line between victimhood and agency is and how one has in fact led to the other.[5]

Despite the demands, pulls and pressures of a conservative, patriarchal society and despite their experience of violence at different levels, these women have made conscious political and personal choices that reflect their commitment to the movement. It is interesting to recall here what both Bakhtawar and Anjum told me with regard to marriage and the fact that they chose to remain single. *'Maine quam se shaadi ki hai, pachees saal quam ke saath guzari hoon'* – I have married my community and nation; I have spent 25 years in their midst, said Bakhtawar while Anjum declared that she had married the movement more than twenty-five years earlier, which gave meaning to her existence and also shaped her life. When Asiya's mother prompted her to get married, she told me that she requested her to permit her not to go in for marriage so that she can continue to do her work, but when the government banned her organisation soon after militancy began and the police were after her like a shadow, she saw how anxious her mother had become and how urgently she wanted her daughter to get married. Asiya agreed, but on condition that she would only marry a mujahid and asked her mother if she could find one. 'I was now willing to marry for my mother's sake', she told me, 'but I had a few conditions: I would marry a mujahid, someone who was part of the Tehreek so that he would be able to understand me and the work I did; that just as he would work, he would also let me do my work.' The mujahid she married in 1990 was a founding member of Hizb-ul-Mujahedeen but has been in prison for 23 years; past the life sentence he was meant to serve. She said that due to current political circumstances

and her underground life, she must have barely spent two years of
her married life with her husband and that even those two 'scattered
years' were marked by the volatile political situation and the
turbulence of an underground life that robbed them of any 'sense
of permanency in our everyday lives.' This was the reason, she said,
that 'our children have grown up without knowing or experiencing
the meaning of family life or what it is to have your parents with you
at home.' Not once did Asiya use the word 'sacrifice' to describe her
own life during our long conversations but she did express a sense of
sadness for what her children had to endure because of her political
life, leadership and her convictions. My conversations with her and
with Bakhtawar and Anjum dwelt on many aspects of their lives but
the substantive part centred on the political exigencies that had led
them into the movement and how this political engagement had
impacted their personal lives – to the extent that it was difficult for
them to separate the two. What shaped these women leaders and
their passion for azadi? What characterised their growing-up years?
What brought them into public life, into the movement to which
they have dedicated nearly thirty years of their lives? Based on my
interviews and conversations with these women, I have tried to trace
the trajectory of their extraordinary lives – converging and diverging
at particular moments in the course of the Tehreek.

Bakhtawar

Popularly known as Behenji, Bakhtawar retired from what she
considered 'active social work' (as opposed to being an active political
worker in the movement) nearly two and a half decades after being
closely and 'dangerously' involved in the movement for azadi. She
spent many years of her life underground as the police and security
agencies were out to arrest her for her militant activities. She revealed
to me that her jazba for azadi was born out of her compassion for
the people of her land, of her community. 'My heart has always been

with the poor of my land. I grew up with a keen sense of justice
in my heart. My mind (*zehen*) does not permit me to ever turn
away from them. Moreover, at home I grew up hearing my brother
discuss with his friends [she mentioned several names of men, some
of whom are now well known separatists and political leaders] the
various problems that ordinary people faced. I was then sixteen
years old. I met these leaders through my brother when they visited
him at home. I heard them talk about the political ferment outside
and what people were going through and it gradually awakened my
own interest and strengthened my resolve to go out and help them,
support them. I have always liked doing social work. I feel that I am
meant for it. '*Mera ishq hai logon se hamdardi. Aur phir hamari ma ki
hamesha yehi dua rahi hai ki hum qaum ki qidmat karen.*' (My passion
is to serve the people and my mother's prayer has always been that
we serve our community and nation).

I first met Bakhtawar at Parveena's house in 2002 and often after
that at her parents' home where she lived. We never met outside
since she had 'retired' from public life and hardly stepped out of her
home. Younger to Parveena and four brothers, she also studied up
to primary school after which both sisters had to give up education.
While Parveena was married at the age of 12 or 13, Bakhtawar
helped her mother in the house. One of her brothers was close to the
JKLF while another was deeply religious and it was a mix of politics
and religion at home that she remembered as quite significant in her
growing-up years. From a fairly young age she believed that the three
main tasks and primary stages in her life consisted of: *quda ki qidmat,
qaum ki qidmat aur ma-baap ki qidmat* (service of god, service of the
nation and service of parents). At the time of my meeting she was
busy with the third stage of her life, looking after her aging and ailing
mother who needed physical care and moral and emotional support.
She spent most of her time by her mother's side. She felt that she

had neglected this aspect of her life during the height of her political
involvement in the movement.

> The police were after me like a shadow even though
> we were doing this kind of work for the welfare of the
> community. They suspected me of having links with the
> militants also because I raised issues of custodial rapes
> and killings of innocent civilians. The police could not
> tolerate this and tried hard to intimidate me in every
> possible manner. Wherever I went I knew that I was
> being followed but they had never seen my face as I was
> always covered in a burqa.

She used it to her advantage and evaded the police. 'Once,' she
told me, chuckling, 'when I was being followed in the narrow by-
lanes somewhere in the city, I entered a house, took off my burqa and
when I came out the police were there and still looking for me!' She
was arrested in the early nineties after she 'led a huge rally of women
to the secretariat against the security forces and their atrocities.' It
was after her first arrest and the subsequent harassment of her family
that she decided to go underground where she remained for more
than three years.

> Remaining underground was the most difficult period
> of my life as I constantly worried that my family would
> be harassed on my account. I have always been very close
> to my parents. My having to go away in this manner
> is one of the main reasons that my mother fell ill and
> has not recovered since. It was very tough for me to live
> without seeing them at all. I did not stop despite all these
> hardships and difficulties only because I believed in azadi.
> I had to break from my family and did not know how
> they were for more than a year until one of my saathis
> arranged a clandestine meeting with my mother, telling

her that she had brought a 'gift' for her. My mother cried
inconsolably when she saw me standing in front of her.

Bakhtawar spoke at length about how she had sacrificed her
personal and family life for the cause of azadi but accepted with
equanimity the third stage of her life that gave her a sense of satisfaction
as a daughter. According to her, this was not a prescription for other
women but a defining and guiding principle in her own life. She is
very close to her sister, Parveena and their mother and believes that
all three of them have one thing in common; compassion for people
and the desire for justice. *'Mera, meri ma aur meri behen ka – hum
teenon ka dil ek jaisa hi hai. Insaf ka jazba bhara hai. Yeh Allah ki
dain hai'*, she said, with a warm smile. (My mother, my sister, and
I, our hearts are alike. We are filled with the desire for justice. This
is God's gift).

Bakhtawar's political activism, which she calls 'social work',
began in the mid-eighties when she and Anjum Habib set up the
Women Welfare Association (WWA) to raise women-specific
issues, and to help destitute women and mobilise them for their
rights. However, once the armed struggle began and the Tehreek
took centre-stage, they could no longer sustain WWA's activities,
which gradually became defunct; this also happened because many
of the Pandit women who were active members of the organisation
had to flee the state due to the escalating militant violence. It was
later when Parveena's son was abducted and disappeared in 1990,
that she started to accompany her sister to jails and other places in
search of her son as well as to meet women from other families of the
disappeared. However, their trajectories took different paths in terms
of the work they undertook, leading to the establishment of APDP
and WWA/MKM, respectively. 'When my sister's son was picked
up I also went to jails and different places with her and saw the
terrible conditions that prevailed there. Wherever we went I saw and
met women and children who were in a pathetic state of health and

impoverishment. I also met destitute women and their unmarried daughters and wanted to do something concrete to alleviate their suffering', said Bakhtawar. Soon after militancy began, the violence escalated and she saw how women suffered due to this and felt the need to work with the affected women and families in a concerted manner. Among the many diktats that the militants then issued, was one to shut down cinema halls and erase film hoardings depicting women. Bakhtawar joined Asiya Andrabi in taking up this call.

> Earlier I used to support Asiya Andrabi of Dukhtaran-e-Millat in her activities that mainly consisted of erasing cinema hoardings in the city. It was quite daring of us, particularly as women, to be out on the streets. We had to do it under cover of darkness to avoid the police. We were following the militant's call to shut down cinema halls. But I soon realised that there were more urgent concerns to attend to such as the problems faced by women and children as a result of the escalating violence. The security forces were brutal in the measures they took to counter armed militancy. People were now caught between the two but they were willing to even sacrifice their lives for the cause of azadi.

She then decided to work with Anjum and it was in 1991, at the peak of militancy, that she and Anjum set up the Muslim Khawateen Markaz. As she described it, the idea was:

> ...primarily to help widows by initiating some income generating activities for them as their men had either been disappeared or killed and there was no one to look after them. We also mobilised women to join us in our protests against the atrocities of the security forces and the frequent clampdown of curfew because of which ordinary people were facing many hardships. Women came out in large numbers. I remember it was

a big rally of women that I led from Mujahid Manzil
to the Secretariat. Women were so angry that they were
not bothered about the security forces surrounding us.
No one was scared then. I always believed, and told the
women too, that we were not doing anything to be afraid
of. We had set up a Relief Trust (Hilal Committee) to
reach out to women victims of both militancy and the
security forces. This also included poor and destitute
women whom we tried to help to enable them to look
after their families. Immediately after the rally the police
took me into custody but within an hour many of my
neighbours, along with all my family members, reached
the police station demanding my release on grounds
of poor health. The negotiations went on till late into
the night when they released me on the condition
that I was brought back the next morning. It was then
that I decided to go underground for the first time for
three years.

It is a 'known secret' that Bakhtawar was actively involved, both
at the political and organisational levels, with the JKLF. I asked
her what kind of support she received from the leadership of the
movement. She did not say much regarding the JKLF except to say
angrily that some of these leaders had gained in stature due to the
sacrifices of ordinary people and that once, when she learnt that
they were visiting a house nearby where lunch was being served, she
went there and confronted them. 'I refused to eat there and told
them to their faces that they had blood on their hands and that they
were contaminating the food.' Regarding the Hurriyat, she said
that they supported her 'but they did not really bother while I was
underground. I am a woman who went through all this hardship
but they were not really bothered as they were quite conservative
in their attitude. Moreover, what really angers me is the fact that

hardly anyone of them recognised or acknowledged our role in the movement.'

Bakhtawar's mother passed away a few years ago but she continues to stay at home even though the passion for social work remains alive in her heart, she told me. She said, 'I wish that I could continue to do social work. My mother's prayer has always been that we serve our community, my community's pain and suffering is always in my heart and one day I will step out again to do this work.' As I was leaving, she embraced me warmly saying, 'you are my Muslim sister; you too should pray for me.'

Anjum Habib

'I have been closely related to the movement and will remain with it till my last breath. Tehreek is a serious path and I am in it with my conscience, conviction and deep commitment. It's a commitment to the movement, to my Allah and to my community and nobody can ever take it away from me. I am married to the movement.'

I have known Anjum since 2000 when I began my fieldwork in Kashmir. I first met her at a large public meeting at Eidgah in Srinagar where I introduced myself to her and sought time from her to meet again. That was the beginning of an enduring friendship between us. We have spent memorable time together both in Kashmir and in Delhi – in protest meetings, processions, MKM meetings, seminars and at each other's homes. The only time I did not meet her was during the five years she spent in the Tihar jail in Delhi (2003-2007) on charges of terrorism. I think I was terrified to meet her personally as I had learnt from her lawyer about the terrible mental and physical condition she was in, as well as the violence she had suffered while in prison. I wondered whether I would be able to bear hearing about it. But if I am to be honest I must also admit that at some level I was nervous and fearful that being so close to her would somehow implicate me too. I had thus failed to keep up my end of the friendship because of which she carried the hurt of my absence and I its guilt – until I met her again in Srinagar soon after her release. Despite the hurt, she greeted me warmly at her sister's house where she was staying. She spoke softly, almost in whispers, ruminating on the five years in jail. It is over now, she said, her confinement as well as her life, as she struggled to find a way to begin again, to start her work afresh 'when so much has changed in these five years.' Her niece, who was visiting, showed me a video she had made recently where Anjum was seen being suddenly accosted by policewomen and thrown into the waiting van as she was leading women in a protest demonstration against the security forces – this was her first public, political appearance after her release. The image was haunting and as I turned to look at her she said, 'I do not wish to waste any more time. I have returned from hell. I have to find my feet again; I have to find meaning in a life that has been ruined.' What she felt certain about amidst great emotional, psychological and intellectual confusion was her conviction that it was work alone that would heal her. In our subsequent meetings, as she shared significant bits and pieces of her experiences inside the jail, we both knew that this – her extraordinary story – had to reach out to a wider audience as it was a 'searing indictment of the draconian state policies and expedient political practices' that targeted her for being who she was – a Kashmiri Muslim woman political activist. Her journey was eventually chronicled in the book she wrote called *Qaidi Number 100*, which I translated into English as *Prisoner Number 100* (Zubaan 2011).

Much had changed in the political scenario while she was away in prison. At the time of her arrest she was the chairperson of MKM, which was split into two factions by the Hurriyat leadership during her years in jail. When she returned from jail she no longer had access to the MKM office.

Earlier it was the United Hurriyat but during my jail
term, it split into two factions; almost every organization
in Hurriyat, including MKM was also divided after the
split. This was really unfortunate. This was done to
marginalise me politically. However, they did not know
that it is not easy to break my spirit or me; I fought
my way back by firstly gathering my confidence and
myself. When Geelani Sahib met me and we discussed
the prospects of MKM, I decided to join his faction; I
also believed that it was important to be politically active
and whatever the faction, I had to work hard on behalf
of and with the women.

Anjum later converted MKM into Kashmir Tehreek-e-
Khawateen (Kashmir Women's Movement) and also started to work
for the welfare of Kashmiri political prisoners whose plight she had
witnessed first hand during her own time in Tihar jail through an
'association for the families of Kashmiri political prisoners.' As with
MKM, the political agenda and activities of the KWM are part of the
Hurriyat Conference as one of the 23 members of the conglomerate.
While WWA had focused its activities on issues related to women,
without reference to the 'Kashmir Issue' MKM and later, the KWM,
included the political resolution of the Kashmir dispute as its abiding
and guiding principle and as part of its constitution. However, as
counter-insurgency measures gained ground and gave rise to grave
human rights violations, the struggle against them became the
fulcrum of the organization and the mandate no longer remained
'limited' to 'women's issues.' As Anjum explained, 'in our male
dominated, patriarchal society, women's rights are seen in accordance
with our religion and although we had taken up these issues earlier,
we failed to resolve them as we met with stiff resistance from the men
and moreover, it was the Azadi movement that gained precedence
over everything else.'

She recalled the circumstances that had led to the formation of WWA in the mid-eighties:

> Soon after graduation, I had begun to want to do something for our community, our women, that would alleviate their suffering. We were all quite agitated due to a recent dowry death in the district (Anantnag), which was unheard of until then. We began to think of building an organization that would take up issues of women's exploitation, unemployment and against the practice of dowry, and to find ways of empowering women. We then decided to establish Women's Welfare Association (WWA) and reached out to women teachers in different colleges in the district. There was a very positive response as this was the first time that such an initiative was being taken. It was as though each one was waiting for this to happen. This was during 1985-86. Within a couple of weeks, we had more than 200 women as members of the organization, many of them from the Pandit community. I really miss that period, as women were so full of enthusiasm. The Pandit women's participation and contribution in WWA was quite significant.

Anjum also spoke about how the MKM was established and how student politics and activism preceded militancy. According to her, there was an organization called the Islamic Students Union (ISU) in Srinagar that existed and functioned even prior to militancy; many of the young men who belonged to this organisation were now actively associated with JKLF (Jammu Kashmir Liberation Front). They had said that they would take the initiative to form a women's organization, as they were aware about WWA and its activities.

> Later, a few women (from ISU) came to meet me and said that they wanted to form a women's organization called

Muslim Khawateen Markaz (MKM) and asked that I join them. I told them about WWA and its constitution, which was similar to what these women had in mind except that WWA did not elaborate on the Kashmir issue. MKM however planned to do so and looked also at how it could be resolved politically, the role women would play in achieving the goal. However, there was no mention of women's empowerment, their education and other social issues that WWA had identified as an integral part of its mandate. I suggested that we should bring these issues to the fore and build MKM accordingly and I was one of the founding members, along with Bakhtawar Behenji.

At the peak of militancy, MKM undertook many activities: these included running a nursing course for women. The training this course provided was meant to address a very specific problem – that of men shot at by the security forces and then left, wounded and bleeding on the streets. People were not permitted to take them to hospital, so women who had received nursing training came in particularly handy. She explained how the women had made an organized effort to help by filling forms along and mentioning their blood group in them to be able to donate blood whenever necessary.

MKM members regularly donated blood for our men who were injured and lying on the streets. Another aspect of our work was to visit the homes of the bereaved families, especially those where a death had occurred due to firing; we would offer our condolences and whatever moral, financial support we could provide to the families. We also acted as couriers, taking messages back and forth for militants and helping them find safe passage from one area to another. We worked at every level of the movement.

According to Anjum, the KWM came into being when she realised that although Kashmiri women had staked their lives in the movement and spoken in a voice that was distinctly theirs, the more visible presence in Kashmir was that of mainstream feminists from India, who came in to organise seminars and discussions. She felt that not only were they heard more than their Kashmiri counterparts, but there was an attempt on their part to superimpose their ideology and perspectives on Kashmiri women, without even beginning to understand the specificities and nuances of their struggle. She wished to establish that Kashmir had its own women's movement, which had a place within the larger movement for azadi. It was with this in mind that she set up KWM.

Anjum was born in August 1961 in Anantnag, 'a beautiful district, surrounded by wonderful lakes.' It was in this mountain valley that the family lived, in their large ancestral home. 'I come from a fairly well to do and educated family, which was considered one of the most progressive in the district; people also respected our interpersonal relationships within the family. My father was the key person in the family, he was a high ranking government employee and was liberal in his outlook. But it was my mother who was responsible for ensuring that we got a good education.' Anjum said that she grew up with a sense of loneliness although she lived in a large joint family with uncles, aunts and many male and female cousins. Describing her childhood, she said,

> My childhood was not an ordinary one; I must have
> hardly ever made a fuss about wanting a toy or new shoes
> and clothes; my father bought me shoes and clothes
> that were the same as my male cousins' with whom I
> grew up. I played with them more than with my female
> cousins. It was only after I became a teenager that I
> became conscious of my femaleness, otherwise I behaved
> no differently from my brothers. However, I had a

different outlook even at a very young age. Now when I
look back, I do feel that I was quite different from other
children of my age. I was a very tender-hearted child; I
would cry every time I saw a beggar woman or an old
woman in need.

She completed her graduation in Political Science, Education,
and Urdu Language from the Women's College and later joined
Kashmir University in 1983 where she did a Masters in Education
and an M. Ed. The eighties were not a period of student activism
and the university did not have a students' union at the time. Anjum,
however, created her own student body: she recalls that the hostel
where she stayed had women 'from far flung areas from different
districts' and she and other members of her cohort established
some sort of control over their peers. The students, she said, 'felt
intimidated by the women, particularly me. They would not even
dare to climb up the stairs if they saw me coming down.' She left the
university after completing M.Ed. and Masters in Education. The
university was not entirely devoid of political activity. Anjum recalls
that in the years leading up to militancy there was some political
churning going on but she and the other women students were not
able to easily comprehend what it was that was going on.

There was something brewing at the university those
days. We were a large group of students who'd spend
considerable time in the Iqbal library and once when we
were returning from there and on our way to the hostel
in the evening, a few male students whom I did not know
stopped and asked us about what we did at the library.
They were somehow trying to tell us something and also
trying to encourage us to take up action and protest as
we had done recently regarding the poor quality of food
in the hostel. Perhaps they were looking for students
who were bold and confident enough to see how they

could contribute towards the movement that was just beginning to take shape. There was a lot of ferment during this period and in 1989 the rumour was that Shabbir Shah had been arrested. He was very popular. During this period, one of my colleagues was also killed along with two other people. There was a lot of unrest everywhere – it was like a fire that spread suddenly and changed everything. The entire community seemed to have risen. My father though was against the use of the gun and would tell the young men to struggle peacefully for azadi rather than take to the gun. But young people were not ready for such advice as they thought that the elders had already suffered and now it was for them to decide what was best for them. They were convinced that the path they had chosen – of armed resistance – was the correct one.

By 1989-90 the protests and processions had become widespread and Anjum remembered the one where

nearly 10 lakh people from all over the Valley had come out on the streets to march in a procession to submit a memorandum to the UN office here in Srinagar. I was leading the women along with Asiya Andrabi and a few others. It is a fact that whenever any protests took place, women came out in large numbers and would be in the front rows to protect the men who were otherwise mercilessly fired upon by the security forces; we women went with a conviction not only for the cause of azadi but also to ensure that our men remained safe. Women became a protective shield for our men; this was a great contribution of women who did not otherwise indulge in any kind of politics. Women did play a very constructive role in the movement and continue to do so even now when the character and nature of the protests and struggle have undergone a change towards more peaceful methods.

I was curious to know what had drawn Anjum to the Hurriyat. She told me that she had not just happened to join politics and the movement, but had made a conscious, thought out choice to do so. The Hurriyat Conference came into being in 1992-93 and soon after it gave a call to all social, political and religious organizations to join to make it a strong and viable umbrella organization. Anjum responded to this call.

> Our *jung* (war) was with a country that was a veteran in politics and unless our own politics and political leaders were mature and capable, how would we take our struggle further? When I joined the Hurriyat Conference I did so to be able to raise human rights issues as well as those concerning women. I also travelled to different countries to attend conferences but I slowly became aware of the kind of arrogance and in some cases, ignorance and indiscipline of the militant leadership. I must say that we still have to work hard for our younger generation to know and learn about our own heroes in the movement and their sacrifices. We have failed to provide an institutional background and understanding regarding this.

MKM became a founder member of the Hurriyat soon after it came into being but unfortunately, as happens in other male dominated, patriarchal organisations, MKM and the women who were in the forefront of the movement were not given due recognition. 'You would never hear any of the Hurriyat leaders acknowledge MKM's contribution to the cause.' It was not only the Hurriyat leadership but also others, mainly men, who ignored or downplayed women's participation or contribution to militancy, as I found during my fieldwork. Anjum had hoped that through

148 SAHBA HUSAIN

the Hurriyat platform, MKM would be able to highlight women's concerns and bring women into active political participation by providing them with a distinct political voice within the movement. However, she found the reality was quite different: there was no space for women in the Hurriyat: 'women's voices, their concerns, the need for their empowerment through specific programmes or initiatives, the need for them to be in decision-making, none of this existed or exists in the Hurriyat.' She had wrongly believed that 'the way to gain freedom for our qaum and to bring in a better reality for our people' was what was at the heart of the political mobilisation. 'This is what I had in mind when I joined. I was quite young then and nurtured a strong sentiment for sacrifice, for azadi, for political change. But I lacked a clear understanding or the wisdom to fathom the complexities of the situation.'

Having spent more than twenty-five years in the movement, I wondered how she saw the movement now.

> I have now developed the ability to understand people, the different aspects of politics and also to see behind the masks. The five years in jail also taught me many lessons. It was a very long period during which much had changed politically and I had to struggle hard to find my bearings again and get back to being politically active and meaningful. After my release, I started life from zero – from scratch, so to say. I have been through hell and was in a frail psychological and physical state after I was released but I have tried very hard to raise a voice that favours azadi and human dignity.

❋ ❋ ❋

Asiya Andrabi
'Our demand for azadi is tied to our desire for the supremacy of Islam and its way of life. For me, giving up my life for this cause is

an ordinary matter and my prayer to Allah is to accept our sacrifices in realising this dream.'

Asiya was born in 1962 and is the youngest of four daughters and three sons. She spent most of her childhood and schooling in district Pulwama where her father was posted as the Block Medical Officer (BMO). The family moved to Srinagar when she was in the Eighth Grade and lived in Khanyar locality where she completed Middle school and Matriculation from Government Girls' Higher Secondary School and later joined the Women's College in the city where she graduated in Biochemistry. Being an 'ambitious girl' she wanted to go to Dalhousie for further studies but her elder brother did not allow her to do so. 'You are still young and you do not know that there is already so much hostility for Kashmiris in India', he had told her, adding that Islam did not permit a young girl to go away from home and that too, in such a hostile environment. He advised her to go to Kashmir University instead and to choose any subject that she wished to study. In a state of utter disappointment, she went into her father's library, there she chanced upon a book called *Aurton Ke Dilon Ki Batein* by Mayil Kairabadi. The cover story was of Marcus Margret, now known as Mariam Jamila (after her conversion to Islam). Asiya described to me in detail how profoundly the book had impressed her and how Islam and its teachings became a rallying cry and a passion for her, and how this completely changed her life and set her off on a path that she had until then not even contemplated.

> When I began to read this book, it was the evening (*asr*) prayer time and I finished reading it by the next prayer time, *maghrib*. This was a turning point in my life. As I was reading, the doors of my mind and heart began to open and I thought to myself, oh my god, I am a Muslim girl from a Syed family and I did not know that Mariam Jamila, a Christian woman by birth, had understood

Islam in a manner that I had not yet begun to do. I felt
very bad and disturbed, rather shocked about how I had
lived my life thus far. I realised that life was temporary
and we would have to face the hereafter when we would
be asked – as Mariam Jamila had narrated – whether we
had lived meaningfully in this world. It is no exaggeration
to say that everything suddenly changed for me as it was
a turning point in my life; the aims and goals of my life
had changed; these were limited earlier but now they
became broader and I started to understand what life
was really about. I had started looking at life in a broader
spectrum, questioning my role and responsibility as
a Muslim woman. It was the first time that I decided
to observe purdah in the manner that the author had
explained and the reasons she provided for it.

Immediately after reading this book, she told me that she
confronted her father and demanded to know from him why he had
kept her in the dark regarding Islam, its teachings and the Islamic
path. Wasn't it his duty to inculcate these values and teachings in his
daughter, she asked.

I went to meet my father who had just returned from
his clinic. I told him, Abbaji, you have provided us with
all the comforts of life and made sure that we did not
face any difficulties but despite being an Islamic scholar,
you never counselled us about the true meaning of life. I
asked him, being a father, is it not your duty to explain
to us about Islam? We are not aware of even the basic
teachings of Islam; we have simply been following the
traditions of a Syed and Pir household without enough
knowledge of Islam; we have been following traditions
rather than the commands of Allah. I realized that due
to a sense of shock, I was being a bit harsh on my father.

However, he said, 'Don't get perturbed, you are still young but do tell me what you wish to do now.' I told him that I wanted to study Arabic and that he should help me in it so that I am able to understand the basics of Islam by reading books that are written in Arabic.

Although practising Muslims, Asiya's parents and brothers were against the idea of pushing the youngest member of the family into an orthodox Islamism. Her father was also apprehensive that his daughter would join the (militant) movement just as his sons had done.[6]

Asiya completed her graduation in Arabic and secured first position in the state of Jammu and Kashmir. Later, she also completed a correspondence degree from Kashmir University. She said she did not have enough time to attend classes at the campus because, 'as soon as I changed the perspective and priorities of my life, I decided to share what I had learnt about Islam. If I learnt and understood the status of women in Islam, then it was my duty to share this knowledge with others.' Asiya roped in other women as volunteers and together they started Islamic teaching centres in Srinagar and elsewhere. It was this that eventually led to the formation of Dukhtaran-e-Millat. She shared interesting details with me of how these teaching centres developed where hardly any had existed earlier.

From her childhood, a girl is socialized to believe that she has to go away to another house and family and even when she is offered food or clothes to wear, she is always told that she will have to leave her parents' home. I began to ask why girls were not taught that if they become good Muslims, they can also be good at managing their homes and families. I think girls must be taught about their rights as Muslim women for without understanding these, how do we expect her to understand the rights

of others, the rights of a husband over his wife, and the
rights of a mother-in-law over her daughter-in-law?

This understanding prompted her to become an Islamic scholar
and to share her knowledge of Islam and its way of life.

> It was in 1982 that, thinking about all this and wondering
> how to use my Islamic learning, I thought of applying
> for the post of a *Maullema* (an Islamic woman scholar)
> in a local girls' school which I had seen advertised in a
> local paper. I was appointed and asked to join the very
> next day. When I arrived and met these innocent little
> girls, I asked them if they had any older women at home
> such as their sisters, mothers, or other women relatives.
> I took permission from the school authorities and told
> the young girls to bring all of them to school with them
> the next day. And so it happened that the next day, all
> the 26 girls came with their sisters and mothers and
> the class was full of them. There must have been 50 of
> them there.

The first lesson Asiya offered the assembled group was on how to
improve the status of Muslim women, as they did not have a say in
any matter, even those that directly concerned them, nor did anyone
ever listen to them. Here is what she said:

> Islam has given us our identity, our status but because
> of our own ignorance, we have lost our reputation and
> dignity. I noticed that many of the women were above
> 40-50 years and some of them were grandmothers too.
> By the grace of God, so many women turned up that I
> had to organize them into five different classes. It was
> the first time that they were listening to a woman teacher
> who explained to them the teachings of Islam and what
> it meant. I advised them to start similar teaching centres

in their own localities where they could teach the local women the basics of Islam on a daily basis and offered that I would come once a week to conduct a class for them. This is how these classes developed into full-fledged teaching centres. Our work grew and continued smoothly until 1987-1988 without any hurdles or hindrance from the government.

It was during this period that Asiya wrote her first pamphlet, addressed to Dukhtaran-e-Fatima (daughters of Fatima). The pamphlet critiqued the practice of a government organised event called Jashn-e-Kashmir in which young Kashmiri girls were taken to Delhi

> …to dance in front of ministers who were in the audience. I was against this practice and exhorted the girls not to participate in such events. I told them, 'You are not born to dance in front of others and exhibit yourselves. You should first and foremost be grateful that you are born as Muslims and thank the Almighty for the same. This is Allah's greatest blessing on us that we are Muslims and not born in a non-Muslim family.' I told them to follow the path shown by the prophet who had bestowed upon women the status of respect and dignity, which they did not enjoy earlier.

According to her, she had written the pamphlet in a simple and appealing manner and she distributed it widely in different localities where the teaching centres were. This brought trouble for her as officials of the Criminal Investigation Department (CID) arrived in her locality asking for her whereabouts. She said, 'I had already stated in the pamphlet that we were the daughters of *Umma* (faith) – Dukhtaran-e-Millat (DM) – the daughters of faith and that any Muslim woman anywhere in the world was a daughter of faith.'

While this galvanised large numbers of women in her support it also raised suspicion among the state authorities regarding her intent.

When Asiya set up DM, she said that it was not in the form of an organization but more like a movement, a platform

> ...to revive our culture, our beliefs, and our conviction regarding Islam which had become eroded over time. This was not anything new in terms of a movement but something that revived our dormant sentiments, our rights that had been snatched away from us and the movement I began was a revival of that. Our movement did not come into existence for the cause of the Kashmir issue; our main aim and goal was to follow what Allah had decreed in the holy Quran, that Islam is not a religion but a way of life. It was for this reason that we did not give it a name of an organization but pledged that a Muslim woman, whether from the East or the West, was a daughter of faith.

Apart from opposing government-organised functions, in 1985-1986, DM took the movement further by making certain demands to the government; the first was a demand for separate, reserved seats for women in public transport as they suffered daily due to men overcrowding the buses. DM conducted a sustained, peaceful campaign around this issue by holding demonstrations and public meetings. Asiya who did not believe that anything could be gained by meeting 'corrupt, mainstream politicians' even decided to meet the then chief minister Farooq Abdullah along with fifty other women and impressed upon him the need for separate buses for women but 'he rejected our demand saying that we were living in the 20th century and DM, with this demand, was trying to take a regressive step which would take Kashmir back to 1400 years ago.' To this, she responded that as far as she was concerned, it would be the 'best for humanity to return to that golden era.'

DM had by now rented an office in Batmaloo, a locality known to be the bedrock of militancy. As DM's activities and protests grew, the police and the security apparatus began to clamp down on the organisation and it was in 1987, after a 5,000–6,000 strong demonstration of women that she had led in Srinagar against the 'display of posters and pictures of scantily dressed women that hung in public places those days', that the police raided DM's office. 'All our belongings were thrown out on the street, including all the books, documents and translations of the Quran and other literature.' It was then that the police started 'visiting' her family, warning them that if Asiya did not stop mobilising women for her anti-India activities, she would be arrested and that they had in fact come with an arrest warrant for her. Her parents were anxious but she spoke to her father and told him that she had 'consciously chosen this path and did not come to it by accident or any compulsion; I know the path I have chosen will be full of difficulties but I will overcome these. I therefore left home and stayed away for 21 days.' This was the first time she left home and remained underground for three weeks, not realising then that the rigours of an underground life would become a 'routine' for her and the family.

Asiya was 25 years old in 1987 when the elections were held in Jammu and Kashmir in which MUF (Muslim United Front) had participated and it was around the same time that the anti-India struggles had also begun. She believed strongly that the movement for azadi couldn't be sustained through the process of elections and that it was a political blunder and a contradiction to want azadi on the one hand and swear by the Indian constitution, on the other. 'Anyway, that is what happened; MUF lost the elections despite having won the seats due to massive rigging of elections by India. This was when the anti-India movement really began here in Kashmir. It was soon after these elections that the first batch of young men (JKLF) crossed the border for arms training and returned with guns.

DM openly supported the armed militancy and provided logistical support to the militants and DM activists also acted as nodal agents in terms of gathering information for the Mujahedeen.'

It was in 1990 that the government officially banned the DM, forcing Asiya to go underground as her house was raided almost every other day. Her father had retired by then and the family had to face many hardships due to the frequent raids. Her parents were now alone at home as her brothers were also underground and one of them was arrested when he was on his way home from Kanpur where he studied. It was also around this time that her mother wanted Asiya to get married. 'I was quite fortunate to have married the person I did, Mohamed Qasim. He had done his B.Com and had just started Chartered Accountancy when the Tehreek began and he left for Pakistan for training. He returned in 1990 and we got married.' According to Mohammed Qasim who had heard about Asiya and was approached to marry her, 'I considered myself wedded to the cause of militancy, and did not want to endanger another person's life. I knew about the exploits of this woman jihadi who had already established a name for herself and had become a household name in the Valley. She brought a wave of change in the lives of Muslim women. Her DM was a vital source of information for the jihadis, working as their undercover agency. Marrying her would be like being wedded to the cause of freedom again', he is reported to have said.[7]

In 2002, the Ministry of Home Affairs declared DM an unlawful organization under the Prevention of Terrorism Act, 2002. A Gazette Notification issued by the Union Home Ministry said that 'the organization is involved in terrorist activities and banned under the POTA [Prevention of Terrorism Act] with immediate effect.' However, she soon started rehabilitation centres for destitute women, providing them skill training after which she would give them sewing machines so that they could earn a livelihood.

There were fifty-six such centres, including in remote areas that were being run by the DM but the government, through the home ministry, had them all shut down. Prior to this, Asiya said, 'there was a massive raid at my house by the Crime Branch from Delhi. LK Advani, then Home Minister of India, had issued a statement that I was responsible for running militant centres and providing women with military training. As a result, all the centres were shut down and all the sewing machines and other things were confiscated. We were not allowed to do even humanitarian work among the women who most needed it.' Despite the government ban, she gained further prominence in 2002, while she was underground, by imposing the Islamic dress code on women with a threat of defacing them if they refused. However, while local reports said that tailors were doing brisk business, large numbers of women defeated her attempt by refusing to 'fall in line.' In 2006, she initiated a drive against 'social evils in society' through a platform called Forum against Social Evils (FASE) and the agenda was to root out 'corrupt western influences' on the youth of Kashmir, particularly young women. Groups of women, known as the Mariam Squads, regularly raided restaurants and internet cafes, intimidating young men and women, 'educating them about the correct code of conduct, dress and behaviour, according to Islam' and blaming the mushroom growth of internet cafes and restaurants for the rise in 'immoral activities.'

When the 'sex scandal' surfaced in Jammu and Kashmir in 2005-2006, Asiya played a leading role in exposing the nexus that she believed existed between the army, the bureaucracy, and the politicians. She and many others alleged that the sex-scandal was a honey-trap laid by the counter-insurgency experts to nab militants. While demanding a thorough investigation and punishment for the 'culprits and the accused' she simultaneously raided many houses that she suspected were running the sex rings, and in some cases, destroyed these houses. She was arrested under the Public Safety Act during this period for 'taking the law into her own hands' but later released due to intense public political protests and outrage against her arrest. Asiya denied the allegation that she had taken the law into her hands and told me that it was in fact the security forces and their personnel who destroyed people's homes in order to frame her and find a way to arrest her.

Despite adopting coercive means to 'eradicate social evils' and playing the moral police, Asiya nevertheless enjoyed tremendous local support that cut across class and politics, and several editorials in the local newspapers eulogised her for her 'pioneering role in society.' She gained public support, respect and sympathy not only for the work she was doing but also because of the many years she had to spend in jails or in the underground. Her first-born son spent the first 22 months of his life in jail with her and remained with her when she decided to go underground for ten years between 1994-2004. One of the main reasons that Asiya decided to come over-ground was the growing concern she had for her two sons who were not able to pursue their education or lead a normal life. She said that due to her frequent arrests and having to be underground for long periods, her sons were 'beginning to suffer from psychological depression and fear psychosis.' Most importantly, she realised that 'they were being exposed to lies' as she had to adopt different names at different times due to her underground life and as a result, they began to believe that it was 'quite normal to tell lies.' She said that they would often ask her 'why we, their mother and father, had to use false names.' It was in 2004 that Asiya took the decision 'to come overground, return to the house and face whatever the consequences for the sake of my children.' However, she was arrested within a few months of returning home. She was in jail again as recently as May 2017 and was released in August after the J&K High Court quashed her detention under the PSA and sought her release.

I was not able to meet Asiya during the first few years of my fieldwork as she was either underground or back and forth from jail. It was only in 2012 that I first met her at her home and once again after a couple of months. Until then I had only seen her photographs, in which it was only her eyes that were visible as she was fully covered in a burqa. As I entered her home, I noticed a golden sticker on the wall of her living room with the following words inscribed on it: *be-pardah aurat per jannat kya, jannat ki khushboo bhi haram hai* (to women who are not veiled, not only heaven but even the fragrance of heaven is denied). I had imagined I would see her in her signature cloak but here she was, looking like any other ordinary Kashmiri woman, speaking softly, ready to share the story of her extraordinary life. When I got up to leave after a few hours, she came to the door to see me off, hugged me warmly, and said with a smile, 'You are an Indian Muslim woman and it is your *majboori* that you have to find ways to maintain your identity and culture as a Muslim woman in India. We are not compelled in this manner, as Kashmir was never and will never be a part of India.'

❊   ❊   ❊

I did not know much about militancy and the movement for azadi until I began fieldwork in Kashmir. These years of engagement with the land opened my eyes to the complexities, the nuances and the triumphs and tragedies of militancy through the different phases of its existence, which spanned more than one generation. I was also not fully aware of the extent of popular support that it enjoyed and how it had captured people's imagination, attention and participation on the ground. That women played such a crucial and inspirational role in militancy and in the movement became more evident as I travelled, met and interacted with them in cities, towns and villages where the dynamics of its social and political consequences were a lived reality. However, women's varied roles and contributions, not only within the movement but also in sustaining their families in the absence of their men did not receive the kind of recognition and acknowledgement that it deserved from the leadership or from other sections of society. While the sacrificing, passive victim woman was someone who was recognized and accepted, those who exercised agency, who stood their ground even in face of the state's military suppression and intrusion into their homes and lives, were not so easily accepted. It is largely due to their own efforts and remarkable work that these women have gained greater visibility in the public realm over the years. It is significant that they did not stumble into the movement, nor were they incidental to it. Rather, as we have seen above, each chose her political path carefully and deliberately.

The combined forces of militarization, patriarchy, and conservatism are a constant challenge for women. As the above account shows, Anjum has been pushed to the margins of the organisation she joined. Despite years of active association with the Hurriyat, she has still not found a place in the all-male executive council, and has been denied the decision-making powers that her male counterparts enjoy. Moreover, when women gain political prominence in the movement as leaders, the state hounds them and their families with all its brutal force as revealed in the above stories. The women we have talked about above have spent a number of years in jail or in the underground, as in the case of all three women leaders, but they have emerged more resolute and courageous each time.

NOTES

1. Bakhtawar. April 2003. Srinagar
2. 'Women of Kashmir a Symbol of Resistance.' March 9, 2017. *The Kashmir Monitor*. Srinagar.

3. I benefited greatly from the many conversations/discussions I have had with Gautam Navlakha over a period of time on the subject.

4. Butalia, Urvashi. 2005. 'Concept Note on Gender and Conflict.' Peace Studies Course. New Delhi: Aman Public Charitable Trust.

5. Ibid.

6. Thakur, Pradeep. 2003. *Militant Monologues: Echoes from the Kashmir Valley.* New Delhi: Parity Paper Backs.

7. Ibid.

chapter four

The Mind and the Body

THE MENTAL HEALTH OF THE KASHMIRI PEOPLE

As I began my fieldwork in Kashmir, I became increasingly interested in the psychological impact of the conflict and the continuing violence on the everyday lives of people. It had become apparent quite early on that the situation posed an unprecedented challenge for people: how could they remain safe and secure? The environment was heavily militarized, the threat of violence constant, and death and destruction stalked people's everyday lives. In this situation the question uppermost in my mind was how and where to begin. How could I even begin to understand the extent to which people and their lives had been affected and altered in a manner that defied imagination? I remember how often people – irrespective of gender, age, and occupation – used the words trauma and tension to describe everyday lives within and outside their homes. As I met and interacted with them closely, I found myself spending considerable amounts of time at the government psychiatric hospital in Srinagar where I met doctors and patients and observed the situation closely. I was struck by the sheer numbers of patients: there were young and old men, middle-aged and older women, but young girls and children were conspicuous by their absence.

At the hospital, large numbers of patients jostled for attention, while the two lone psychiatrists and their post-graduate interns struggled to keep up with the demands on their attention. The Outpatient Department (OPD) records registered a steadily increasing number of patients, with 100-300 visiting every day. Many of them were women. I was told that among 100 patients with acute depression, nearly 70-80 per cent were women, even though more men than women visited the hospital. Nearly twenty years later, in 2018, I found during a visit to the hospital that the number of patients had continued to escalate, and had crossed 100,000 by 2012. There was visible infrastructural improvement and more awareness among people about psychiatric ailments and the availability of mental health services, but the tragedy continued. While these numbers were deeply disturbing, I knew that was not the full story and I was keen to see what they masked.

In what follows, I speak about how violence and its aftermath has had catastrophic implications for the health and well-being of the Kashmiri people; I also look at how it has impacted their educational opportunities, their livelihoods and family relations. Many of the women I met were anxious about losing men in their family either to militancy or to the state which, because of the suspicion its agencies harboured against them, could randomly target them. They could be picked up, disappeared or killed at any time. Women were vigilant and protective of their men.

Despite heavy militarization and counterinsurgency measures that target men and women in specific ways, militancy today is in a resurgent mode with many educated youth taking up arms in defiance of the militarized state's brutal repression. Their anger

and rage is now accompanied by fearlessness and defiance as can be
seen at encounter sites where the young, along with many women
from the neighbourhood, gather in large numbers to help find a safe
passage for militants, even at the risk of their lives. With the spurt
in the ranks of the militants and their killings, the J&K police and
the army came up with a plan to involve the parents, particularly
the mothers of militants, to issue appeals to their sons to give up
arms and return home. The emotional ties that bound mothers to
their sons, they thought, would help bring them back.[1] The police
claimed that 'mothers are playing a vital role in ensuring the return
of their sons. In a majority of cases, the boys agreed only after talking
to their mothers.' Indeed a few did return, but the reality is that
the entry of such young men into the ranks of the militants is a
new phenomenon compared to the earlier phases of militancy. The
discrimination, constant harassment, the contempt and suspicion
with which the state treats young Kashmiri people is what drives
them towards militancy which they embrace with a sense of
commitment, and with fearlessness and defiance. Those who opt to
pursue life elsewhere are not spared either as there are reports of how
Kashmiri youth, be they students or employed are treated outside –
basically as suspects and enemies. While the government claims that
unemployment is a major cause for the youth joining militancy,
many of the educated youth have also abandoned their jobs and even
education to become militants.

While much is written in the media regarding the rise in militancy,
what is the reality within homes where the family members mourn
the loss of their young sons who are killed battling the security forces?
What about the women – their mothers – whose grief at the loss
of their young sons remains unaddressed? How do they cope with
their everyday lives, where love and loss has left its mark on them in
profound ways? One of the things I heard from a psychiatrist at the
hospital was that the essence of trauma is how one experiences it and

where women were concerned, he said that their unwavering belief in the hereafter helps them cope with the tragedy. Burhan Wani's mother prayed and waited for her son to return home and lead a 'normal' life but gradually reconciled herself to the reality of his being a militant. After he was killed, she expressed her gratitude to all the mothers who had provided her young son with shelter that enabled him to live safely for six years until he achieved, as she told a local reporter, 'what he aspired for – martyrdom.' Her only consolation was that he had lived up to his own aspirations and become a martyr for a cause that was so close to his heart.

Let us begin by looking at the recent past to understand how the issues of violence and loss are interlinked with mental health and how the character of the Indian state has remained contentious, treating 'its own people' as second-class citizens or enemies. I have also drawn from my field notes from earlier years to show the continuity that exists in terms of the violence and loss people experienced and how it is reflected within the family and the community, in the records of the hospitals – where doctors and other health professionals too have been affected in different ways – and in the government's own records and its attitude towards the crisis.

The 2016 Uprising and the Aftermath

Kashmir witnessed a massive uprising – described by a local journalist as the 'most intense people's uprising for the first time since 1990' – following the killing of Burhan Muzaffar Wani by Indian security forces on 8 July 2016. A young, educated, and popular militant commander of Hizb-ul-Mujahedeen who joined militancy in 2010 at the age of 15, Burhan became an icon for the youth, as he was active on social media and had posted his picture along with a group of other young militants holding their guns proudly and prominently. Apart from the guns, the smiling faces of the men in the group also held out hope to a young generation that has grown up in the context of pervasive violence and brutal repression by the security forces. In the words of an online news report, Kashmiri youth angered by the 'never ending militarization' of the Valley were drawn to Burhan Wani: 'Prior to Burhan Wani's killing, when two of his associates were killed by the security forces, tens of thousands of local Kashmiris came out to attend the funerals and the funeral rites had to be repeated six times to allow all the mourners to participate.' For Burhan Wani's funeral, an estimated 200,000 people are reported to have come even from remote parts of the Valley where forty back-to-back funeral prayers were reported to have been offered. This, despite the state imposed curfew that lasted 56 days.

To 'control' the sudden outpouring of unarmed protestors onto the streets of Srinagar, the 'JK Police and Indian paramilitary forces used pellet guns, tear gas shells, rubber bullets and assault rifles. This resulted in more than 90 civilian deaths and over 15,000 pellet injuries.'[2]

Many local doctors feared that at least 117 civilians were likely to lose their eyesight while others suffered partial blindness as a result of injuries caused by pellet shotguns (billed by the government and Indian forces as 'non-lethal' means of crowd control). It was widely reported and shown in the media how, in the first month of the uprising and widespread protests, even medical services and hospitals were attacked and raided by the forces, including ambulances carrying pellet injury victims to hospitals. Despite the acute shortage of eye specialists, hospitals remained crowded with affected people seeking attention. Shri Maharaja Hari Singh Hospital (SMHS) reportedly admitted more than 200 patients with eye injuries within the first five days of protests. A team of three eye specialists from the All India Institute of Medical Sciences (AIIMS) was brought to Kashmir to help the local doctors treat the pellet injuries and perform surgeries where needed. The visiting doctors are reported to have described the traumatic scenes at the hospitals as a war-like situation.[3]

Apart from the physical injuries and intense psychological trauma, everyday life was disrupted for months as Kashmir witnessed the longest curfew of 56 days and strikes/hartals for 115 days. A senior local journalist mentioned how, during this period, people shared food, offered shelter to protestors from other towns and districts, made announcements from mosques, and sang songs of freedom. Despite the brutal crackdown, and the trauma, people remained spirited and defiant.

As the protests continued, in May 2017, the Indian army launched 'Operation All Out' (named after the popular mosquito repellent) with an aim to kill all militants by the end of 2017. Even as the operation kicked in, more militants surfaced. According to a local correspondent, even after killing 215 militants – total strength at the beginning of the year – there were about 200 more militants at the end of the year.[4] To nab the militants, the Indian forces, he said, conducted 800 cordon and search operations in Kashmir in 2017 alone. According to the Jammu Kashmir Legislative Assembly, 11,290 protestors were arrested on charges of stone throwing between 2016–2017.[5]

The violence and killing have not stopped. As recently as April 2018, 11 young local militants were killed in encounters in Shopian and Anantnag districts, along with 4 civilians and 3 soldiers, all in a single day. The army and the J&K police claimed this as a major success of 'Operation All Out' but failed to comprehend the extent of people's support to militancy, which was evident at encounter sites where they turned out in large numbers to help militants escape – despite the obvious risk, to themselves, of physical injuries and even death. Nearly 40 civilians, including women were reportedly shot dead during these protests at and near these encounter sites.

The security forces, including the army, came down heavily on residents who were accused or suspected of shielding militants, torching or blowing up several homes allegedly used as hideouts by militants. In the past 15 months, security forces under Operation All Out have reportedly killed more than 250 militants.[6] One of the fathers of a slain militant, talking about the impact Burhan Wani had on the youth, told a local correspondent that for the youth, 'the life Burhan Wani lived was more worth living for than this *zulum* [injustice]…the sentiment runs deep in the district… we suffered oppression silently but they will not – they have decided to stand against it.'[7] The anger on the streets was not going to die down soon, he warned. Shopian district alone saw more than 15 encounters in the 18 months between late 2016 and early 2018. According to the superintendent of police, Shopian, there were eight militants in the district before Burhan Wani was killed but after his death, the district witnessed a dramatic rise in militancy: 'their number kept increasing and at one point in 2017 it was four times more than total militants in 2016.' In the words of a professor at the Central University of Kashmir, 'each killing whether of a militant or a civilian is adding to the anger and rage in the valley.'[8]

The State of the People's Mental Health

One of the direct consequences of the nearly three-decade long political conflict and the continuing daily violence is the impact it has had on people's health, including their mental health. This is deeply enmeshed with the abuse of their privacy, the daily violations of their fundamental rights and the consistent denial of justice to victims and survivors. Issues of mental health and trauma have to be understood in the context of the overall human cost of conflict that has claimed more than 80,000 lives since militancy began.

So widespread and common is the direct and indirect experience of violence in the lives of people that doctors believe that a majority of the Kashmiri population suffers from common symptoms of stress and a large number have been diagnosed with clinical depressive disorders.

Dr Arshad Hussain, professor and senior psychiatrist at the government psychiatric hospital, told me recently how patients visiting the hospital before the 1980s had more neurobiological and genetic disorders where the environment played a *minor* role, but today patients mostly suffered from psychological disorders where the environment played a *major* role in what they felt. Post Traumatic Stress Disorder or PTSD, panic and phobia, sleep disturbances, somatoform disorders were some of the common psychological ailments in the present scenario and these were found to be more in the case of women.

A survey conducted by Medecins sans Frontiers in 2015[9] revealed that 99.2 per cent of the adult population in Kashmir reported experiencing or witnessing at least one traumatic event during their lifetime[10] and also showed that mental health ailments have emerged as one of the most pressing public health concerns in Kashmir with 100,000+ patients visiting the psychiatric disease hospital in Srinagar annually. Combined with the psychiatric department at SMHS hospital, the number of registered patients went up to 150,000 by December 2014.

While the numbers are alarming, it is worth noting that unlike in previous years, mental health issues are now coming to the fore as general awareness regarding the availability of psychiatric help is growing among people. 'Earlier, when we had a huge mental morbidity, particularly post-traumatic stress, patients did not come to psychiatrists; many went to faith healers and spiritual places. But now, psychiatry and shrinks have become a reality in Kashmir and therefore, mental health issues would increase with time rather than decrease.'[11]

Dr Mushtaq Marghoob, senior psychiatrist and former head of the department at the government psychiatric hospital described how the MSF findings confirmed a 'serious mental health situation, with highly prevalent common mental disorders and distress having continued to increase to reach epidemic levels among the traumatized population of Kashmir.' Given such a scale of mental ailments, what were the coping mechanisms that people turned to? The MSF survey found that the common coping strategies were prayer, talking to friends and family, keeping busy as well as, for some people, social isolation. Interestingly, Dr Mushtaq Marghoob referred to himself as a faith healer, saying 'people have absolute faith that whatever tragedy strikes them is the will of god, so they do not give up.' He added: 'Their faith is a support system and it helps me treat them too. Without it, psychiatric disorders in Kashmir would have turned into an unmanageable problem. Where medicines cannot work, these traditions do.'

The mental health survey, as well as the post Burhan Wani protests, point in the direction of an increase in psychological ailments among people directly affected by the violence as well as their families and the community. As a recent report on the community-based prevalence of mental health illness in Kashmir points out, mental health issues do not remain limited to those who suffer but also lead to generational trauma through a cycle of increased stress in families, declining socio-economic conditions, health care burdens, the breakdown of families, marital issues and domestic violence.[12]

Over the years, hospitals and mental health services saw some improvement in overall infrastructure and facilities. But the records continued to show a steady increase in the number of patients seeking treatment from the decade of the nineties on, with the last few years showing a considerable surge. But whether then or now, one thing remained constant, and that was the increasing burden on women. They continued to be prime caregivers in the family, while at the same time remaining vigilant for their young sons' safety and this often meant that they neglected their own health. In addition, because medical services were difficult, if not impossible, to access in rural areas, this added to women's health burden.

Soldiers Control the Cure: The Militarisation of Health Services

During my fieldwork and on many subsequent visits it became apparent that the conflict had led to a structural breakdown of the social service sector, particularly the health infrastructure. In rural areas, you could often find buildings meant to house health care facilities but which were empty of doctors, nurses and other health personnel and that had virtually no medicines. Some vacant buildings had been occupied by the security forces. In Kupwara district for instance, according to a local newspaper report, 'for the past several years, troops are camping at PHCs in Handwara, Kupwara, Karnah, Teetwal and Lolab areas. Several deaths have taken place in this frontier district due to the occupation of the buildings.'[13]

The official argument that only vacant buildings were used for the troops did not carry much weight: more important was the question why the government had failed to provide a safe and secure environment that would encourage doctors and nurses to do the work they were meant to do. During one of my visits to Budgam (in mid 2000) I found that there was one district and four sub-district hospitals where doctors were meant to be on duty 24 hours but nowhere was this the case. Many doctors from the peripheries had moved to the maternity hospital in Srinagar. A Block Medical Officer told me that Budgam had once had a large number of women doctors but now most of them were not able to work, particularly at night, because things were so unsafe. 'Even as a chief medical officer of the district, I cannot insist that they report for duty, especially at odd hours. It is well known that a woman doctor cannot even cross a stretch of half a kilometre without the threat of being molested or assaulted by the army. How can their presence be ensured when their security is in danger?' The only two nurses on night duty were there 'mainly because their husbands were also on duty, and were able to provide the much-needed sense of security.'

In my meetings with women health workers – Auxiliary Nurse Midwives (ANMs) – in tehsil Chadoora of Budgam district one afternoon, another problem surfaced when we began talking about the difficulties women faced in their day-to-day work in the community. One of them spoke out about the threats they received from the militants. She pulled out a letter she had received from a local commander of Hizb-ul-Mujahideen asking her to 'immediately stop the family planning campaign in the community or face dire consequences' as this was an 'insult to Islam and its great values' (my translation from Urdu). After repeated written threats sent to her through his own messengers, she sought a meeting with the commander to 'negotiate with him and settle the issue once for all' but the meeting did not take place although her consistent refusal to succumb to the threats 'forced the militants to retreat but only after subjecting a young man who had undergone vasectomy, to brutal torture as a lesson for others in the village to abstain from family planning. This instilled terrible fear in the community, which had to be overcome. We women community workers had to constantly express our resolve to work even as we faced challenges not only from the militants but also our own community's resistance to our work as well as the security forces' intrusion into the privacy of our lives,' said the health worker. Dr Asma Khan, a senior gynaecologist at the maternity hospital in Srinagar told me that prior to militancy, 'there was a growing awareness of contraception in the state and vasectomies and tubectomies were routine. But for several years now, no vasectomy had been performed and tubectomies were attempted only in cases where another pregnancy could be life-threatening. The number of illegal abortion centres had also increased.'

Basic facilities at health centres were also in a dismal condition. Primary Health Centres (PHCs) in the districts were ill equipped to provide even basic health care services. There were no anesthetists, no blood banks and not even enough medicines in store to meet an emergency. A majority of patients from such PHCs were routinely referred to other hospitals in the city whereas women patients were referred to the only maternity hospital in Srinagar, whatever be their illness. In such cases, it was the responsibility of the district medical officers to shift patients. While a few ambulances were available at the block level, patients had to pay for fuel and travel to the block to avail the facility. This often proved hazardous for women, particularly expectant mothers, as soldiers on duty would also stop them for security checks and frisking, leading to stress and anxiety, explained the Block Medical Officer. In one PHC located on the main road, there was one medical assistant, one compounder and one nurse at the time of my visit. According to them, they were on duty only till 2 o'clock in the afternoon. The medicines were not only in short supply but also of very poor quality. Many patients had to leave without proper treatment. To make up for the bad quality medicines, 'patients had to be given bigger dosages. This also meant prolonged treatment', said the nurse. If this was the case of a functioning PHC on the main road, what would those in the interior of the districts be like, I asked the medical assistant. His response was that access to something as basic as primary health care was a major problem. They could not even begin to think of specialized care, he said.

The situation in the subsidiary health centres was no better. I visited one in Pattan, Baramulla where there was one Block Medical Officer and one nurse on duty. This is what I was told by the BMO:

> The doctors are not willing to work any more in the villages. They prefer to be in urban centres. Many of them have started their own practice, while drawing government salaries at the same time. At this sub-district hospital, we have a ten-bed capacity, which remains vacant most of the time, as patients prefer to go to the city for treatment. This building has remained the same whereas services have diminished steadily. Accommodating patients here has been a problem. We admit delivery cases but any indication of a complication is enough for us to send the women to hospitals in the city. The few doctors that we have do not give time to patients here and call them home or to their private clinics instead. The majority of patients cannot pay the fee that is demanded. There are cases of abortions and miscarriages but given the situation they are considered normal. God's management is not so poor that mere depression or shock will cause a woman to miscarry or abort. People must have faith in God.

At this, the woman medical assistant in the room suddenly left and when I followed her outside she had an angry outburst. 'Do not believe him,', she told me, 'he is a liar, hiding the truth. People's suffering here has nothing to do with God, as he said. It has to do with a violent reality.'

The Institute of Mental Health and Neuroscience (IMHANS) community-based survey of 2016 also found that the primary health services have seen little improvement with hardly a component of mental health care. The secondary and tertiary care government hospitals also have inadequate numbers of psychiatrists. But virtually all the districts are overwhelmed with the number of patients approaching hospitals for treatment.[14] Of the 50 psychiatrists available, only a few were able to attend some of the major district hospitals on designated days. However, the increase in the number of psychiatrists has also seen a rise in private psychiatric clinics; patients who attend these are significant in number but go unreported as records are not maintained in private clinics.

As far back as in 1982, the Government of India initiated the National Mental Health Programme (NMHP) which was meant to ensure that mental health services would be available and accessible for everyone, but in particular for those from vulnerable and underprivileged backgrounds. In 1996 a district mental health plan was launched to provide community-based mental health services and to integrate these with general health services. This programme was subsequently expanded to 123 districts in India. Four of the districts selected for its implementation (2004-2005) were in J&K, but despite the fact that mental illness had increased drastically in Kashmir valley in the last two and a half decades, *all the selected districts were in the Jammu region* (my emphasis). The community-based survey also found a 'disturbingly high treatment gap of 88 per cent with only 6.4 per cent of the suffering population having received treatment from a psychiatrist.[15]'

A Fragile Solution: The Government
Psychiatric Disease Hospital IMHANS

The only government hospital for psychiatric diseases in Kashmir, located in Srinagar that provides psychiatric services to the entire Kashmir Valley, was established in 1957 as an integral part of the Central Jail and mainly admitted patients recommended by the jail authorities. It was initially known as a mental asylum and later as a mental hospital and since mental health services began in a 'mental asylum' people felt stigmatised to be known or treated as psychiatric patients. Today, the hospital has been upgraded and is now known as the Institute of Mental Health and Neurosciences (IMHANS). The change in nomenclature was particularly directed towards helping patients overcome the social stigma attached to visiting a psychiatric/mental hospital. In a recent conversation I had with Dr Arshad Hussain, he informed me that the infrastructure for mental health services had improved greatly, with the hospital building being renovated and expanded, with added facilities and more doctors on duty.[16] Moreover, the SMHS hospital with its psychiatric department also provided psychiatric services and when I made a visit there recently (2018), the OPD was overcrowded with men and women patients waiting their turn, with Dr Arshad and four young women psychiatrists on duty. Infrastructural improvements notwithstanding, the number of patients has continued to increase over the years because of the prevailing atmosphere of political instability and the constant threat of violence.

The Wards

With a capacity of 100 beds, the hospital only admits those diagnosed with severe psychotic symptoms. Despite the shortage of space, many more patients were admitted than there were beds for, which led to sometimes as many as three sharing one bed. Little is known about these patients, who are often abandoned by their families and by society. During one of my initial visits, I accompanied Dr Sadaqat Rehman, a clinical psychologist at the hospital, who routinely visited the wards to monitor the welfare of the patients.

Adjacent to the hospital there were four wards in a large compound with high walls, one for female patients and the others for male patients. The female ward had 22 patients; one of them tied in chains to her bed in a corner. 'She gets violent fits during which she attacks other inmates. We have to keep her chained for others' safety', explained the doctor. It was noon and the women patients had just finished their lunch and were moving around in the courtyard as the ward had just been cleaned. 'We are forced to have the open latrine system inside the ward as patients do not have the cognitive sense of space', said Dr Sadaqat. After lunch, every woman was given her dose of medicine and locked inside the ward till late evening when they were brought out for dinner and a few physical exercises. Another round of medication and they were locked in again for the night. According to the doctor, this was meant for their own safety, as they were vulnerable to sexual assault, both from the male inmates as well as the Border Security Force (BSF) jawans whose headquarters were adjacent to the ward. The male wards were in the same premises without a door or a wall to separate them. A high-rise wall had been erected next to the windows of the female ward 'to keep off the BSF men who used to take advantage of the mental state of these women and sexually abuse them.' The windows now had heavy metal grills that opened on to the walls. Many of the patients were either in a state of delirium or stupor due to the high dosage of medicines. I was nearly mobbed as some of the women inside the ward pleaded with me desperately to be released, with one of them scribbling her name on my palm. Many of the patients had been languishing in the ward for years, as their families had not returned to take them back home, even after the doctors had declared some of them to be normal.

Similar conditions prevailed in the male wards where there were 80 patients, far beyond capacity. One ward with seven beds was specifically meant for patients recovering from drug addiction. This and the other wards were also filthy, even though they had just been cleaned. Many of the patients refused to wear clothes and when made to do so, tore them off. 'This is because of the heat generated in their body due to the kind of medicines they have had to consume over the years and also because many of them are completely divorced from reality so it hardly matters to them whether they wear clothes or not', said the doctor. Here too, their families had abandoned them and they had nowhere to go even when some of them showed signs of recovery. They also remained locked inside the wards except at mealtimes and recreation, lasting about an hour. 'We have to lock them in so that they do not wander into the female ward' (Just then I saw a male patient enter the female ward and the attendants had to physically drag him out). The conditions were dismal and deplorable but as the doctor said, 'they are better here than out on the streets as they have nowhere to go.' The hospital tried and succeeded a couple of times in tracking down the patients' families and taking those who had recovered back to them. However, there were reports that they were abused and beaten up when they returned to their families and in such cases; they eventually found their way back to the hospital for shelter.

My impression as I first entered the premises of the hospital was that it was a war-ravaged place, not a hospital. I was struck by how it was in a state of complete disrepair and neglect. I learnt that it had been gutted twice during the past decade – 1990 – and it still bore traces of the destruction. In the large compound surrounding the building, I noticed the charred remains of burnt vehicles that seemed to testify to the violence that had engulfed the place earlier. I wondered how such remnants of the violent past must affect those who visited the hospital, in search of treatment that they hoped would cure them of their trauma and suffering. Wouldn't the surroundings traumatize them further, I wondered? The inner path leading to the hospital was full of rubble and garbage, stacked against the broken walls of what were earlier the cells where prisoners were lodged. No more part of the central jail, the hospital was now located close to the barracks of the Border Security Force. (Many years later, when I shared my first impressions with Dr Arshad, he responded by saying that the hospital in those years had reminded him of the 'war-ravaged Tora Bora' and how difficult it was for the doctors to work in those conditions).

One of my visits to the hospital in 2003-2004 coincided with the OPD hours and there was a tremendous rush of patients. The corridors and the doctor's rooms were full but it provided me with an opportunity to sit with the doctors and listen to the patient's complaints. Not much had changed from the time of my first visit in terms of the nature of complaints that patients came with, nor was there any visible improvement in the physical conditions of the hospital. Shortage of staff remained as critical a problem as the rush of patients. When I entered a room belonging to Dr Mushtaq Marghoob, senior psychiatrist, he threw up his arms in exasperation and exclaimed, 'this is not psychiatry because this is not how it is practised. This is not even psychology…Just look at the number of patients in this room. There are so many waiting outside too. I do not know what to call this. It is sheer madness.' Outside and inside his room were tired and anxious looking men and women, some of whom had come with their sons who needed treatment. They held onto their prescriptions as though these were sacred documents and as one of the women told me, losing them would mean starting all over again, a cumbersome procedure. 'It is humanly impossible for us to treat such large numbers of patients. Our own health is at risk in such a situation as the stress level is so high. We are understaffed and overworked. We have to take long leaves at times to protect our own sanity', said Dr Marghoob. Outside, in the open courtyard other patients were queuing up in front of a tiny, wired window with their prescriptions to get the free medicines available at the hospital.

The hospital records showed that until 1992 there was no reported case of PTSD but such cases had gradually begun to outnumber the others.[17]

The doctors mentioned how patients tended to neglect PTSD symptoms for far too long. This resulted in various complications and needed prolonged treatment and this was compounded by the high degree of ignorance among people regarding psychiatric symptoms or treatment. The social stigma attached to visiting 'what is commonly known as a mental hospital' also inhibited timely diagnosis and treatment, particularly in the case of young women whose marriage prospects would get jeopardized. Sixty per cent of the patients preferred to first visit general physicians, cardiologists and faith healers for treatment. Those who could afford it went to private psychiatric clinics that have mushroomed in the city over the last few years.

Doctors believe that the majority of the population is suffering from 'not ordinary but catastrophic stress.' This is induced when people are witness to the sudden killing of a close relative or when their loved ones are tortured in their presence. This has been a common occurrence since militancy began. According to the doctor:

> One patient who witnessed the killing of a family member continued to see it happening all the time – even in his sleep. Such patients displayed psychotic symptoms such as delusions and hallucinations and what made it worse was that they remained ignorant and unmindful of their own illness. Not to relive the trauma or be reminded of it, they would avoid visiting the place where the event took place. One individual's psychotic state often led to family illnesses where all members, particularly women, would begin to suffer from acute depression, anxiety and sleep disorders. Women had the added responsibility of providing special care to members of the family suffering from psychological disorders, resulting in the neglect of their own frail health. The quality of life among such families was close to schizophrenic.

If there were crossfire or a sudden shootout, such patients would suddenly stop going out and refuse to meet people. They led their lives in the constant shadow of fear and under the threat of violence. 'One patient who had to be admitted in the hospital for two years was released but the psychological impact of the event was still so deep that he was not able to lead a normal life even after being discharged. He eventually lost his job, the only source of income for the family.' During one of my visits to the hospital I met a distraught mother who had brought her young son for treatment. As they entered the doctor's room, her son collapsed to the floor and had to be helped to his feet. She told the doctor that he often suffered from fits when he would smash everything he could lay his hands on and had to therefore be locked away in an empty room as the mother feared for the safety of other family members. Her son could not be treated that day, as the hospital did not have the medicines he needed. He could not be admitted, as he would have posed a danger to other patients in the wards. The mother turned to me and said, 'What shall I do? Most of our household belongings are now ruined. He does not say a word. I know he is very angry because he saw his father being killed. I cannot go out to work, as I cannot leave him alone at home. Bringing him to the hospital is a problem and now we have to return without any help.' I learnt that this was not a lone case and that many women shared a similar predicament.

According to doctors, all age groups were now exposed to PTSD. Before 1990, only those above 40-45 years would come with complaints of high blood pressure, hypertension, and heart ailments, the age group with similar symptoms was now between 18-35 years. I personally saw how desperate and frustrated young men had become as I met many of them in a village I visited in Baramulla district one afternoon. As I was talking to a woman near her house, some of the young men approached me and said that they wanted to share their problems. It was mid-afternoon but all of them were at home; not one of them went to college – many having discontinued – or had any employment. While a few other women also came out, young girls had either gone to school or were busy with household chores. A young man with thick grey hair came up to me and said, '*Mein bayees saal ka budha hoon*' – I am an old man of 22. He elaborated by saying that he had been undergoing heart treatment for the past two years and added that he was not alone, that there were many others like him in the village. Other young men complained of throbbing pain in the heart, frequent headaches, general weakness and anaemia. 'We are the worst affected people. There is a lot of anger in us but we cannot express it. The army will finish us. We just have to bear it. The army is always on the prowl. There is so much repression. Many of us feel that death may be a better option than living like this. In our village there have been ten crackdowns in one year. Many of us are educated but unemployed. We work in the fields, in the few carpet factories and also do odd jobs for survival, earning 30-40 rupees on a good day. Unemployment is a big problem here. The sense of insecurity does not leave us even for a moment. The government claims that it has provided jobs to 45,000 educated young men but from our village, not a single person has found such employment', said one of the young men.[18] When I mentioned this to a local doctor he said, 'Young men are seething with anger today as they are always viewed with suspicion by government forces. They are picked up arbitrarily by the army, frisked, tortured, humiliated and then expected to lead normal lives. What are their choices and options? What use is education when unemployment stares them in their face? They feel insignificant and useless, not being able to either look after themselves or their families. Tried and challenged by circumstances on a daily basis they can and do take to arms. In fact, even parents find it difficult to trust their young sons, as they may actually be militants living in the midst of the family. Why not? How can one tell?'

In my meetings with other young people, their sense of anger and frustration was clearly visible as they spoke of different factors that impinged on their lives – unemployment, army repression, ill health, and the breakdown of social networks. As one of them said, 'our homes have also become like prisons. We are afraid to even open our windows for fear that firing may take place and we'll fall prey to the bullets. As you can see, we have covered our windows with iron mesh as a safety measure. We make sure we are back home even before it gets dark.' His mother added, '*hum toh taazi hawa ke bhi haqdar nahin rahe*' – we are not even entitled to a breath of fresh air. Large-scale unemployment coupled with a crippled social life where there was hardly any source of entertainment or space left to fulfil one's aspirations has led to intense frustration among the youth. One village elder said, 'There is no distinction between the young and old in the life that we lead here. It is so harsh and claustrophobic, what is the difference between the old and the young here? We live in a suffocating environment.'

For young women, the threat of sexual violence was a constant worry as 'soldiers on the streets stare and pass lewd comments.' According to a doctor in a district hospital:

> Young boys and girls do not experience normal life as they are confined to their homes once dusk falls. Unable to cope with the prolonged state of stress and depression resulting from an abnormal environment, they take to drugs and in extreme cases, even attempt suicide. They have got accustomed to taking drugs on a daily basis, and many have thus become addicted to them. There is no drug control policy here, which compounds the problem. Antidepressants and other such drugs are often sold without prescription. In this situation of an unprecedented demand for these drugs, chemists are known to sell them at higher prices, charging three times

more than the actual cost. The sale of Corex (cough
syrup), popular among the youth, is at a peak. A bottle
costs twenty rupees but chemists are known to sell it for
as much as a hundred. It has become a lucrative business
for them, as they take advantage of these young people
who have lost their ability to think rationally. The daily
humiliation faced by them has taken a toll on their lives,
which they consider to be devoid of any meaning. People
may appear to be healthy but they carry symptoms of
severe mental and physical illnesses. Their sense of fear
is so acute that even the sound of utensils in the kitchen
can upset some of them. There is no peace of mind any
more. Those who stay home are as scared and vulnerable
as those who have to step out.

Women's health has suffered in specific ways due to this situation.
When this is combined with their lack of access to basic health
facilities, things become much worse. Among older women, anxiety
and high levels of stress during pregnancy are reported to have led
to premature deliveries as well as abortions. However, these were
not always recorded as such in hospitals but entered as 'miscarriage
due to haemorrhage.' Gynaecologists admitted to an increase in such
cases, combined with prolonged depression and anaemia among
women. According to the records of the Lalded Maternity hospital in
Srinagar, the peak period of such cases was 1990-1995 when counter
insurgency measures such as crackdowns and cross-firing were a
routine matter. 'Cases of premature deliveries and abortions were
entered in the records as cases of accidental haemorrhage', said the
superintendent of the hospital. 'Being the only maternity hospital,
patients come here from all the districts of Kashmir. Three to four
hundred women visit the OPD in a single day. Only seriously ill
patients and those ready for delivery are admitted. Against a 450-bed
capacity there are 700 patients at times.' Since many women travel
long distances to come to the hospital, they cannot come alone and

are often accompanied by relatives who then take over the corridors, cook, eat and sleep there.

According to the ward-in-charge, the poor quality of medicines meant that women had to be given larger doses for prolonged periods of time. During my visit one afternoon, there were nearly 300 women waiting their turn to meet the doctor. The OPD closed at two in the afternoon and the majority of women feared they would have to make another trip, another day. The maternity ward (emergency) had only seven beds with three women sharing one, all of them in advanced stages of pregnancy. Attendants in the ward admitted that it was difficult to maintain hygiene or prevent infections and that this affected women's lives and their health in significant ways. At home, as prime caregivers, attending to those who were ill in the family, women bore the maximum burden, often at the cost of their own health. 'Women are biologically predisposed and psychologically more vulnerable. Conflict is one of the major reasons for increase in psychological problems in Kashmiri women. They are the commonest survivor group left behind with the responsibility of their children,' said Dr Arshad Hussain.

Given the mismatch between available health and mental health services and the widespread prevalence of health and mental health problems, Kashmir has witnessed a proliferation of private clinics and health practitioners. An inadequate health care budget, combined with the increasing number of patients, has led to malpractices in the form of unnecessary investigations, casual diagnoses and tedious procedures in private clinics. Already traumatised, the people have also to bear these increased costs. One of the alarming consequences, particularly for women, which have arisen out of this and the somatisation of psychological disorders among women, is the increasing number of hysterectomies performed every month. These take place in private clinics and are performed not by gynaecologists but by surgeons, without a single consultation with a gynaecologist and even young women of childbearing age have not been spared. Many women of perimenopausal age where menstrual disturbances are common were found in a 'low mood, with complaints of aches and pains. In many such cases, during investigation, doctors would find incidental fibroids that are normally present in 40 per cent of women but most of the women patients would opt for hysterectomy because of an unfounded belief that the uterus is unwanted after childbearing age and is responsible for all their ailments. However, in most cases the pain persists despite the surgery as the problem is psychological in nature and can be treated only through proper counselling.'[19]

The Mental Agony of Women

More men visited the hospital than women and children even though women were more prone to depression and anxiety. 'If 30 per cent women are affected, only 5 per cent would come to the hospital. At any given time at least 15 per cent women suffer from prolonged trauma and stress resulting in physical symptoms such as frequent palpitations, deep and overwhelming sorrow, lack of interest and concentration, sleep disorders and loss of appetite. Dr. Arshad pointed out that of 100 cases of acute depression, 70–80 are of women. In a patriarchal society women's health is not treated seriously and they are not taken to hospital even though the symptoms may require urgent medical attention.'

The continuing violence has forced women to face the challenge, on a daily basis, of single-handedly restoring a semblance of normalcy to their lives as well as ensuring their family's wellbeing. As in most conflict situations, women play a crucial role in the effort of reconstructing broken homes and hearths and healing the psychological and physical wounds of their loved ones. With large numbers of dead and missing men, often the sole earning members of a family, women have had to take on new and challenging roles to sustain their families. Evidence of this can be seen in the increased number of female-headed households. In a traditional, patriarchal society, this has imposed both a social and a psychological burden on them, particularly as most of them do not have the kind of social or economic skills that are needed to cope with this reality. Despite this, large numbers of women have stepped out of the privacy of their homes to negotiate a life of dignity for themselves and their families. As survivors, they have borne the brunt of the trauma of the sudden death and disappearance of their men, and they suffer from many stress related ailments. Doctors believe that this is one of the major causes of depression among women. Dr Zaid Wani, psychiatrist and specialist in PTSD related illnesses at SKIM hospital, found that 62 per cent of women suffered from PTSD compared to 38 per cent of men. However, women's health remains one of the most neglected aspects of state policy. The psychiatric disease hospital is witness to the health costs of the conflict and the brunt that has been borne by women. Of the 60,000 patients registered in the year 2005–2006, 60 per cent of them were women from all walks of life – urban, rural, married, unmarried, rich and poor. But doctors at the hospital believed that this was only the tip of the iceberg. According to them, the women who managed to come to the hospital had done so despite the social stigma, the shame and exclusion that they would have been subjected to. They believed that there were many others who did not have the strength to do this and therefore remained within their homes, living with their ailments, unable, and sometimes unwilling, to speak about them.

Unable to recognise or articulate the symptoms, women complained of somatic problems such as headaches, palpitations, and loss of appetite, gastrointestinal problems and insomnia. Instead of seeking timely treatment for clinical depression or PTSD, they

would go from cardiologist to neurologist to haematologist and
to faith healers, leading to avoidable complications and prolonged
treatment. Besides all these disorders that can be diagnosed and
measured, some women also complained about symptoms that are
not so easily defined such as the Midnight Knock Syndrome, where
they apprehend that someone will knock at their door, and that
knock will presage violence, perhaps even death. It is a common
experience of Kashmiris to be suddenly woken up in the night either
by the security forces or the militants knocking at their doors to
search the premises or seek shelter. Another such condition was the
Empty Nest Syndrome where women experienced intense isolation
and loneliness after sending away their children to safer destinations.
Doctors found it difficult to treat such patients, as 'these symptoms
did not fit into any specific psychiatric entity.' In such cases doctors
could only provide non-clinical/medical techniques to cope with or
overcome what they described as 'indigenous disorders.'

Children: The Inheritors of Trauma

In an environment where the threat of violence followed everyone like
a shadow, doctors found that children were particularly susceptible
and vulnerable and would begin to display behavioural disorders,
ranging from a state of fearfulness, crying, irritability, instability and
refusal to be left alone. Despite the alarming symptoms, 'there is
no psychiatric care available for children even though psychiatric
disorders are as common in children as in adults. There are additional
problems among children of mental retardation, autism, conduct
disorders, pervasive developmental disorders, as well as the traumatic
stress that causes all these.' There is reported to be an increase in
the number of cases of attempted suicide among children, including
young girls. I met a girl of 12 years who survived a suicide attempt

and was brought to the hospital. Doctors found her mental health was so fragile that treating her with medicines would have taken a minimum of two weeks to show any results and to avoid this delay, she had to be given electric shocks. This treatment requires a patient to undergo general anaesthesia but since the hospital did not have this facility at the time, the treatment was going to be far more painful. I was struck by the lack of options and how the doctors felt compelled to provide this life-threatening treatment to the young girl, particularly as there was no paediatric psychiatrist in the hospital.

In the case of the district block medical officer's daughter (in Budgam) he told me that, 'she was four years old when violence first began in the Valley. She used to vomit at the sound of firing and continued to do so even after she turned ten. She could not be left alone even for a moment. All of us in the family, particularly her mother, were traumatized because of her mental and physical state. The doctors told us that if she was not cured now, this affliction would remain with her all her life, leading to further complications, even premature death.' He informed me that this was not a rare case and that there were many such families living in deep anguish and trauma. Tragically, children are conspicuous by their absence among the patients who throng the hospital. The reason, as explained by an intern on duty, was that the children would be further traumatized given the situation at the hospital: 'It is not at all conducive for them, especially as we do not have a paediatric department here. Parents of young children are also anxious to protect them from the social stigma. Many of them go to neurologists and cardiologists in their clinic, even though the problem is psychiatric in nature.' The question that has found no convincing answer is: where do the rest of the traumatized children go to seek help and recovery? Expressing grave concern for the children, the intern said that the epidemiologists predict an epidemic of psychiatric disorders in the paediatric age group if timely care and action were not taken.

A study conducted on 100 children diagnosed with mental health-related disorders pointed out the impact of armed conflict on the mental well being of children.[20] As a chemist in a busy shop in Srinagar explained to me:

> Children born in 1985 are now young adults. The worst effects of violence, fear and tension can be seen among these youngsters who have spent their most impressionable years living and coping with repeated traumatic experiences. This has also cast a long shadow on the normal activities of growing children – education and play. Not for them the carefree games in the neighbourhood parks or lanes. Having grown up in this hostile and violent environment they have not seen or experienced normalcy here. This abnormal situation is what they perceive as normal until they go out of Kashmir and see the difference. *Sirf bandish ka mahaul dekha hai, azadi ka nahin* – they have only seen a life of restrictions, not freedom. Most children of this age had not seen life outside the valley. Parents had to constantly find ways of dealing with their children to keep them from militancy as well as to protect them from the security forces.

This had also led to disruption in their education, particularly in the first few years of militancy. Subsequently, many have had to terminate their education to be able to supplement the family income, as there were thousands of families where the only male earning member had either been killed or was missing.

Orphans in Search of Shelter

Children constitute nearly 38 per cent of the state's population and although there is a disparity in figures, it is well known that today there are as many as 25,000–50,000 orphans. The state has not been able to intervene effectively as there were only six government orphanages at the time of my visits, housing less than a hundred children in each due to 'limited capacity and resource crunch.' According to recent reports, the number of orphanages had now increased to 17 – six for girls and eleven for boys.

While hundreds of orphans are reported to have taken shelter in the homes of relatives, the majority of them remained uncared for. The more fortunate among them have found shelter in private orphanages run by local NGOs. There are reports of children suffering from malnutrition and mental degradation with no recourse to social, legal and emotional protection. Continued disruption of their normal lives has meant that children are exposed to unforeseen risks and hardships. According to Dr. Basheer Ahmed, Kashmir University, 'the culture of violence has distorted the values and outlook of children and youth. A large number of them today believe that they can get anything they want with the power of the gun. This has corrupted family relationships and altered their dynamics. Children no longer respect their parents, as we have known them to do. They have become distinctively aggressive in their attitude to family members. While this is one reality, its inverse is that affected families also depend on their young children for a livelihood, as there is no other option for them. In both rural and urban areas, children are therefore kept out of school so that they can work and contribute to the family income.' I was told: '73 per cent of the orphans gave increasing poverty after the death of their fathers as the reason for them dropping out of school. Facing acute financial constraints at an early age had devastating effects on their young minds as an increasing number of them went out to earn a living or support their families. A majority of orphans worked in the handicraft sector, some took up petty jobs in different shops, automobile workshops, in homes as domestic workers and in tea stalls. They were often not paid a full wage and payment was not done on a regular basis.'[21] In this demanding situation, made worse by government apathy, children have had to pay a price with their physical as well as emotional health. Along with other basic health services, immunization of children had also collapsed during the last decade and this has resulted in avoidable diseases and ailments. Doctors have also reported an increase in neurological and heart ailments among children.

One government run orphanage for girls that I visited in Srinagar, housed 25 orphans in the age range of 5-18 years. According to the woman warden, the government provided Rs 15 per day per child for their dietary expenses, which included tea and two meals a day. According to a government notification, the orphans are entitled to Rs 750 a month, per child up to the age of 18 years, with an additional Rs 150 per month for children undergoing vocational and technical training.[22] The warden said that the 'inmates' were given two pairs of clothes each, for winter and for summer. There were no provisions for medical aid (except for a first aid box), transport or communication (no telephone). There were stray visits by government doctors to the orphanage. Only 'verified' relatives were allowed to meet the girls once in two weeks. There was no cook in the kitchen, as older girls were required to cook and clean the utensils for which they took turns every twenty-four hours. 'This is to train them for their married life,' said the warden to me, proudly. Absence of medical, transport and communication facilities meant extra hardships for children as well as the staff. A six-year-old girl who was brought here by her grandfather had to be discharged within three days, as she would not stop crying. She was brought in a state of shock as the security forces had shot down her father in her presence. When the warden took her to a private doctor he refused to attend to her even though she was in a hysterical state: 'If the orphanage had a resident doctor and a counsellor, the girl could have stayed here and been treated. Her grandfather was the only surviving member of her family.'

A study on the mental health status of 76 inmates in the age group of 5–12 years in a girls' orphanage in Srinagar found that 42.10 per cent had suffered from different mental health disorders, PTSD being present in 13 and major depressive disorders in 8 of the children. All the girls had lost their fathers at a young age and belonged to lower socio-economic classes, risk factors associated with mental health disorders.[23]

I also visited an orphanage for boys that housed 55 orphans in the age group of 8–16 years. A majority of the boys were from villages around Srinagar. According to the warden, a middle-aged woman, 'fifteen years ago we had to search for orphans but today the demand exceeds our capacity here. All the children are from violence-affected families. Due to limited capacity and as a rule, these children have to leave the orphanage after their matriculation is over. An exception is made in the case of destitute children who have no relatives. However, their relatives take most of them away as their qualifications make them a potential asset for them. As long as they have stayed here, I've looked after them as though I was their mother and father.'

According to her, the provision of Rs 15 per head, per day was instituted in 1982 and had not been revised since (2002), despite a tremendous increase in prices. Even this meagre amount often did not reach the beneficiaries as corruption had made inroads even in the orphanages. 'It is not possible to give young children even a glass of milk or an egg as the money is not enough to cover the expenses. We are required to give them a balanced diet of 100-grams of meat, 150 grams of vegetables and 210 grams of rice twice a day. However, meat is given only once or twice a week', said the warden. In this orphanage also there were no medical, transport or communication facilities, with the government doctor making a visit twice a month and a rusting first-aid box for emergencies. In both these orphanages, children went to the local government school. They were taken on a recreation trip to 'one of the many gardens once a month.' A majority of them spent their vacations in the orphanage as relatives seldom came to take them home.

The conditions in the oldest private orphanage in Srinagar were appalling. Established in 1973, it had a capacity to house 10–15 children whereas at the time of my visit it had forty children in the age range of 6–18 years, living in its three cramped rooms. According to the young, male warden, 'Before militancy began, this orphanage housed only children from poor and destitute families. But now most of them are from violence-affected families. If we were not so short on space and resources, we could have taken in many more.' All the children were from surrounding villages as 'they are able to adjust better here than children from the city who are accustomed to better conditions. We have bare minimum facilities of food, shelter, books and a pair of uniforms for the children.'

Two to three children shared a single mattress on the floor. 'If one fell ill the others also would fall ill. Any infection in a child leads to all of them suffering from similar symptoms. We are not able to ensure even basic hygiene as there is only one bathroom for all of them to use.' Since there were no wardrobes or trunks, children used a string on the wall of the rooms to hang their clothes, with the result that the walls were always covered with clothes collecting dust. Mattresses that were used at night were folded in the morning to create enough space for the children to sit down to study. Books and bundles of clothes were piled up on the floor and children had to keep an eye on them to ensure that they did not get mixed up. The front courtyard was used as a playground as there was no other space available for games or sports. The kitchen walls were covered in soot and the utensils were washed in the back of the courtyard. The children dreaded the rains as they would have to stay indoors, and the only available space outside would be full of slush for many days. According to the person in charge of the orphanage, the social welfare department, through a grant-in-aid of Rs 100.000, financially supported the orphanage whereas the actual annual expenditure was 275,000. 'The problem is that the money is not released regularly. This year we received only rupees 38,000 as grant-in-aid because we are told that the government coffers are empty. We receive maximum donation through *zakath* during the month of Ramazan.' One of the founding members added that before 1989 they did not need any NGO for this work as the community took care of children in need of help but today they had to depend on other sources to be able to meet the demand at least partially. The situation was such that even children in the orphanage were not safe: 'The BSF raided our orphanage five times in the last ten years. Boys of 18 were beaten on suspicion that they were militants. This added to the children's insecurity and fear. We need to have a counsellor as children suffer from depression, low self-esteem and lack of confidence. We have doctors from HRC who visit once a week or whenever we need their help but the government is least concerned with the plight of these children.' Two of the orphan children who had completed their education were now working as teachers in the orphanage on a minimal salary. One of them said, 'I do not have a family other than this. I am able to understand children and their fears when they first come here as I myself have grown up in this orphanage. Forty per cent of the children here are full orphans (both parents having died) and sixty per cent of them are half-orphans, that is, children whose fathers are either missing or disappeared.'

While the government does have schemes for the welfare of orphans and widows, their implementation suffers from various loopholes, mainly due to incompetence. Below, I detail some of these schemes.

The Hand of the State: Government Schemes for Relief and Rehabilitation

The Rehabilitation Council was set up in 1996 under the State Social Welfare Department (SWD) 'to rehabilitate victims of militancy under the militancy victims' scheme (MVS).' To avail of this, victims had to bring a copy of the First Information Report (FIR) registered at the local police station and signed by a gazetted officer, to the tehsil office of the SWD in Srinagar. The next step was for the victim to fill in a form provided by this office. Based on this information, a verification officer would visit the home of the victim and file his report at the tehsil office of the SWD. The report would then be sent to the district office for clearance of sanction after which, it had to be signed by the Chief Medical Officer, the Assistant Divisional Commissioner and finally the Divisional Commissioner. This procedure could take from two months to a year and whether the victim was able to avail of the benefit 'depended on the resilience of the victim', said one of the officers.

The verification officer told me how 'these cumbersome rules deterred many women from claiming these benefits. They feel nervous to visit a police station, as there have been cases of sexual harassment there. As a majority of the women are illiterate, the police take undue advantage of them. They are asked not only to prove their dead son or husband's innocence but also to narrate clearly the sequence of events that led to their loved one's death. Already traumatized, women often break down under such pressure and this kind of routine harassment. Women are often asked to meet the Station Head Officer (SHO) to register their FIR and there have been cases when the busy SHO had asked women to visit his home to get the work done.' This description reminded me of what a widow had earlier told me at the tehsil office when she had gone there with her young daughter – that the SHO had asked her to come to his house in the evening as he was too busy to attend to her then. 'We would rather starve than go to his house', she had said. The verification officer continued, 'It is traumatic for these women who are accustomed to staying within the confines of their homes to be suddenly confronted with this kind of terror. It is worse for those who are left with no male relative at home and have therefore to be accompanied by young daughters, daughters-in-law or any other female member of the family. In such a situation the threat of sexual abuse and harassment is that much greater.'

What are the benefits of the scheme? Widows of forty years and above were entitled to receive Rs 500 per month, later increased to Rs. 750 per month. Those below forty were covered under the remarriage scheme for which a one-time grant of Rs 10,000 was made to them. Women were required to first submit an affidavit to prove their marital status. This payment was made through a cheque and therefore women seeking this benefit had to first open a bank account in their names.

The militancy victim scheme did not cover those who were victims of the excesses committed by the Security Forces or families of the missing persons. 'Those women whose husbands are killed by the Security Forces and those whose husbands are missing and not established as dead are not entitled to the same benefits as there is no FIR to prove their death. They are not even entitled to the Integrated Social Security Scheme (ISSS).' Under this scheme, widows living below the poverty line (with a family income or Rs 500 or less) are entitled to Rs 150 per month. However, widows with an earning member in the family or a son twenty years and above were not entitled to this, no matter that the son may not have had any employment at the time. Many of the women had no option but to take up whatever employment was available. The assistance provided under the scheme lapsed after completion of five years, as the validity period was over and the entire procedure had to be gone through again, including re-verification of the person's credentials.

At the tehsil office of the SWB and in families that I visited, widows complained that they did not receive the money on a regular basis. In fact, some of them had not received any money for over six months as their files revealed. 'This meagre amount of five hundred rupees can also be of great help to us considering the level of poverty we live in. But in the hope of receiving this money we end up spending more than half of it on transport expenses as we have to visit the office several times in a month.' Officials at the tehsil office attributed the problem to the government's financial crunch but according to the verification officer, 'corruption was the main reason. Even widows and orphans were not spared. Funds meant for their welfare hardly ever reached them. This was an endemic problem at all levels in the government.'

Women had to make several visits to even claim this pittance, added the verification officer. As one of the women told me in a tired voice, 'I have already spent half of this amount on transport. I also wasted my time and energy. I feel tired and humiliated.' According to the former Director of SWD, 'if rules are relaxed, there will be no end to claimants. Everyone will come as a widow to claim the money. The government has to see to its own resources.'

Many of the women for whom these schemes were floated were not aware of them and therefore were not able to benefit from them. While I was sitting in the tehsil office of the Social Welfare Department, a student of Class X came with her widowed mother with a copy of an FIR and the application form to claim the compensation. Her father was killed in 1990. He was called out of the house one morning and shot dead. She was then five years old. She said she did not know about the scheme until recently when someone in her locality told them about it. Her mother looked pale and exhausted. She was barely able to speak. We sat outside the crowded room and tried to talk. She was married at an early age and had two daughters. She said she did not know how old she was – maybe 30, she said. When her husband was killed, she was suddenly left with her two young daughters and no one to support them. She had never worked for an income earlier. She took her two daughters and went to live with her parents. But when her father died a few years later, she had to move back to her one-room house with her children, as it was difficult for her mother to support them on her own. To earn a nominal amount of Rs 500 per month, she now had to spend hours at home on the charka (spinning wheel). She said her only hope was that her daughters, once educated, would be able to find some employment and take care of their own lives. 'My life changed suddenly one morning. I have grown very old since then. I also feel worried for my young daughter. As I have no male relative she has to accompany me to the police station and different offices. I can only pray for her safety.'

In this climate of fear and anxiety, people did not have access to information that was supposedly meant for their benefit. There was no transparency in the governance or implementation of schemes, which led to wastage of precious resources and reinforced women's insecurity and vulnerability. Even the 'field staff' of the Women and Child Welfare Department (WCWD) of the SWB, such as the Auxiliary Nurse Midwives (ANMs) who worked at the community level, were often ignorant of the various government schemes. This was clear in a training programme for ANMs organized by the WCWD that I attended. There were more than fifty participants who had attended the three-day training programme in preparation for their 'field work.' During my interaction with them I shared the information I had regarding the different schemes run by their department. When I asked how many among them had any knowledge of this, not a single hand went up. The group leader mentioned that it was the first time they had even heard about these schemes. Without adequate publicity or regularity in payment, the government's apathy was more apparent than its professed concern for the 'poor widows.'

❊ ❊ ❊

The above account reflects the government's apathetic and inadequate response to the catastrophic health situation in Kashmir. Unless it intervenes with urgent measures and initiatives, the situation can deteriorate further and cause avoidable hardship to people. It was clear to me during fieldwork that the government had shifted the burden of its responsibility to local and outside non-governmental organisations (NGOs) to cater to the basic health needs of people. Until a few years ago, there was hardly any outside non-government organisation or agency working in Kashmir but today there are hundreds of them filling in the vacuum created by a negligent and incompetent administration. Moreover, the privatisation and outsourcing of social services has further marginalised the government's role. It is a fact that NGOs, with their package of social service goods and opportunities for a people in need cannot and must not replace a government whose obligation it is to deliver. However, the more the NGOs have advanced, offering basic health, education and income-generating programmes, the more the government has retreated, brushing aside questions of its own responsibility and accountability. Despite a state rehabilitation policy for women – the militancy victim scheme – and a designated budget to implement it, the administration has largely failed the women of Kashmir. This was clearly reflected in the findings of a survey we conducted in three districts of Srinagar, Kupwara and Baramulla where the supposed women beneficiaries stated that many of them had not even heard of any government scheme, let alone availed of it. In many villages, no official had ever made a visit to ascertain or assess people's needs or the implementation of any of the stated schemes. The situation was such that, as mentioned earlier, in one of the villages in Baramulla, the village community offered us (Aman and the local team) a plot of land to build a primary health centre as none existed over a distance of more than twenty villages. With the help of Aman, we were able to do this. Soon after its inauguration in September 2003 in village Mattipora in Baramulla district, the hospital became one of the most successful community-based health initiatives in the area where, in one year, more than 12,000 patients, including women and children, had availed of the basic health services that were being provided daily by a team we had built of local health professionals who volunteered their time. Similarly, in the absence of any specialised psychiatric care for children, we managed to set up, in collaboration with a local NGO (Help Foundation), and a team of psychiatrists from the government medical college – who also offered their time and expertise on a voluntary basis – a Child Guidance Clinic that catered to the mental health needs of this vulnerable group.

Mobilising and receiving local community support for such constructive programmes was possible mainly because government health facilities were so inadequate and the state administration had failed its people. More importantly, in the midst of widespread death and destruction, building local teams of professionals and volunteers with the village community's participation, and addressing their problems proved to be a cathartic, healing process, even for those of us who were involved in it.

NOTES

1. *Greater Kashmir*. March 2, 2018. Srinagar.
2. Ibid.

3. By 22nd July, within two weeks of protests, SMHS hospital had conducted 137 eye surgeries and by end-August, 570 injured were treated and 425 eye surgeries performed

4. Mir, Hilal. 'Kashmir's Everlasting Insurgency.' January 30, 2018. *TRT World*.

5. Ibid.

6. *The Wire*. April 7, 2018

7. Jameel, Yusuf. April 8, 2018. *Asian Age*.

8. Ibid.

9. The survey comprised 5600 households from 400 villages across the ten districts of Kashmir.

10. Over 11 per cent of adults reported taking benzodiazepines (anti-depressant/sedative) – 90 per cent through doctor's prescription. It further revealed that 45 per cent adults in Kashmir Valley had significant symptoms of mental distress. Approximately 41 per cent adults were reported to be living with significant symptoms of depression with 10 per cent of them meeting all the diagnostic criteria for severe depression.

11. Hussain, Arshad. 2014. *ABC News*. Srinagar.

12. Institute of Mental Health and Neuroscience, Srinagar (IMHANS 2016).

13. Greater Kashmir, March 2006

14. Hussain, Arshad. Srinagar, 2018. There were at least 100 patients visiting the district hospitals per day, per district – among which 60 are women and 40 men, mostly young.

15. IMHANS 2016.

16. The number of psychiatrists had now increased to 50 compared to two in the decade of 2000.

17. Marghoob, Mushtaq. 2004. Srinagar. 'By 1993 there were 10-15 cases of PTSD per day. The number of patients who presently visited the hospital with symptoms of PTSD ranged between 100-300 daily. Interestingly, their number varied, he said, according to the changing seasons, peaking in June, July and October when 250-400 patients visited the OPD in a single day.'

18. According to a survey by the Ministry of Labour and Employment 2012-13, Kashmir had the highest youth unemployment rate across India. At the state level, the number of registered job seekers increased by 190 per cent between 2008-13.

19. Hussain, Arshad. 2018. Srinagar

20. Khan & Marghoob 2006. Forty nine per cent of these children had experienced traumatic events such as killing of a close relative, 15 per cent witnessed arrest and torture of a close relative, 11 per cent had witnessed night raids, 14 per cent were caught in cross-firing and 4 per cent were beaten up/tortured.

21. Dabla, Ahmed Bashir. 1999. 'Impact of Conflict Situation on Women and Children in Kashmir.' Department of Sociology, Kashmir University. Srinagar.

22. Department of Jammu & Kashmir Affairs, Ministry of Home Affairs, Government of India. 5 June 2008.

23. Marghoob et al, 2006

chapter five

The Tyranny of Silence

SEXUAL VIOLENCE AND IMPUNITY IN KASHMIR

In 2013 I returned to Kashmir to do some research for another project I had become involved in: a five-country study[1] on the structures of impunity that made for a complete lack of accountability for sexual violence. My task was to try and unravel the complex layers and forms of sexual violence that were visited upon women and men as a deliberate strategy of counter-insurgency in the state and also to trace the different kinds of silences that have surrounded the issue. When I began fieldwork, I was apprehensive that people may not be willing to share their experiences as victims/survivors of sexual violence – as had been my experience in 1999-2000 with the Kunan Poshpora[2] tragedy still fresh in people's minds – but I soon realized that something had changed. Whether it was individual men or women, victims or survivors, or a group of civil society members, people, and more specifically, women seemed now to be willing to speak and share their experiences. Two and a half decades had passed since militancy, and since then people had lived with fear, brutal military repression and violence. The time had come to speak, demand accountability, redress and justice.

While reaching out to women victims and survivors in their homes, I also met a cross section of people, such as former militants (in villages of Baramulla, Kupwara [Lolab], Budgam and in Srinagar), male survivors of custodial torture and sexual abuse, senior journalists, lawyers, gynecologists, and psychiatrists. To understand the perspective and the dynamics of the local women's organisations in dealing with those who approached them with complaints of sexual violence, particularly at the hands of the militants, I met women leaders of Dukhtaran-e-Millat and Muslim Khawateen Markaz.

Silence and the Search for Justice

The deliberate/strategic use of sexual violence by the armed forces makes it a powerful subtext in the conflict, a subtext that is often suppressed or silenced (for different reasons) by the authorities, the family and the community, or by the victim herself. The social construction of gender whereby women (and their bodies) are seen mainly as repositories of family and community honour makes it difficult for women to break the silence that surrounds the crime, and this results in creating a culture of impunity. While families may remain silent in a bid to protect their women, the state's consistent refusal to recognise or acknowledge the crime results in denial of justice to the victims and impunity for the perpetrators. Yet, while silence promotes impunity, silence and the pursuit of justice cannot go hand in hand and it is this factor, along with other structural factors, that determines the moment of 'disclosure' for the victim, family and community or their desire to break the silence. The victim/survivor's pain and trauma are too overwhelming to sustain silence. At the same time, for many of them, their disclosure is often met by hostile and negative reactions from the authorities and society as they are further victimized or are assailed by self-doubt and the fear of reprisals.

Silence and denial were the two expressions, two sides of a coin that I was confronted with whenever the subject of sexual violence against women was raised, individually or collectively. I remember being in a conference in Srinagar, some time in mid-2000. It was organized by local women activists and young professionals to debate the social consequences of militarization, particularly as it impacted women's lives and gender relations. When a participant from Manipur raised the question of sexual violence against women, the room fell silent until one of the Kashmiri women said, 'This does not happen in our society.' Although many instances of women having been subjected to the worst forms of sexual violence – including the mass rape of women by the soldiers of Rajputana Rifles in the twin villages of Kunan and Poshpora (Kupwara) in 1991 – were public knowledge, women were reluctant to talk about it, the refrain being: 'It is a matter of shame for us to discuss this.' We, the women from 'outside', were reminded of the cultural sensitivity that prevented many of the local women from either raising or discussing this critical issue with 'outsiders.' Silence was deeply valued over speech in this regard; as a way of protecting the women or keeping community relations intact at a moment when the social fabric of society was being torn apart.

Then, Shopian[3] happened – where two young women relatives were raped and murdered allegedly by soldiers of the paramilitary – nearly twenty years after the mass rape of women in Kunan Poshpora. This gruesome incident became a turning point (as investigations in the case were deliberately botched by the authorities as well as the perpetrators, and justice was denied to the victims' family) in the lives of ordinary people – women, men, the young and old – as they

took to the streets of not only Shopian but all of Kashmir, demanding
justice and accountability from the state and the armed forces. As
popular agitations and protests gained momentum throughout
the state during summer, the town was laid under siege as the
government imposed a curfew that lasted more than forty days,
causing severe hardships to the already aggrieved people but also
bringing them together in solidarity; people continued to protest
even in the most adverse circumstances. People's solidarity during
the prolonged curfew cut across class, gender, and occupation as
local men and women from other towns collected food and other
essential commodities for the besieged population of Shopian, both
to assist them as well as to sustain the agitation. The struggle for
justice for the two women victims and their family stretched across
the state, unifying people and giving them a voice; this was no
longer a time for silence or for shame, although silence, in certain
situations, is also used as a strategy of protest. This was a time to
break the silence, to use speech as a strategy of resistance, to be vocal
and challenge the state's institutionalized impunity and its lack of
political will to provide justice to victims of violence/sexual violence
and punishment to the perpetrators.

As the head of the gynecology department at Lalded Hospital,
Dr Shehnaz Teng told me in an interview in 2013, 'Shopian has
brutalized our entire society and our collective psyche. It has brought
the question of sexual violence against women to the fore once again,
after Kunan Poshpora.' Although the long summer of discontent
and protests did not result in delivering justice to the victims, 'it
demonstrated the complex interplay between legal authority, social
protest and political power under conditions of occupation in
contested Kashmir. On the one hand, it reveals how state power
functions in the region, not only through the heavy militarization
that routinely exposes residents to violence, but also through the
legal system that promises, but systematically denies, possibilities of

accountability and redress. It makes visible ways in which groups struggle to engage with the formal legal system and work to establish alternative forums for the pursuit of justice in their efforts to challenge state violence and institutionalized denial.'[4]

The case of Kunan Poshpora also demonstrates this, where after a lapse of twenty-two years, silence was broken again when the case was reopened for fresh investigations. Those instrumental in breaking this silence, in filing the petition and bringing the case back on the 'national agenda', were young, third-generation local women professionals[5] who have joined the continuing struggle of the victims and survivors for justice. Here was a renewal and reinvention of a collective voice and struggle. Revisiting the twin villages, building bridges of trust and hope with victims and survivors and bringing their voices back to the courtroom and the streets, these young women opened new ways of challenging the culture of impunity and taking the struggle to its logical end. What motivated these women, most of whom were not even born when the incident took place? It is interesting that the mass agitations that erupted all over the country following the gang rape and death of a young woman on a moving bus in Delhi on 16 December 2012 became a catalyst for the young women in Kashmir. As one of them explained to me, the mass rape of women in Kunan Poshpora had not evoked a similar response in the country as the Delhi rape case had done and it became 'clear to us that we had to break the silence and raise our voice here and shape our own struggle.'

The passage of time – between Kunan Poshpora and Shopian – has witnessed many more instances of sexual violence, abuse, rape and torture, as the state and army repression continued, resulting in large-scale violence, death and material destruction. Less than a year after Shopian (2009), another violent incident occurred that became as much a catalyst for the intense agitations that erupted in the summer of 2010: the Machil fake encounter, in which the personnel of the army and J&K police killed three young civilians, claiming that they were militants. It was later established, beyond doubt, that these men were, in fact, local youth who had been lured by the security forces (SF) on the pretext of providing them employment but who were then killed in cold blood. The intense protests that followed saw the wrath of the security forces come down heavily on the protestors.

At the same time, these two brutal incidents provided a fresh impetus to the movement for azadi and intensified the 'resistance' that began to reinvent itself and took new and different forms – from violent to non-violent means of protest, from bullets to stones. The prolonged agitation where men, and particularly young men, pelted stones on the highly armed security forces resulted in 112 of them being killed by the latter and many others thrown into jail under the Public Safety Act. The large numbers of outraged civilians on the streets included women and there were instances where they were seen and heard exhorting their men – sons, brothers and husbands – to join the protests and demand justice. As the agitation began to claim lives and the death toll mounted, women stormed the streets to protest and to publicly mourn the dead.

Breaking the silence around violence, including sexual violence, recognizing such violence as an act and strategy of war, and shifting the burden of guilt and shame from women survivors on to the perpetrators was perhaps one of the significant aspects of this resistance and protest. The need for accountability and justice, that had been systematically denied all these years, had now become an urgent quest for people, including for victims and survivors, their families and the community. Interestingly, the structural and socio-political circumstances and factors that led women and others to remain silent have not changed in any significant manner, but most importantly, the barrier to seeking justice – silence – had been broken. What then are the challenges, the implications for those who are now fearlessly raising their voices, asking questions, protesting loudly on the streets, demanding justice with renewed fervour? Could there be increased surveillance, more military repression, reprisals, violence and prolonged curfews? And the realization perhaps that justice and reparation might still be denied by the state and its institutions, including the biased/unsympathetic criminal justice system that further engenders impunity.

Here, it is important to acknowledge another kind of silence that has continued to persist in the country regarding sexual violence and rape of women in Jammu and Kashmir by the armed forces. As the young women mentioned, the issue has not found much resonance in the rest of India where a sustained struggle over the years by women led to significant amendments to the rape law a couple of decades earlier, as well as a set of stringent laws that were adopted by Parliament (post 16 December 2012) to prevent crimes against women more recently.[6] A young local woman's poignant question whether it was legitimate for Indian soldiers to rape Kashmiri women, assumes significance in this context. The failure of the democratic opinion in the country to raise the issue of sexual violence and impunity in J&K has only exacerbated the situation.

Strangely, where the armed forces are concerned, ideas of patriotism and national security are invoked to justify mass violence and the crimes of sexual violence in the name of protecting the sovereignty, integrity and unity of the country against an 'enemy' nation, and against a rebellious people of a state who deserve to be taught a lesson. Women's honour is pitched against national honour, and the unequal gender relations are reinforced and perpetuated militarily. It is this social sanction and our acquiescence in what gets carried out during military suppression of people that further generates impunity and allows it to intrude upon every aspect of people's social life, private or public. The threat of sexual violence that results in palpable fear amongst people as they negotiate their daily existence, fully aware that they could be assaulted or picked up and tortured any time is also indicative of how social impunity operates in the everyday lives of people. The experience or the sense of shame and emasculation that haunts men who have been sexually tortured and those who live with the fear of meeting the same fate becomes routinized in such a situation. It is well known that during armed conflict, men are as much prone to sexual abuse and violence by the military, and it is as difficult for the male victims/survivors to break the secrecy and silence that surrounds the crime. 'Sexual violence against men during war/conflict remains largely invisible. Like violence against women, sexual violence against men is nearly unspeakable in its brutality.'[7]

Militarization is not only about numbers, but how it impacts individuals and groups, men and women in their everyday lives, and how it begets violence as well as people's resistance to it. A former militant I met told me how he had been subjected to the worst kind of violence but used it as a means of resistance: 'Violence in general and sexual violence in particular is bound to happen when there is such a big deployment of armed forces; it will happen even if these soldiers were locked up in a room or barrack – there will always be violence perpetrated by them and public resistance against such violence.'

In this scenario, the distinction between a street and a home is breached irreparably as both become a site and arena of violence. Women are targeted both within and outside their homes as mothers, wives, sisters and daughters to avenge the actions of their men, be they militants or mere suspects. Ironically, in the battle between the armed forces and militants, the latter too have not refrained from resorting to the same tactic of targeting women for being related to men who are suspected to be informers or traitors to the cause. As Khurram Parvez of JKCCS pointed out to me in a conversation, the heightened surveillance regime that operates in the state also accounts for the increased vulnerability of women where even a telephone conversation with a male relative or friend who is suspect may invite the wrath of the SF and result in blackmail or other forms of harassment, including the threat of sexual violence.

Impunity in Daily Life

While there is much in public knowledge regarding institutional impunity in terms of the role of the state, the security forces, the police and the judiciary, there is a need to understand the structural aspects of impunity as it impinges on gender relations, the family and the community. At the same time, it is also important to understand how impunity challenges the cultural sensitivities of people by itself creating or generating a culture of silence as well as people's defiance and resistance to it.

How do we understand the meaning of impunity as it operates in daily life? An important aspect of this research was to document the role and experience of women during militancy and to pay attention to the voices of women who belonged to militants' families, as wives, mothers, daughters or sisters – women whose men had crossed over for arms training. It was also important to talk to men – both militants and civilians – to gain some understanding regarding their own experience of being victims/survivors of sexual abuse and violence during custodial interrogation. How did they and the women cope with this situation and the sexual violence that many of the women suffered as a result? How did they protect themselves from such violence? How did they manage and sustain their family's survival, including their children's education and caring for aged parents? In many a home where a child was born after the father crossed over, how did women keep alive the absent father's existence and memory for their child as he/she grew up? And how did life turn out for these women and their families after the return of the 'Mujahid', were they and their homes any safer now? What mechanisms did these women use to seek justice for themselves and punishment for the perpetrators?

While the SFs remain the main perpetrators of violence and enjoy impunity, it is also important to look at the role of militants not only as victims but also as perpetrators – to highlight how impunity operates at this level through social sanction, validation, silence and sympathy. During an informal conversation with a senior army officer in 2012 in a border district of Jammu where I was doing research[8] he said, 'When a woman victim approaches me in search of her male relative, I can go on philosophizing to her about life but the moment she asks me about the whereabouts of her husband or son, I am silent because I really have no answer.' When asked about the Armed Forces (Special Powers) Act, impunity and its implications, he simply brushed our questions aside saying:

> There is so much hype about AFSPA and its protective clause for the army. As far as we are concerned, this afspa-waspa means nothing to us, it is not at all in our psyche when we step out on duty. I may be killed for all I care but I must have the power and authority to enter or raid any house or location any time of the day or night, if my duty is to eliminate militancy. I must be able to show that I am the strong arm of the government, of my country. I must get the militant, even if I have to kill him. It is too bad if he chooses to hide inside a home amongst innocent family members, including women.

Such arrogance of power demonstrates the height of impunity and the limits of the justice system. It also shows the unequal relations that operate between unarmed civilians and the empowered military, resulting in fear of reprisals and a heightened sense of insecurity among civilians.

A press release by the Jammu Kashmir Coalition of Civil Society (JKCCS)[9] on the occasion of the twenty-third anniversary of Kunan Poshpora stated that:

> Rapes and sexual assaults, which are internationally recognized as a war crime, and a form of torture, have been extensively and routinely used as a weapon of war in Jammu and Kashmir. All the organs and agencies of the state have deliberately impeded processes of justice and truth for victims, and have colluded to ensure impunity to armed forces. They have specifically fostered and endorsed impunity for sexual crimes, within the wider culture of impunity that prevails in Jammu and Kashmir. The Kunan Poshpora case is emblematic of both this pervasive culture of impunity, and of the long-standing resistance against such atrocities.

Outside Kunan Poshpora too, women bore the brunt of the impunity of the armed forces in their everyday lives, but their experience of sexual violence and their resistance to it and the aftermath of such violence needs to be acknowledged.

Coercive laws, particularly the AFSPA, with its inherent clause of impunity, exempt the armed forces from punishment for crimes and empower them to carry out any counter-insurgency operations, including shoot to kill, on mere suspicion. It is this institutionalized impunity and lack of accountability that is responsible for the perpetration of mass violence, including sexual violence, in the state and for derailing or impeding the process of justice even where credible evidence is available. When homes are raided during the day or the night, when men are forced out of their homes for search-and-cordon operations or taken away for interrogation, women become an easy target for sexual abuse, including molestation and rape. The human cost of conflict goes beyond numbers as violence touches and alters lives in fundamental ways for women, men and children.

The violence and its aftermath are a transformative experience for women as they set out to search for their men and means of livelihood, or cope with the loss of their loved ones.

The Meanings of Sexual Violence

'A woman is worth dying for. When she is assaulted, not only her family but also our nation is assaulted', proclaimed a woman doctor.

Are there any linkages between sexual violence and the notions surrounding male and female sexuality, the construction of gendered roles and expectations arising out of it, as well as issues of power, domination and patriarchy? Does sexuality have any social, cultural significance that would lead to a better understanding of sexual violence? Men, who may otherwise feel or be seen as strong are made to feel vulnerable due to the constant threat of detention, disappearance or custodial torture and women are specifically targeted sexually by the armed forces to punish their men. Men in the family and community hold the women in high esteem and try hard to protect their 'honour' that is routinely threatened, violated.

Until recently, there was not much documented information available, both at the official or unofficial levels, regarding the number of women victims/survivors of rape or other forms of sexual violence. While a few local civil society organisations have begun to undertake district-wise surveys on the subject, the state government released preliminary data on the floor of the Legislative Council in March 2013, according to which there were 7,000 cases of crimes against women, including rape, kidnapping and molestation registered in J&K during the years 2011–12, with Kashmir accounting for 6,873 cases. Molestation of women accounted for the highest number of total cases at 2,516, followed by kidnapping at 2,100, 'eve teasing' at 698, and 685 cases of rape and four cases of gang rape.

Interestingly, cases of abetment to suicide (in the case of a woman victim) have also been listed at 366, but the correlation between these crimes and whether they led to suicide/abetment to suicide has not been examined.

What these figures do not include are the numbers of women who have risked their own lives, fractured their limbs or suffered severe injuries in an attempt to protect themselves from being sexually assaulted by the SF. The shadow of fear and the threat of sexual violence adversely impact the everyday lives of women. As one of them said, the threat of rape was always present, an ultimate punishment for women belonging to a militant's family and harbouring him. She continued: 'Apart from the soldiers who threatened us with rape, even IB (Intelligence Bureau) officials would often come to the house and threaten me that they'd take me away and rape me if I did not tell them where my husband was. This fear of being raped was paralyzing; I have had nightmares and could not sleep, except with the help of tranquilizers.'

I heard many instances, eyewitness accounts, particularly in villages, where women jumped out of a building that was raided by the SF or a woman jumped down 30 feet from a hill in a forest where she had gone to collect firewood and suddenly found herself surrounded by soldiers. Death was a better option for them than their 'ismat rezi' (rape), said the man who narrated these incidents. A former militant commander who witnessed how a woman had jumped out of a window to save herself from the grip of the soldiers who had raided the building shared this story with me:

> It happened in Kohlin, Baramulla sometime in 1991.
> We had received information that the village was going
> to be raided by the forces, I urged my battalion to move
> but I stayed on, planning a combat strategy. While I was
> in a hideout, I heard a woman screaming and saw that

the soldiers were trying to grab her near a window of a 3-storey building and she was struggling to free herself from them; she was wearing a *pheran* which the soldiers had grabbed but she wriggled out of it and dashed out of the window. She survived although both her legs were fractured but it was better than the fate she'd have met had the soldiers captured her. Unfortunately, I could not even intervene and save her, as they would've captured me. This was the worst mental torture I suffered, watching this incident.

In my interviews and informal conversations with women and men, different forms and types of sexual violence emerged, including molestation and rape, custodial torture, child sexual abuse and incest. The last two crimes may not be specific to Kashmir in the sense that, like elsewhere, the victim knows the perpetrator, who is usually a family member or a close relative. However, it acquires a different connotation in an armed conflict situation that is marked by mass violence, frequent and indefinite curfews, and the rupture (due to violence) in interpersonal relations within the home. According to Dr Arshad, a practising psychiatrist at the government psychiatric hospital, seven cases of child sexual abuse were brought to the hospital for treatment where, except in one case, the rest were abused by a close relative. 'Cases of child sexual abuse are not usually reported in our clinical settings easily' he said, adding that 'the survivors were brought to the hospital only after they had attained adulthood' to protect the children from further trauma and shame. It also led him to believe that the 'incidence of incest may not be so rare in our society as is commonly believed.' The specificity of the incidence, according to him, was related to the fact and reality of prolonged curfews being clamped down by the government, due to which families are confined to their homes day and night, resulting in 'increased physical proximity and familial isolation' and in smaller homes, 'crowded, common sleeping area for all members of the family; male and female, children and adults.'

Among the many other incidents of sexual violence against women, the Dukhtaran-e-Millat leader Asiya Andrabi's narration of an incident where a teenaged girl was raped by her own father and became pregnant brought into focus the complex dynamics of the aftermath of such violence, and the role and expectations of leading women political activists, such as her. What is their response to such incidents? Are they able to provide any moral, emotional or material support to the victim? Or are they bound by their own prejudices regarding gender roles, religion and patriarchy? According to Andrabi, the young girl's family contacted her and since there was no other option but for the girl to go through an abortion, she 'consulted the local mufti [religious head] who refused to believe that such a thing could happen in our society and said that Islam does not permit abortions. However, I myself could not take responsibility as a life was indeed growing inside that girl and I too believe that it is haram to abort it. I therefore advised the family to take a decision on their own, as I could not be directly responsible for it. I later learnt that the abortion was carried out in the secrecy of their home. The girl's future was thus destroyed, ruined.' She further elaborated that violence against girls/women was rooted in the co-educational system 'where boys and girls mixed freely'. According to her, schools did not need to impart sex education to children because, she said, 'sex was as natural an instinct as thirst. Just as we reach for water when thirsty, so it is with sex', adding that what needed to be taught to girls and boys were the negative aspects of sex; not what is natural. 'That is why there is no need for sex education. *Gunahon ke safe tareekhe kaise ho sakte hain?* How can there be safe ways of committing sins', she asked? Regarding the threat of sexual violence by militants, she did not say much but observed that following Islamic laws strictly to punish the perpetrators, as done in Saudi Arabia, would check the menace of sexual violence against women.

The leader of MKM, Anjum Habib, emphasised the fact that women victims/survivors did expect women leaders in the movement to play a definitive role in safeguarding their honour, particularly where militants were concerned: 'It is a challenge for us because women survivors of sexual violence feel upset with us that we have failed to prevent militants from targeting unarmed, innocent women. "Why didn't you stop them?", they would ask me.'

The woman doctor I had earlier interviewed stressed the moral dilemma that the victim/survivor's family faced regarding abortion, particularly as a result of rape. She narrated an incident where a mother had brought her young pregnant daughter to the hospital for an abortion. 'Seven years ago, I had personally met a 17-year-old girl brought here by her mother. According to her, two [Maruti] Gypsy vans full of Indian security forces had suddenly stopped in her way and abducted her daughter. She was raped and abandoned. [The] mother was reluctant to report the case and had [brought her to have an abortion]. The girl was psychologically destroyed and emotionally distraught. Her future was finished.' However, the hospital (Lalded) did not maintain any records of unmarried women brought for abortions. According to her: 'The police bring women victims here for medical examination for rape, once an FIR [First Information Report] has been registered in a police station. Women victims of sexual violence do not visit the hospital by themselves. There were many such cases during militancy but now it is sporadic, maybe two to four cases in the span of a year.'

According to Dr Arshad Hussain: 'I see a spectrum of patients at the hospital, including women victims of domestic violence and abuse, but never in my career have I seen victims of sexual violence or rape. Women come with different symptoms of depression, anxiety and many other ailments, which, as a doctor, I would say are related to the problem of sexual violence, but they do not talk about it because of the double trauma they would suffer and also because there is a cultural sensitivity regarding the issue of sexual violence.' 'How do women cope with the trauma if silence is maintained?', I asked. He replied, 'No, they are not able to cope and, therefore, they suffer from all the ailments and symptoms that I earlier spoke about. People fail to understand that sexual violence, including rape is a crime of power and domination, not a crime of lust or passion. This understanding could pave the way for people to break their silence regarding sexual violence.' He said that ideally, a woman victim/survivor should be brought to the psychiatric hospital for counselling, but it is a culturally alienating experience for a majority of the women and their families to do so. Even to file an FIR at a police station, it is not the women victims but their male relatives who would do it on their behalf, claiming that 'the family's honour had been robbed', said Khurram Parvez.

It is well known that in an armed conflict situation, women are sexually targeted to punish their men or to coerce them to disclose their whereabouts. Stories of sexual violence are, then, routinely suppressed both by the authorities as well as by family members, and the problem is compounded in J&K due to militarization as well as patriarchal gender relations. Given the situation, many women suffered threats, violence, as well as raised their children and managed their family responsibilities on their own; neighbours would not come anywhere close for fear of reprisals; not even when, as a former militant's sister said, 'we screamed or cried during an army raid.' Having been related to the militants, the women and their homes were marked, leading to a life of isolation.

They were not spared from being sexually abused and tortured as homes and neighborhoods were raided. At the same time, men who were picked up by the SF – on suspicion of being militants – were not spared either as they were subjected to torture, including sexual abuse, in custody. While there is one kind of silence on the sexual violation of women, another kind of silence, much more deeply encoded for a range of complex reasons, is the one that relates to the sexual violation of men, leading to a deep sense of humiliation and the fear of being socially ostracized and rendered unfit for sexual activity with their wives once they return home. However, in an armed conflict situation, where men, be they militants or not, are routinely picked up for interrogation and torture, the victim could well turn into perpetrator, further vitiating the already complex web of violence and its 'methodical' use against a 'suspect.' According to Anjum, the SF's role regarding sexual violence against women is well known as there are public protests and outrage but the role of militants in relation to sexual violence is neither documented nor have there been public protests against it, mainly for fear of reprisals on other family members.

Some women and men did talk about how militants sometimes took advantage of families that provided them shelter and food to sexually abuse the women. According to a local journalist:

> One militant of a commander level regularly took shelter in a particular home for over two years. Word spread that he was having sex with a young woman in the family but when he was confronted, he claimed that the woman herself had taken the initiative and all he did was to fulfill her desire. The woman, on the other hand said that she was coerced into it but she refused to file an FIR or to take up the case in any other manner; even her family remained silent about it. This also laid the ground for a contest between consent and coercion; did the women consent or did armed militants coerce them into it?

Was the refusal to register an FIR to do with shame and stigma, or did they not wish to betray the movement? No, it was mainly due to the woman and her family's fear of reprisal, he said. When confronted

with this question, a former middle-aged militant acknowledged the
fact but hastened to add that it was nothing compared to the 'sins
of the SFs.' He further said that militants were human too: 'we have
committed such mistakes in the past but certainly not as a routine
practice' – *hum bhi insaan hain, hum se bhi kabhi kabhi aisi ghalti hui
hai* – we are human, we too are guilty of committing such crimes
occasionally. A former commander with a battalion of 40 'comrades',
he had picked up the gun and joined the armed struggle at the age
of 18 in 1991. 'I gave up college but did my graduation in armed
struggle,' he told me. After a decade, he gave up the gun because his
family members, including his old parents and young sisters, had
to face constant harassment at the hands of the security forces. He
said that the security forces would raid his house repeatedly and get
violent with family members; his sisters were threatened, beaten and
dragged by their hair, while his old father was picked up and tortured
and was found a week later in a dazed mental condition. When we
brought him home he told his son to kill him first if he were to ever
'go back.' His neighbour, another former militant told me that he
went *'taar ke us par'* (across the border) in 1989 and belonged to the
first lot of militants to have crossed the border for arms training. His
son was three months old then, and while seeking blessings from his
parents who also gave him some money, he left without informing
his wife. According to her:

> When he returned after six months, he was barely home
> as he was now a Mujahid. Two years later he was arrested
> and tortured, my son was three years old at the time and
> I also had my second child. Those years of his detention
> were terrible; there was no money to even buy food. I was
> stressed and worried all the time and fell ill frequently.
> Before he was arrested, my house was raided several times
> and the soldiers would beat us up and scatter everything
> around. I was beaten up twice as I refused to disclose my

husband's whereabouts. Even his sister was beaten badly. They'd use their lathis to beat us. I always remained inside the house, locking the doors and windows; it was terrifying as the army could raid any time. When he was detained in Srinagar jail, I'd visit him there with my two small children and one growing inside me. I would walk the distance till my footwear came apart as I had no money to travel any other way [weeping]. I would visit him in any jail that they shifted him to. My mother would accompany me at times to different interrogation centres. When he returned two years later from jail, his beard had grown down to his waist.

Her husband was a contractor prior to crossing for arms training. When the family's financial situation worsened her young sons also went out to work part time as daily wagers in nearby apple orchards. She said that during jail visits, she met many other women in a similar situation; it was far worse for some of them as they had absolutely no support from their families whereas she remained steadfast as she shared her husband's and his parents' sentiment for azadi. She had lost two of her own brothers to the cause, she said. 'My two brothers became *shaheed* for the cause. One of them was part of a group of 45 boys who were crossing but they were shot dead near Uri. He was 16 years old then. The other brother crossed after the *shahadat* and returned after three years and was an active militant until the SFs killed him too during cross firing.'

When I visited another former militant's home, he told me how during the early period of militancy, there were frequent raids and crackdowns by the SFs in their village and how insecure the family felt. He mentioned how vulnerable his ageing father felt as he was now the only remaining earning son in the family. He said that his father once tried to physically prevent him from rescuing his niece from the 'clutches of the soldiers.' The father was worried about the

family's plight in case his only remaining son too were picked up
by the soldiers, just as his other son was: '*chup raho warna tumhein
bhi yeh utha kar le jayenge aur phir hamara kya hoga*' – remain silent
or else they will pick you up too; what will happen to us then? His
younger brother was picked up several times although he was only
a civilian doing carpet work in Sogam. The constant suspicion, due
to which he was repeatedly picked up, detained and tortured, turned
him to militancy in 1996: 'That was the last time we saw him. After
three years of his disappearance, he was shot dead by the SFs in a
nearby village. When we heard about it and went to identify the
body, it was my brother. We tried to file an FIR against the SFs but
they prevented us by claiming that he was an outsider, a Pakistani.
However, we managed to bring his body home and slowly, as word
spread, villagers began to gather outside our house. My mother
collapsed when she saw the body of her son who she remembered
as a healthy, young man who had "gone away" and had now been
brought home dead. She has not recovered since then and has lost
her mental balance completely and also lost her vision in both eyes
due to the stroke she suffered as a result of the sudden shock.' She
was helped to come out and sit with us but she simply stared into
space and screamed incoherently every few minutes. She had to be
hand fed and cleaned. The widow of the son now had the main
responsibility of looking after her and the rest of the family including
her own young daughter and son. She too was inconsolable, even after
17 years. The widow was a young woman then and the daughter was
barely four years old. She was expecting her second child when her
husband 'went away' and the son was born after his father was killed.
The daughter, who was sitting silently all the while and listening to
the story, mentioned how she only had a vague memory of her father
as compared to her brother. She said she had studied up to Class X
and given up as she'd then have to travel outside to study further and
it was not safe for her.

A little distance away, as we walked from his home, Nazeer pointed to a deserted, abandoned house where a young married man had been picked up by the SFs and killed on suspicion of being a militant. His parents had died a few years ago but when his younger brother saw his brother's dead body, he died of a massive heart attack due to shock. Now it was only his young widow and a small child. Who would look after them? She was married to her husband's cousin in a nearby village so that he would take care of her and the child. When he was introduced to me, he barely spoke and seemed dazed. I later learnt that he was not mentally sound but the widow was still married to him so that he could 'at least provide for the widow.' Hardly anybody visits them, as they believe that the dead haunt the house in which they live. 'She leads a life of isolation at home. Every house here has a *dardnak* (painful) story to narrate,' he said.

A militant's own experience of violence and victimization at the hands of the armed forces had far-reaching psychological implications, not only for himself but also in his interpersonal, social relations; in particular, the experience of brutal sexualized torture that led to feelings of inadequacy and emasculation amongst them. As revealed by a study, such methods of torture were meant to 'destroy the victim's sense of self and relation to others.' The assault on the victim's body, 'while shaming and demoralizing, also destroys his sense of autonomy and agency at its most basic level, by the scrutiny and control of the victim's body and bodily functions.'[10]

A former militant who experienced brutal torture in custody told me how his body had more or less healed but the psychological, emotional scars remained. The memory of torture persisted including the kind of tools that were used, the humiliation, the pain and powerlessness of that moment. In his own words: 'There were many things the soldiers used, at times the torture tools also consisted of thin leather and metal strips that would peel the skin with each lash.

The bare body would soon begin to bleed. The metal strips had lines etched on them of famous Bollywood songs that the soldiers would hum while lashing us, exchanging notes on which songs were more suitable, sniggering and giggling all the time.'

He also pointed out that silence prevailed around the issue of sexual violence against men – people hesitated to discuss openly the nature of violence against men by men – sexualized violence and how rampant it is during custody. 'The silence around male sexual violence during (conflict) raises critical questions about male bodies, gender and power (relations). Social norms of masculinity create and enforce relations of power on multiple levels – between men as individuals, between men and women and within larger social institutions -military, workplace (and) nation state' (Vodjik). It is a fact that this form of specific sexual abuse against men is often disguised under the more generalized category of torture – thereby 'normalising it as a natural, if unspoken part of war' (Vodjik).

Women in the family spoke, although hesitantly, about how their men had suffered due to the brutal torture inflicted on them where sticks and iron rods were shoved into their rectum as well as electric shocks used on their genitals. According to them, this kind of sexualized torture often left the men in a dysfunctional state, both physically and emotionally. Moreover, some of the men were haunted by feelings of guilt; for the losses and sacrifices suffered by their family, particularly the women. One of them recounted how he was assailed by feelings of guilt and shame as he had lost seven of his family members including his sister, all of whom were killed by the SF. 'My mother died waiting for me, she had cried so much that she fell ill and passed away, my old father was also not spared. In fact my entire family suffered due to my involvement in militancy and I am solely responsible for my family's suffering and loss.' Interestingly, this former militant later became an active human rights defender.

The Aftermath of Sexual Violence

According to a survey, sexual violence has impinged on the mental health of people more than physical violence has done in the years since militancy began (MSF 2006)[11]. Sexual violence against women has been used as a common strategy by the army and paramilitary to terrorize and intimidate people. While nearly 12 per cent of the respondents said that they had been victims of sexual violence, 64 per cent had heard of cases of rape in the same period, and one in seven people had actually witnessed rape. A local newspaper reported that more than two rapes or molestation cases have been reported in J&K per day over the last twenty-four years, but the conviction rate in these cases during the same period has been a dismal 3.26 percent.

A recently published report[12] on impunity in J&K has highlighted nine cases of rape by the armed forces in different districts of the state. While the location is different in each case, there is a certain pattern that emerges in terms of the nature of sexual violence against women (for being related to the men that the army was seeking to punish) and the clause of impunity that they used to escape either investigation or conviction despite documented evidence against them. In all these cases of torture and sexual assault, including rape, the soldiers targeted women irrespective of their age or marital status – from a teenaged girl kept in custody for days of torture and sexual abuse to a mother raped inside her own home. In the case of the young girl, she had to be hospitalized for weeks and had to undergo a hysterectomy as part of the treatment. Nine years later, the family awaits justice that remains elusive, as in all other cases. According to the report, some of the alleged perpetrators even claimed that it was consensual sex rather than rape. As in many other cases, the coercive environment and the fear of reprisal that perhaps led to silence was falsely seen as a woman's consent. The report also documents how some of the perpetrators were, in fact, rewarded and promoted by the state as part of its policy to acknowledge and reward the personnel/ officers for their 'meritorious' record of service, while denying justice to the aggrieved women/men.

How Impunity Traps Women: The 'Sex Scandal'[13]

Consider the case of the 'sex scandal' that had rocked the valley in 2006. As details emerged, it showed a clear nexus between the elite political class, the bureaucracy and the top army brass, where young women (including a teenaged girl) were lured and coerced into providing 'sexual favours.' According to a senior local journalist, 'The sex scam that shook the state was mainly due to the fact that women were desperate to have their men released from jails/interrogation centres. These women were then exploited and sexually abused both by the political establishment and the SF.'

The 'scandal' brought agitated and angry people – men, women, and children – out on the streets for days and months, demanding investigation into the case and punishment for the guilty. It was the testimony of a teenaged girl that brought the heinousness of the sexual crime to public knowledge. Asiya Andrabi told me how she was instrumental in unearthing the scandal by carrying advertisements in the local dailies asking people to contact her on a given number to report cases of sexual violence/prostitution. One phone call carried this terse message for her from an unknown man: 'You have put your hands in a snake pit. Go for the big crocodiles rather than the snakes.' She understood the import of the message regarding the corrupt and powerful nexus that existed at the top and how it was used to exploit women.

After the initial enquiries, the case was handed over to the Central Bureau of Investigation (CBI), which found enough evidence against many influential men in the government as well as the army.

The majority of the accused government officials were not only bailed out of jail but were reinstated/promoted in their official posts, while the army justified it as a 'honey trap' they had set up through which to reach the militants. A national daily[14] carried the story under a headline that captured its essence: 'An Old Counterinsurgency Weapon Comes Back to Haunt the Valley under State Patronage' (2006). The news report traces the scandal 'to the time when a network involving sex lords, intelligence officials, political leaders and militants began to take shape.' Recognizing the benefit of 'honey traps', the intelligence agencies had begun to use it by early 1990s. The report quotes a senior Central Reserve Police Force (CRPF) official in Srinagar: 'A majority of militants were ordinary Kashmiri youth aged 18–22. The young militants displayed a penchant for prostitutes... [and the] sweet nothings whispered to the prostitutes by the militants found their way to intelligence agencies.'

According to another news report, the usefulness of 'honey traps' began to decline by 1996, but the women already being used in this 'racket' then turned to provide their services to high-profile people. Interestingly, 'the accused have pleaded before India's supreme court that they have been indicted because of their role in fighting terrorism in JK.'[15] The petition filed in the Supreme Court lauds the role played by some of the high- ranking accused in 'creating a situation of peace and tranquility in the Kashmir Valley as is now existing.'

The Battles that Women Victims/Survivors Fight

What happened to the women victims/survivors? Despite going from 'pillar to post' in search of justice, despite their testimonies (to a commission of enquiry), these women were abandoned by the state – which was clearly in collusion with the accused whom it had to rescue and protect – for voluntarily being in the 'sex trade' for livelihood purposes. The only social and 'moral rehabilitation' in the case of a few women survivors came from Asiya Andrabi, who counselled them and advised them to seek 'Allah's forgiveness': 'I offered whatever help I could, including getting two, three girls married to the men in the same trade as no one from respectable families were willing to marry the girls due to the stigma of their previous profession. The men, being part of the chain, agreed to marry as I explained to them that they would be able to understand each other better and be sympathetic to each other,' she told me.

As far as the 'queen-bee' of the scandal was concerned, it is believed that she had started wearing a burqa [when she was released from jail] but the local people in the mohalla would not allow her to do it, as they would not know of her whereabouts if she wore one. According to Andrabi, [the] 'local people were closely monitoring her every move. When it was brought to my attention, I went to the locality and met people and asked them, "If she is willing to give up the evil path and lead a better life, how could you remind her of her past and force her to return to it?" They told me that they wouldn't allow her to live in the same locality, but I tried to convince them by saying that the risk of her reverting to the same activity was much greater if they did not allow her to stay here. Sharia does not allow you to displace her, I told them.'

In the words of the survivor herself, 'When everybody abandoned me, Baji [Asiya Andrabi] came to my rescue. She helped me transform into a God-fearing woman.' Despite this, she has been forced to lead a life of seclusion, on the outskirts of the city, where she lives with her husband and son 'in permanent confinement' as, she said, 'no relatives visit us and there is no contact with the neighbours.'[16] When I asked Andrabi if she helped these women survivors return to public life by becoming members of the DM, she laughed and said that these women had to first undertake their own journey to become 'pious Muslims' before they were able to join the organization led by her. The case illustrates clearly the limited options that women had in the given situation and how they were simply cast as either 'good' or 'bad' women.

The 'sex scandal' and its repercussions reveal the complex layers within which sexual crimes against women are mired – how the culture of impunity has crept into different social domains and institutions, leading to protection of the guilty and further victimization of the victims. The incident also illustrates the double exploitation of women by the militarized state as well as by the patriarchal community, as the victims themselves were held responsible for their plight and pushed to the margins of society. The objective of rescuing and protecting these women was either to have them 'married off to men in the same profession' or turning it into another form of 'moral policing' whereby these women were exhorted to abide by their own cultural values and not be corrupted by the 'evil Western influences.' A former militant reiterated this by saying that 'prior to militancy women were not safe due to Western influences and therefore we shut down alcohol shops and cinema halls; women are much safer now.'

Concern for women's safety and security in a militarized environment can thus have negative repercussions for women. Militarization perpetuates and reinforces patriarchal values that not only control women's sexuality but also undermine their role and status in society. According to Andrabi, 'Allah has given women the status of mother, wife, daughter and sister; that is her identity. It is the father's status that determines her own; husbands may change, women may be divorced, but fathers remain the same [and that is where women draw their identity from].' Far from the Valley, in the border town of Rajouri, a woman principal of a girls' higher secondary school echoed similar thoughts when we[17] met concerning women's safety and security in relation to the threat of sexual violence in a militarized environment. In her official capacity as principal, she had earlier managed to have a paramilitary camp removed from the school premises. 'How does it really matter if the army is all around? It depends upon the woman to abide by the prescribed role to stay away from any trouble or harm,' she declared. She asserted that she herself had always encouraged girls to come out and study, and even mobilized them to enrol in the school. She had completed thirty years of service despite the restrictions imposed on women by 'our male-dominated society.' For women to remain safe and secure, she believed that they must not loiter around and should restrict their mobility to school and home, adding: 'It depends on how a woman conducts herself to gain respect in society by adhering to certain rules and codes of conduct that have been laid down for us as women.' According to her, *'Aurat ko mehfooz rehne ke liye do zaroortein lazmi hain – chadar or chardiwari* [The two most critical needs for women's safety are the veil and the four walls of their homes]. Women's social status in society has nothing to do with patriarchy.' She added: 'According to the Koran, it is men who have first been told to keep their gaze down in front of women, it is only then that women have been advised to cover themselves fully.'

❀   ❀   ❀

Just as violence, sexual violence or the threat of it is a lived experience for women and men in J&K, impunity, in all its different dimensions, permeates all aspects of their lives, be it social, political or personal. So it is with the dominant patriarchal ideology that tries to subjugate women. By breaking the silence, by engaging in the struggle for justice, by acts of defiance and resistance, ordinary people and women victims/survivors challenge impunity in their everyday lives with resilience. The imposition of coercive laws, prolonged curfews, detention and custodial torture, or the fact that women are specifically targeted by the armed forces have, rather than subjugate people, brought them closer in solidarity and reinforced their resolve to resist and challenge injustice in myriad ways, from the streets to the courts of law. The state's lawlessness in the name of 'law and order' is manifest on the ground where people wage their struggle. The failure of the state to provide justice to victims of armed conflict is further compounded/exacerbated by the failure of the democratic opinion in the country to urgently raise these issues and create enough pressure on the Government of India to do the needful – end the reign of violence, terror, injustice and impunity, and be accountable to the people. Unless this silence is broken, and this social sanction is revoked, we continue to promote rather than challenge the culture of impunity through our acquiescence.

NOTES

1. Zubaan and IDRC (International Development Research Centre) study on 'The Sexual Violence and Impunity in South Asia.' This chapter mainly draws from my earlier version titled "Breaking the Silence. Sexual Violence and Impunity in J&K, published in 'Faultlines of History: The India Papers II.' Ed. Uma Chakravarti. 2016

2. On the night February 23, 1991, battalions of Rajputana Rifles raided Kunan and Poshpora villages in Kupwara district. Men were herded out of their homes and locked up elsewhere and tortured while 40-50 women of all ages irrespective of their marital status were systematically raped through the night. Later the government instituted a one-man inquiry commission that categorically denied the charges of rape despite the victims' and witnesses' testimonies, giving a clean chit to the army. It was after 22 years that the case was re-opened for fresh investigations when a group of young local women approached the State Human Rights Commission and later filed a petition in the Srinagar High Court.

3. International People's Tribunal for Human Rights and Justice in Kashmir. 'Militarisation with Impunity: A Brief on Rape and Murder in Shopian, Kashmir.' July 19, 2009.

4. Duschinki, Haley; Hoffman, Bruce: 2011. 'Everyday violence, institutional denial and struggles for justice in Kashmir.' Ohio: Sage Publications.

5. A group of five women, who also volunteered work at JKCCS, got together and filed a petition in the state human rights commission (SHRC) and later in the Srinagar High Court demanding that the case be reopened. They mobilised nearly a hundred women to sign the petition along with them, of whom fifty women agreed to do so. The group of 5 women later wrote a book 'Do You Remember Kunan Poshpora?' which was published by Zubaan in 2014.

6. Verma, Justice J.S.; Seth, Justice Leila; Subramaniam Gopal (January 23, 2003). *Reports of the Committee on Amendments to Criminal Law.*

7. Vojdik, Valorie K., 'Sexual Violence Against Men and Women in War: A Masculinities Approach' (July 1, 2013). *Nevada Law Journal*, Forthcoming; University of Tennessee Legal Studies Research Paper No. 217. Available at SSRN: https://ssrn.com/abstract=2271222 or http://dx.doi.org/10.2139/ssrn.2271222

8. This was during research undertaken for Women Regional Network, on the social consequences of militarization, with Rita Manchanda. Rajouri. 2012. This excerpt is taken from my field notes.

9. Jammu Kashmir Coalition of Civil Society. 23 February 2014.

10. Sonpar, Shobna, 2007. *Violent Activism: A Psychosocial Study of Ex-Militants in J&K*. New Delhi: Aman Public Charitable Trust.

11. Medecins Sans Frontieres. 14 December 2006. 'Kashmir: Violence and Mental Health.' Available at: http://www.msf.org/article/kashmir-violence-and-mental-health

12. International People's Tribunal for Human Rights and Justice in Indian-administered Kashmir and Association of Parents of Disappeared Persons. December 2012. *Alleged Perpetrators: Stories of Impunity in Jammu and Kashmir*. Srinagar.

13. The 2006 'sex scandal' hit headlines after the JK police discovered two video CDs showing Kashmiri minors being sexually exploited. The police questioned the minor and the 'kingpin' Sabeena and gathered names of 56 people involved in the scandal. The case was transferred

to the CBI in May 2006 after names of two JK ministers; MLAs and other influential men emerged in the case. Given the sensitive nature of the case, the trial was held in-camera.

The judgment in the infamous 2006 Jammu and Kashmir sex scandal is available at https://timesofindia.indiaties.com/city/chandigarh/ex-bsf-dig-gets-10-years-in-prison-for-rape-of-minor-articleshow/64487266.cms

14. *Sunday Hindustan Times* (New Delhi), 14 May 2006.
15. *The Times of India* (New Delhi), 28 August 2006.
16. 'Kashmir's Sex Racket Kingpin Takes to Hijab.' *Free Press Kashmir* (Srinagar), 3 August 2012.
17. WRN. With Rita Manchanda. Rajouri. 2012. This excerpt is taken from my field notes.

Conclusion

How do I conclude a book like this? A book about Kashmir that is an ongoing 'story' – unresolved, festering, unrelenting and fighting – how to end it when reports continue to come in about the daily death toll, the uncertainty and insecurity that mark every single day in every individual's life? Today, in Kashmir, ordinary people's priorities, their political and social aspirations continue to be overlooked and deliberately neglected by a belligerent state. Restrictive and oppressive laws are used against a defiant people whose struggle for azadi, and for justice is visible on the streets and within homes. Today, in Kashmir, men, women, the young continue to courageously face the physical, social and psychological onslaught and the consequences of state violence and militarization. Trust and respect which should have defined the relationship between the state and its citizens, have disappeared and been replaced with suspicion and complete disregard for human life, liberty and dignity – is this a repairable breach, I wonder?

Seven decades have passed since Partition when the state was divided between India and Pakistan in 1947. The two countries, with their respective claims over Kashmir's territory, have fought three full-scale wars and the relations between the two continue to hinge on this contentious issue that remains unresolved. While India uses the question of Accession to its advantage by claiming Kashmir to be an integral part of the country as it 'willingly' acceded to the Indian union in 1947, Pakistan's claim over it is based on the fact that Kashmir is a Muslim majority state. Both countries have reneged on their commitment to hold a plebiscite/referendum (according to the UN resolution) thereby failing their 'own people' on either side of the divide. Pakistan's role in providing moral and financial support to Tehreek-e-azadi in Kashmir is well known, what India refers to as the 'proxy war.' India prides itself for the successive elections it has held in the state and believes that people have exercised their democratic right in electing a government of their choice. One such election of 1987, mainly remembered as the rigged election, became a watershed year in the contemporary history of Kashmir where people's agitation, hitherto peaceful, turned into an armed uprising.

The armed resistance/militancy that began in the 80s, ebbing and escalating at different points of time, has now taken a new generation of men and women into its fold, who are demanding azadi from what they perceive as a forced/illegitimate union with India. In the nearly three decades of conflict the Indian state has maintained and tightened its grip over not only the territory of Kashmir but its people, militarily. During this time justice has been consistently denied to those who deserve it: the victims/survivors of mass violence. And this is one of the many reasons for the young being increasingly drawn into militancy, as well as for unarmed civilians to challenge the heavily armed Indian security forces with little other than stones in their hands.

Violence has impacted everyday life and human security in profound ways and could linger for generations. The records of the psychiatric hospital in Srinagar reveal an increasing graph of mental health ailments in Kashmir with senior psychiatrists terming it as a catastrophe; the number of patients has crossed 100,000 a year, with women making up a larger number than men.

The impact of violence on women is particularly severe as living through conflict means the loss of their loved ones, the threat of physical and psychological abuse, increase in domestic violence, and the double burden of struggling for survival and sustaining their families. Undoubtedly, such violent conflicts push women beyond the end margins that they already live in, and yet it requires them to take on new and challenging roles in everyday lives. Responding to grave tragedies and emergencies in the family, community and society, women adapt themselves to new roles, as first-generation workers, heads of households, and once in the public domain, as negotiators for justice. Their experience of large-scale violence on a daily basis has left an immense psychological and social impact on women who live through it, at times in silence but also through public, political mobilization.

Despite women's participation and visibility in the movement in varied ways and their experience/efforts in rebuilding family and society, they tend to be marginalized. At the same time, having crossed the threshold of their homes in such extraordinary circumstances by breaking norms and many social shackles, life can never be the same again for these women, touched as it is by violence, loss, uncertainty and resistance. All this has altered their lives and their worldview in specific ways while also opening unexpected political/social spaces for them. The reality of living in a society that is largely governed by conservative and patriarchal norms makes it that much harder for women – within their homes or in the public realm.

It can be seen that whenever women are targeted – be it in villages, towns or cities – it somehow leads the conservative and patriarchal forces in society to believe that this will push women back into their homes, perhaps back into covering themselves up for self-protection. However, it is significant that in reality, women have repeatedly challenged this assumption and refused to either stay within their homes or cover themselves up thereby questioning and resisting conservatism in society at different levels, while not losing sight of the larger political reality. This assertion on the part of Kashmiri women could and does come into conflict in the public realm given the various demands, pulls and pressures of society that women often find themselves in. On the one hand, women are determined to carry on with their enquiry, to break as many shackles as they can; but on the other, this self-assertion often comes into conflict with the movement for azadi where women-specific issues are relegated to the background in the belief that once azadi is achieved, these issues will be taken care of and resolved.

Over the years I have seen a new generation of women who have stepped into the public arena, exuding confidence while dealing with financial or health emergencies at home. Like many other young women I have met, Rasheed Bhai's two young daughters come to mind here. Both are first generation graduates in the family and are able to take on the responsibility or rather the challenge of meeting the family's financial needs. After their father fell ill and died, they found jobs, travelled, met new people, and explored possibilities for a more secure future for themselves and their family. Belonging to a family of houseboat owners, they grew up on Dal Lake, surrounded by men and women relatives and after their father's death recently, remained under their close scrutiny. Notwithstanding this, it is quite significant how confidently they deal with their lives on a daily basis, whether at home or outside. When the younger of the two decided recently to marry someone of her own choice, the older one took on the entire responsibility of not only convincing the relatives but also arranging the marriage on the boat and two days later, seeing off her sister to Baramulla where the bridegroom's family lives. Rasheed Bhai had often shared with me the recurring dream he had regarding his daughters' future – 'I wish to see my daughters live and work on land rather than the lake', he had told me many years ago, believing that the land would provide more opportunities for the girls and improve the quality of their lives compared to the lake where life remained constricted, particularly as tourism declined steadily as the conflict raged. While one of his daughters has now moved away from the lake to begin a new life on land, the other manages the houseboat along with her mother, Hafiza and looks after her own small business initiative in handicrafts. As I have seen them from their childhood and now as young women with various responsibilities, it fills me with hope that despite the long years of conflict and violence, they have stood their ground just as the other women in Kashmir have all through these years. This kind of convergence of the personal and the public realm, the dynamics of personal quest and social/political reality now seems far more widespread than before and certainly not a transient or passing experience or phase. It is more than a generation of women that has gone through this sustained experience and it has profoundly changed them. Women, including the ones I have mentioned above, have learnt to take on various roles outside the home also because circumstances have forced them to step out and confront not just one but many realities that the on-going conflict unfolds on a daily basis.

Each chapter in the book reflects how this conflict and violence have caused human and material devastation and also looks at ways to understand, the ability of ordinary people to cope with, or resist its diverse consequences, whether it be the crime of enforced disappearances, targeted sexual violence, forced displacement/dislocation, or the lasting, collective psychological trauma that results from years of living with violence. While the struggle to find the whereabouts of the missing men continues and women break their silence to report sexual violence, the governments, both at the state and centre, remain unmoved, unconcerned by the plight of the victims and their families, refusing to set up a commission of inquiry or acknowledge the extent of this crime. Instead, they claim that the missing men had either crossed over for arms training or were killed in combat. In the case of targeted sexual violence against women by the state forces, rather than punish the guilty, the state rewards the perpetrators with medals and promotions for their 'meritorious service.'

Another serious breach on the part of the state concerns the displaced Kashmiri Pandits. While promising their honourable return and rehabilitation for nearly three decades, the governments have failed them, as many families continue to live in the 'shame accommodation' of camps in Jammu, most of them having given up the hope or the will to return, while the younger generation does not even entertain the thought, having lived and grown up away from the land of their parents and grandparents. Some of the lasting impressions I have carried from the camps are of women trying in multiple ways to bring a semblance of normalcy to their own uprooted lives as well as that of their families – with hope and humour alternating with anger and despair. At the same time, the 'resident' Kashmiri Pandits, who made a conscious decision to stay back despite the height of militant violence, continue to feel neglected by successive governments as their welfare remains beyond the pale of official policies and benefits – whether regarding educational or employment opportunities or financial assistance. When fear and insecurity caused the sudden displacement of the majority of the community, those who stayed back recall how they had to overcome the fear and how they shared a similar reality with their Muslim neighbours – of violence and vulnerability, as well as a firm belief in the close bond that existed between the two communities. I am reminded of what a Pandit woman had said to me about how she had dealt with the very real fear she felt at the time and taken a decision to stay back. She said, 'I visited a Muslim saint in the neighbourhood who I had tremendous faith in and decided to stay back on his advice that no harm would come to me or my children. Once you have such faith, all fear disappears.'

❀ ❀ ❀

I have often been asked why I took so long to write this book. My friends suggested it may have been easier to write when I was younger. While broadly agreeing with them that I should have done it long ago, I also knew that it could not have been written any sooner. Was I too looking for some kind of closure, since my relationship with Kashmir includes varied experiences, of love, loss and hope where one tries to make sense of the ambiguity of mass violence generally and the specificity of it at a personal level? The deaths of close ones, the near fatal injuries to friends, the detention and incarceration of long years that women and men I have known have suffered, as well as happier occasions such as marriages, births and many other celebrations, all these formed part of my experience. I was perhaps looking for just enough distance from the place that had come to mean so much to me in so many different ways, but the more I tried, the harder it was. My seven year old grandson, Jahaan, would call me frequently from Dubai telling me how long it was since I had visited him and his sisters – my daughter had told him that I was writing a book. 'Naanu, are you still writing that story? Please stop and come soon,' he would implore.

When I first began work as one of the consultants with Oxfam way back in 1999, I was told that the work needed to be humanitarian and apolitical in nature, but it did not take long for me to understand that nothing in Kashmir could be apolitical given the nature of the dispute and the conflict that is rooted in the political – the politics of nationalism and national sovereignty, the politics of patriotism and subordination that continues to be challenged by Kashmiris, despite the vast humanitarian crisis. I must admit that over the years, Kashmir has radicalized and politicised me further, both in terms of my intellectual as well as my emotional understanding of its reality. Writing this book is perhaps a small political act compared to the many courageous everyday acts of defiance, rebellion and resistance that ordinary Kashmiris have come to symbolise as they fight for dignity and their right to azadi.

Acknowledgements

I have a long list of people to thank but let me begin by describing how I ended up writing this book. As weeks of fieldwork turned into months and years, my field diaries piled up, with notes, observations, interviews, and random thoughts. I was then part of a team of consultants with Oxfam (India) Trust where we shared and discussed our research findings regularly and also presented them elsewhere. A memory from the time that stands out for me as I write this: I had returned to Delhi from my first field visit and a few weeks later, I was at a 'round-table' conference on Kashmir where I made a presentation based on my handwritten notes from the field. Among the large audience were a few friends too, including Urvashi Butalia who later came up to me and suggested that I write a book! I looked at her in disbelief since I had never written a book or imagined that I could, but she persisted in her own way while I simply filed away the thought until a year and a half ago when she came up with a deadline for me to deliver the book. If not for her abiding faith in me, and the confidence that she reposed in me even when I lacked it myself, I do not think this book would have been possible. She took keen interest at every stage of writing, investing precious time in reading the first and many other drafts subsequently along with meticulously editing and shaping the manuscript – into this book. Thank you, Urvashi. I am also very grateful to the young and vibrant Zubaan team, particularly Ishani, Meghna, Sukruti and Adreeta for all their help and hard work that has gone into making this book.

For what the book contains in its pages, I owe a deep debt of gratitude to all the women and men who shared their life stories with me in different parts of Jammu and Kashmir over many years despite the pain and discomfort it caused them in recounting traumatic events that shaped or altered their personal lives and homes. I will always cherish the warmth and love with which each one of them welcomed me in their homes or places of work and perhaps unknowingly they also helped me towards an understanding of the complex realities of everyday life in a highly militarized, 'conflict zone'. There are so many people to thank, several of them mentioned in the book and some who remain unnamed for the sake of privacy. I acknowledge my heartfelt gratitude to each one of them, including Parveena Ahangar, Anjum Zamarud Habib, and Bakhtawar – for their friendship and many conversations. Asiya Andrabi for welcoming me in her home and for spending so much time with me, despite her busy schedule.

Many thanks to Nighat Shafi of Help Foundation for her support and collaboration and for her hospitality and friendship that I cherish, along with Pandit Shafi who engaged my attention with interesting snippets of the 'Kashmir story'. Parvez Imroz of JKCCS/APDP, and his team, unravelled the poignant world of the 'disappeared' that was hitherto unknown to me and helped me work closely with the families. Sajjad Hussain, Gowher Hussein and Basheer Ahmed of Husseini Relief Committee, along with their volunteers, helped me greatly in different ways – from visiting hospitals, villages and towns to organising workshops on the health needs of people in remote villages. I am fortunate to have spent so much time – both happy and tragic – with Sajjad, his wife, Razia and with his parents to whom

I offer my Salaams with a deep sense of gratitude. Special thanks to the entire team at Mattipora Health Centre, particularly Sheikh Sahab and Shaheen for the much-needed health care they provided to people from twenty neighbouring villages and for successfully implementing the Aman project.

Gowhar Fazili, Sarwar Kashani and Idrees Kanth for undertaking the research and writing a detailed report on the impact of conflict on the student community in Kashmir; they also helped me in bringing together students from different districts for workshops and animated discussions in colleges and even on shikara rides on the Dal Lake.

Thanks to Sanjay Tickoo of the Kashmiri Pandit Sangharsh Samiti (KPSS) who I first met with Motilal Bhat of the Hindu Welfare Society. They helped me understand the implications of the Kashmiri Pandit migration from the valley and also the situation of resident Kashmiri Pandits. Sanjay, with his encyclopaedic memory vis-a-vis the resident Pandits, accompanied my colleague, Juhi Tyagi and me to places from where the Pandits had left, introducing us to the families who had decided to stay back, not only in Srinagar but in other districts too. Professor Basheer Ahmed Dabla and Professor Noor Baba of Kashmir University shared with us their findings on the sociological and political implications of displacement that helped us greatly. I also wish to thank Kumar Wanchoo, Neerja Mattoo, Dr SN Dhar and Vimla Dhar for sharing their stories and views with us, as well as all the women and men we met in neighbourhoods that witnessed the sudden mass migration of their community.

In Jammu, we began each morning with a visit to the *Kashmir Times* office to meet Ved Bhasin, Anuradha Bhasin and Prabodh Jamwal as we prepared to visit the migrant camps. Ved Bhasin was generous with his time and enriched our understanding with his knowledge of the subject and gave us the much-needed historical perspective. While Anuradha Bhasin shared with us some of the salient findings from her own work on migration, Prabodh Jamwal shared stories with us of the larger humanitarian crisis resulting from the conflict, which helped greatly. Also, much love and salaam to Anju Bhasin and Saba for hosting us on many an evening as we returned from the camps. Balraj Puri, Rekha Chowdhry, Indu Killam and Dr Sushil Razdan also gave us much of their time for which I am grateful to them. Balraj Puri's classic book *Towards Insurgency* was always at my table as I referred to it countless times.

I also wish to thank and offer my salaams to the many journalists I met at different newspaper offices in Kashmir to make better sense of all that I was discovering – Muzamil Jaleel, Shujaat Bukhari, Zaheeruddin, Iftekhar Geelani, Parvez Bukhari, Aasiya Jeelani and Zafar Meraj, to name a few. Thanks also to Zafar's wife, Naseem for her hospitality and for reading out some of her beautiful poems to me.

I owe deep gratitude to Dr Mushtaq Marghoob and Dr Arshad Hussain who let me spend a great amount of time with them at the hospital for psychiatric diseases while patiently deepening my understanding of the mental health scenario in Kashmir. Dr Sadaqat Rehman took me around the hospital, including to the in-patient wards, and comforted me any number of times when I felt distressed at what I saw.

Once I met Rasheed Bhai and Hafiza, life began to get less complicated for me. It was Sajjad who first brought me to stay at their houseboat – Kashmir Hilton – in 2000 until it gradually became my home-away-from-home. The houseboat hosted most of our memorable meetings and workshops with the entire family, including Zarina, Yasmeen, Rehana and Aijaz taking on different responsibilities. Salaam also to Hameed, Nissar and Riyaza whom I met at the houseboat, and who became my driving companions, taking me far and wide in and outside Srinagar, and for the interest they took in my work.

My friends Sushobha Barve and Shobna Sonpar have been co-travellers in Jammu and Kashmir for many years and we have often shared and exchanged notes, which has contributed to my learning. Shobna Sonpar conducted several of the workshops I organised in Kashmir on 'trauma' with different groups of people. Being a practising clinical psychologist, her observations on my work in Kashmir and her analysis on mental health issues were invaluable. I am grateful to her for sharing these with me, some of these have found their way into this book. Thanks are also due to Amrita Misra for the workshops she conducted in Mattipora and to Shelja Sen and Amit Sen for working with groups of 'affected' children with us.

I hardly knew anybody when I first arrived in Srinagar but I was pleasantly surprised to see Arjimand Hussain Talib waiting for me at the airport, although I had booked a hotel to stay in. I had only met him once at the Oxfam office in Delhi but he immediately took me home saying that I couldn't be staying in a hotel when he had his home and family in Srinagar. This was my first experience of the warmth and hospitality that Kashmiris are known for as I met his parents, sister and grandmother all of whom welcomed me as though I was one of them. I am also reminded of the affection with which Ahmed Wani and Shaista took me to their home on one of my visits and insisted that I stay with them, an offer I did not resist, also because their small son, Nabeel, stole my heart!

While Parvez Imroz and Zaheeruddin introduced me to the many aspects of the phenomenon of 'enforced disappearances' it was Parveena Ahangar who took me inside the homes of many of the families including her own. I was deeply touched to see how families had coped with their loss. Apart from my own learning, I also gained Parveena's love and warm friendship over the years. A big Salaam to her, Saima and all the other women I met over the years in different districts. I also wish to offer my thanks to Parvez's wife, Rukhsana who always welcomed me in what used to be their office-cum-residence, offering me food and some respite from the turbulent world outside. Sohail Shehri accompanied me on many of these visits. His company alerted me to the possible risks faced by young, educated men like him from different state agencies, and despite my constant worry regarding his safety, he accomplished the work as though in a 'normal' situation. Salaam and Shukriya to Sohail for this and the much-needed support that he and his family gave me.

I wish to thank Khurram Parvez of Jammu Kashmir Coalition of Civil Society. He was always just a phone call away, never failing to provide me with whatever information or help that I needed. His organisational skills ensured that JKCSS always buzzed with the energy of the young interns who worked there. Thanks also to Karthik and Shrimoyee at JKCCS – who turned a tiny boat at Nageen Lake into their home for seven years – for their insights and inputs and for the many lovely evenings we spent together.

It was Oxfam (India) Trust and later, the Aman Public Charitable Trust that provided me the opportunity to undertake this work. I still remember the morning in 1999 when Dilip Simeon, who was then director of the Violence Mitigation and Amelioration Project (VMAP) at Oxfam, visited me at home and suggested that I join the team of research consultants that he had managed to bring together to look at the specific ways in which political conflicts and mass violence in the country impacted ordinary lives. He persuasively dismissed any doubts I might have had then and managed to convince me to accept the challenging offer. Thank you, Dilip for opening up a new world of research for me that has proved to be a life changer! And for all the travels, the animated discussions as well as the many highs and lows that the team experienced and shared in terms of the rich harvest of data from different parts of the country. A big thanks to the team members, including Jamal Kidwai, Yamini Misra, Yoginder Sikand, Urvashi Butalia (again!), Vrinda Grover,

Teesta Setalvad, Kavita Punjabi, Satyakam Joshi and Purushottam Aggarwal. In all the years that we worked together both at Oxfam and Aman, I never saw Jamal lose his cool as project coordinator despite the many challenges and even during the cacophonous meetings with all the consultants under one roof.

For this he deserves kudos. So also Yamini who efficiently managed the various timelines and helped prepare budgets for each one of us. Thanks also to the support staff at Oxfam and Aman for helping us: Radheshyam, Aslam and Shiv, to name a few. Marcus Thompson of Oxfam deserves many thanks for being the taskmaster at the helm and for ensuring that deadlines were met and each one of us had a convincing answer to the many queries he always had regarding our research. His passion for India also meant that he got closely involved with our work and helped us along the path with humour and warmth. He also helped us transit smoothly from Oxfam to Aman. I also wish to thank him for his warm friendship and for having patiently waited for my book.

Thanks to the few younger researchers who joined me at Aman during different phases of my work in Kashmir, and at times also accompanied me there. Notable among them are Richa Singh and Juhi Tyagi to whom I owe much. Richa had earlier done research in Palestine for her PhD and brought interesting insights and a special sensibility to our portfolio on gender, mental health and conflict at Aman. I also thank her for our enduring friendship that is a result of our work at Aman. Juhi Tyagi – exactly half my age – brought so much energy, joy and enthusiasm to the work that I looked forward to doing fieldwork in her company. Tirelessly persevering, and level-headed in the face of extremely difficult situations, she was with me throughout the time we spent working on the Kashmiri Pandit study, taking copious notes during interviews that she would later type out and organise in different files. Our host in Anantnag, Adil Khursheed, and his family continue to inquire about her even after all these years and I wish to thank them here for their hospitality, also on behalf of Juhi. The chapter on Kashmiri Pandits echoes Juhi's voice too, and I wish to thank her sincerely for bringing so much happiness with her wherever we travelled and for finding the time to read the first draft of the chapter and give me her feedback even while being thousands of miles away.

My close friends-like-family, Rajni Palriwal and Vidya Rao brought in much cheer and reassurance to me while I spent months in near isolation writing the book. My heartfelt thanks to them for prodding me on and for the many discussions I have had with them that added clarity to my thoughts. Also to Indu Agnihotri, Kirti Singh and Ranjana Narula. It is my friend Sunayana who has seen me most closely through the entire period of writing! She and Sayantoni, despite being busy with their own work schedules breezed in and out of my house any number of times with so much cheer and laughter that it always left me feeling rejuvenated. Much love and thanks to them, Kriti, Gaurav, Girija, Nishant, Arjun Mattoo, Lara, Ramya and Nina – my young brigade of wonderful friends. Also, thanks to Anil Persaud for our conversations around my research and writing.

My close friends of many years, Rita Manchanda and Tapan Bose had earlier worked in Kashmir and their insights and ideas were of immense value to me and I think they know this well. Many thanks also to Navsharan Singh, Laxmi Murthy, Uma Chakravarti, Srilata Batliwala and Warisha Farasat for their continued interest in my work in Kashmir and for the conversations and discussions we have had over the years in Delhi and elsewhere.

My family: what a tough task to even begin to thank them! In a bit of a role reversal, Atifa my elder daughter, provided me with the much-needed respite and comfort whenever I needed it, keeping my room ready in her house in Dubai, with more than whatever she thought I needed and making sure that I had a relaxed time – just as my own mother did for me in Hyderabad many years ago. Jatin Suri, my son-in-law is known for being one of the best chefs and hosts in town and that added to my sense of well-being in no small measure. Thanks also to Reshma, Riyad, Upasana, Reaz, Ajoy and Shilpa.

I realised, during the course of writing, that the best stress-busters are my grandchildren and here I wish to thank Saiesha, Amairah and Jahaan for taking great care of my tiredness, without even knowing how magically they nourished me.

It was at my younger daughter, Saema's house in Milan that I completed the first draft of the introduction while she herself was away at work. I am so glad, indeed thrilled, that she has designed the cover for this book and as I reminded her, this was one of the dreams I had nourished since the time I began to write this book. Heartfelt thanks, Saema for this and much else.

I am also greatly indebted to Suman for managing the house in her own quiet and efficient manner and to Madhu who took over effortlessly in her absence.

It is only appropriate that I bring in this bit of gratitude at the end, although it deserves a much earlier mention in my acknowledgements. Each time I returned from Kashmir, it was always Gautam Navlakha with whom I first shared my research findings and my fieldwork experiences. Our relationship is infused with this 'Kashmir passion' and I would have been poorer in understanding had it not been for his insights, observations and the many conversations and arguments we have had over the years. I thank him with much love and deep appreciation – or with deep love and much appreciation!